D0307936

THE
PALIN EFFECT

*****************************THE*****************************
PALIN EFFECT
MONEY, SEX AND CLASS IN
THE NEW AMERICAN POLITICS
****

SHANA PEARLMAN

Biteback Publishing

First published in Great Britain in 2012 by
Biteback Publishing Ltd
Westminster Tower
3 Albert Embankment
London
SE1 7SP
Copyright © Shana Pearlman 2012

Shana Pearl[...] [...] [...] author of this work

All rights [...]ed. No part of this publication may be reprodu[...]d, stored in
a retrieva[...] [...]m or transmitted, in any form or by any means [...] [...]ithout the
publisher's prior permission in writing.

This boo[...] [...]dition that it shall not, by [...]ay of trade
or other [...] [...]e, be lent, resold, hired [...] [...] otherwise circulated [...] [...]ithout the
publishe[...]s prior consent in any for[...] of binding or cover othe[...] han that in
which it is [...]ublished and without a [...]milar condition, including [...]is condition,
being imposed on t[...] subsequent purchaser.

Northamptonshire
Libraries & Information
Service
NF

Askews & Holts

ISBN 978-1-84954-150-3

10 9 8 7 6 5 4 3 2 1

A CIP catalogue record for this book is available from the British Library.

Set in Garamond and Placard by Namkwan Cho
Cover design by Namkwan Cho

Printed and bound in Great Britain by
CPI Group (UK) Ltd, Croydon, CR0 4YY

CONTENTS

ACKNOWLEDGEMENTS

I am grateful to so many people who've made this book possible. First of all, I'd like to thank my mentors: Blanquita Cullum, Griff Jenkins and Tony Snow, who taught me so much about not only politics but life. I'd also like to express my gratitude to everyone at Biteback, especially my incredibly patient and helpful editor, Hollie Teague, and the redoubtable James Stephens.

This book emerged from years of conversations with friends and acquaintances who helped me shape my thinking and I must thank all my inadvertent research assistants.

The actual writing would have been impossible without my parents, who spent a lot of time helping me test my ideas and thoughts. Finally, I want to express my appreciation to my long-suffering husband, Dan, whose support and help, both in a material and intellectual sense, made the writing of this book not only pleasurable but feasible. Thank you.

INTRODUCTION

American presidential elections are, without the shadow of a doubt, the greatest shows on earth. They combine the delectable storylines of soap opera with the expert character craft of professional wrestling, topped by healthy garnishes of self-righteousness, piety and morality. These quadrennial affairs have become a Manichean struggle between good and evil, where we root for 'our' candidates to uphold the banner of uprightness against the barbarian horde on the other side. We tell ourselves that the office of the President of the United States is the most powerful position in the world, with truly global implications, and we solemnly aver that we need to take the election seriously and talk about serious issues. But for the twenty-one months in which we actually weigh which candidate might do a better job as President, instead of talking and thinking about these serious issues, most of the time we're snickering about one candidate's weird accent or fretting about another candidate's middle name. We do this because the United States is almost alone on Earth in electing its head of state in a popular vote, even if only indirectly. Most other modern democracies are parliamentary democracies, in which the party itself votes for its leaders, not the voters. An American presidential election is the world's biggest, longest and most expensive popularity contest. And like any popularity contest, the candidates – and their supporters – are more than happy to say or do anything, anything at all, to get you to pull the lever for them.

There's no question that this urge to do anything to get

your vote can result in some pretty funny moments, like when Massachusetts Governor Michael Dukakis, who had a reputation as a bit of an academic lefty, decided he needed to look more martial during the 1988 election and posed for pictures while driving a tank, which effectively killed his candidacy. Or when Bill Clinton betook himself to MTV in 1992 to try to capture the youth vote (a vain attempt, it turned out) and submitted himself to questions like 'Boxers or Briefs?' The answer: 'Usually briefs',[1] giving George H. W. Bush ammunition to deride his opponent as unserious and not really ready for the Oval Office. When you put people under this kind of pressure – with all eyes looking for any gaffe at all hours – ridiculous things are going to happen, some of which will define you for the rest of your political career. Dan Quayle found this out to his cost when he insisted to a New Jersey twelve-year-old that the word 'potato' had an 'e' on the end and found himself defined for ever more as stupid and dim.

This is standard political technique and has been practised in American elections, as well as those around the world, since time immemorial. Presidential campaigns are so long now – at the time of writing, the current crop of candidates have been going at it for a year and they've got nearly another year to go before anyone casts their vote. People literally can't keep the interest up for the entire length of the process; they can't talk about marginal tax rates and farm subsidies and entitlement reform for twenty-one months – we'd all go mad with boredom. So every presidential campaign will be leavened with human interest stories, which might not have a great effect on policy but keep us, the electorate, entertained. Despite news programmes solemnly intoning that they are going to keep us all informed on the issues, what producers are really hoping for is a nice juicy gaffe that will make great video and keep people talking about what happened on their show for months and months. And this kind of gaffe isn't going to happen when you're broadcasting candidates having an in-depth discussion of the inflationary risks of quantitative easing.

But something has irrevocably changed in American politics since the 2008 election. It's not that politics is more contentious than it used to be; American political discourse has always been ugly and hard-fought. It's that the desperation to win power at any cost has made us divide ourselves into enemy camps, riddled with pointless conflicts that make real leadership and actual improvement of the country almost impossible. This hunger to win has made us tear down fellow human beings, destroy reputations, hurl unfounded accusations at each other, and encouraged ordinary, tolerant people to spout forth either wildly bigoted or brashly violent language at each other. What's happening to us?

In the late summer of 2008, we were heading into the home stretch of what seemed like an interminable election. We'd been through the epic Democratic primary battle and the slightly less epic Republican scuffle. George W. Bush was an unpopular president and the lamest of lame ducks; the media, particularly after the Republicans lost Congress in 2006, piled on him with no mercy. It was almost guaranteed that the Democratic nominee for president that year was all but a shoo-in – the Republicans were weak, George W. Bush was widely disliked, Americans were hungry for something different. And without rehashing the mess that was the Democratic primary that year, when Senator Barack Obama emerged as the nominee, it was clear that the Republican nominee would have a pretty tough row to hoe.

On paper, Obama wasn't a terrific nominee for president of the United States. When he started running, he'd spent just over two years as the junior senator from Illinois, and had gained a reputation of being rather petulant and impatient. He had only one signature legislative accomplishment to his name – a resolution supporting democracy in the Congo – though he'd co-sponsored (i.e. put his name on but not written) numerous other Bills. A number of other initiatives that he proposed went nowhere and, when he felt particularly aggrieved about them, he'd write whiny op-eds in the *Washington Post*. But he was young and cute and had given a great speech at the 2004 Democratic convention and many people felt voting for him would heal the wounds caused during the Jim Crow era.

At this point, the political media, the Beltway commentariat and most progressives themselves, would have preferred it if the Republican nominee, Senator John McCain of Arizona, had given up right then and there. Old, cranky Vietnam veteran against adorable Obama with thousand-watt smile and his sweet family? Please. It shouldn't even have been a contest. But McCain, an old Senate hand, wasn't going to give up that easily. His signature political move, which had served him well on more than one occasion, was the Hail Mary pass. In American football, a Hail Mary pass is when the quarterback, under intense pressure, hurls the football as hard as he can at his receivers, hoping against hope that somebody will catch it and convert it into a touchdown. And that's exactly what McCain decided to do for his vice presidential nomination – he was going to do something unexpected and go for it hard, and hope against hope that it would work.

On 28 August 2008, McCain surprised everyone when he announced his running mate. Up until then, the chattering classes had assumed he would pick someone like Senator Joseph Lieberman of Connecticut or Governor Tim Pawlenty of Minnesota; a moderate figure, at any rate, not unlike himself. However, he chose the relatively unknown and recently elected Governor Sarah Palin of Alaska. Governor Palin enjoyed the highest approval ratings of any governor in the country at the time – hovering around 80 per cent (and it had been as high as 90 per cent) – and she had a reputation of not only being a reformer, but a person who'd stood up to and beat the Republican establishment in Alaska. She'd made big strides in clearing out the corruption in her own party and had negotiated with oil companies for better deals for Alaskan citizens. For someone like John McCain, whose political trademark was being a 'maverick', Palin was a good complement; she embodied McCain's vision of what an elected official should be and do. In addition, she was young – younger than then Senator Obama – and a woman, and it was hoped that her addition to the ticket would capture some of the female vote lost when Hillary Clinton failed to gain the nomination, and that her youth would take some of the shine off of Obama's cool. My old boss, the former White House Press Secretary Tony Snow, called her 'the future of the Republican Party'.

Her first speech in Daytona, Ohio, was very well received; *The Times* called the reception 'raucous'. And in the first few days after McCain made the pick, the reaction was overwhelmingly positive. On 30 August 2008, a Zogby poll showed that Palin neutralised the Obama convention 'bounce', the rise in the polls that traditionally happens after each candidate has their convention. McCain raised $7 million in the twenty-four hours after the pick happened. *Time* magazine endorsed the selection of Palin, saying that she would 'help McCain make the case that he was a different kind of Republican'.

So for people who supported Obama, Palin was a threat that needed to be taken out in case her youth and charisma imperilled the Obama candidacy. It was less than three months till the election, and this woman was starting to have a serious negative effect on the Obama-Biden ticket in the polls. The way Obama supporters decided to do it was not by investigating her policy positions; remember, people get bored of politics easily and Palin's policies, which were largely moderate and focused on rooting out corruption, weren't going to set the house on fire. Instead, the public discussion began to turn to Palin's children, her looks and her personal background. CNN's John Roberts wondered whether a mother of a child with Down's syndrome should even run for such a demanding job.[2] Eleanor Clift expressed her concerns about Palin being able to make the transition from governor of a small state and, prior to that, mayor of a small town, to a national political role:

> She's been in the Governor's office since 2006 and before that, her elective experience was in the Wasilla City Council where she then became Mayor. Population five thousand, five-hundred and five. I guess that's where she learned about the budget.[3]

New York Times columnist Maureen Dowd likened the selection to a 'vacuously spunky and generically sassy chick flick', and imagined a President Palin saying to her husband, 'how 'bout I cook you up some caribou hot dogs and moose stew for dinner, babe?'[4]

And then it started getting weirder. I want to apologise for the very coarse language that's to follow, but I want you to understand how violent, sexist and bigoted the political discourse became about Palin, illustrating how the new American politics has evolved. Canadian columnist Heather Mallick called Palin 'white trash' and said she had 'a toned-down version of the porn-star look'.[5] Comedian Margaret Cho said, 'Even though I would never, ever vote for Palin, I'm kind of obsessed with f*cking her … seriously – I wanna eat her Alaskan pussy from behind.'[6] Gary Kamiya, a columnist for *Salon Magazine*, reflected on her 'doability', and called her a 'whip-wielding mistress'.[7] Comedian Bill Maher is still getting laughs on television every night simply by saying 'Sarah Palin is a dumb tw*t'. Sarah Palin's been called 'good masturbation material' by comedian Tracy Morgan; she's been designated a 'c*nt face jazzy wonder girl' by comedian Louis C. K.; a 'bad Disney movie' by actor Matt Damon; a 'cuckoo clock' by television anchor Chris Matthews and 'Sarah bin Palin' by radio host Tom Hartmann. Has there ever been any losing vice presidential nominee that has gotten people so hopped up? Do people publicise their sexual fantasies about Sargent Shriver or compare Jack Kemp to terrorist leaders? (Hint: no.)

When Sarah Palin was picked as John McCain's running mate, there is no doubt that one could ask serious questions about her experience as an elected official and as a state executive. Of course, one could have asked those questions about Barack Obama and John Edwards as well, but strangely no one did. One could also have asked legitimate questions about her policy positions and her approach to governance. But nobody did; they were too busy obsessing about her looks, her kids and having sex with her. You could point out that the language about Obama was equally rough, and in some cases, it was. But nobody publicly explored their rape fantasies about Barack Obama. Nobody cursed him on television night after night. They might not have been the nicest to him on talk radio, but nobody called him the N-word, whereas Palin got called the female equivalent all the time. And most importantly, reasonable criticism of Obama (as opposed to crackpot stuff like the location of his birth certificate) was based in fact – his twenty-year membership in Jeremiah Wright's Church, his lack of executive experience, his enthusiasm for redistributive income systems. Palin didn't get that courtesy.

I'm not so naïve as to think that 2008 was the first time propagandists made stuff up for their own political advantage. One of the reasons that Napoleon has the reputation of being short, despite evidence that suggests he was slightly taller than average men of his day, is because of English propaganda. What's different in this case is its extent. Before August 2008, Sarah Palin was an intelligent, competent governor of Alaska. After August 2008, she became, in the public imagination, a scheming, conniving, evil, stupid, sexually voracious, redneck, anti-feminist, domi-natrix out to destroy America and turn Washington into a Christian Tehran-on-the-Potomac. This is the Palin Effect. The Palin Effect now means that in order to ensure political victory, facts and rational analysis of evidence no longer matter. If you have the levers of the popular imagination, you can make people believe whatever you want, whether or not it's actually true. The smears that emerged about Palin in that election reached epic proportions. No, she never banned Harry Potter books when she was mayor of Wasilla. No, she didn't cut funding for facilities for unwed teen moms. No, she didn't spend taxpayer money on a tanning bed for her governor's office. No, she didn't force the Republican National Committee to spend six figures on designer clothes for her. No, she didn't want creationism taught in Alaska public schools. No, Alaska schools don't teach abstinence-only sex education. No, the baby she gave birth to wasn't actually her daughter's child that she adopted to ameliorate the shame of a teenage pregnancy.

The 2008 election set out the new rules of American politics; you can say and do whatever you want as long as it achieves the ultimate aim of winning. As long as you can get the majority of people to believe it, it's OK – in fact, encouraged. Suddenly, the line between fact and fiction is blurred to the extent that now even people we trust don't really seem to know the truth anymore. To this day, people believe fictions about Sarah Palin. A BBC radio programme I worked on introduced a piece about her in 2010 by saying, 'Sarah Palin believes she can see Russia from her house', and I had to talk to the producer so the introduction could be corrected. The people who produced this programme are intel-ligent, rational people, whom we trust to get good, accurate infor-mation, yet they were able to believe and, scarily, were illing to tell their audience things that were just plain false. The funny thing is that people are now beginning to realise that the Sarah Palin prior to the 2008 election would have actually been a decent candidate for vice president. In 2011, *The Atlantic* published an article called 'The Tragedy Of Sarah Palin', in which the author lamented that she had actually been a good governor of Alaska, and had actually made positive steps towards bipartisan reform and ending crony capitalism in the state, but that something had happened to her in the 2008 election. But something didn't happen to *her* – the person running in 2008 was the same person who'd done a good job in the Juneau state office. *The Atlantic* and everyone else who'd bought the Palin bill of goods were just too busy calling her a blithering idiot and a right-wing fundie maniac to notice. If she'd been given a chance, she could have contested the election on her own merits. But thanks to the Palin Effect, she wasn't able to get that chance.

Every political candidate deserves to be judged by the American public on their policies and beliefs, not on innuendo, rumour and speculation on their private life. Many people believed invented stories about Palin because doing so made them feel good, because doing so made them self-satisfied, not because the inventions were true or based in fact at all. The Palin Effect has created a situation in which people believe in false dreams and idols because of point-less political divisions; instead of using our critical thinking and rational investigation skills, we retreat back into tribal cultures, only poking a head above the parapet to insult the enemy.

Palin is the illustrative case of this effect, in which normally rational people, who used to call themselves the 'reality-based community', hold certain beliefs because they feel good, not because they're actually based on fact. Now that the Palin Effect exists, as long as any particular candidate or advocacy group can get the smear right, it doesn't matter to large swathes of the population whether or not it's actually based on reality or on psychological manipulation. The same people who were angry at George W. Bush for whipping up fervour for the war on Iraq based on things that weren't true are the same people happily spreading rumours about Sarah Palin, Michele Bachmann, Mitt Romney, Newt Gingrich, and anyone else they perceive as a political threat.

In 2009 I was at a training session with a number of BBC journalists, when the conversation turned to the 2008 election and all of them began lamenting what a racist campaign John McCain had run. 'Really?' I inquired. 'What did he say that was so racist?' They ummed and ahhed and finally one of them said, 'Well, he used Obama's middle name all the time.' I corrected, 'Actually, McCain never used Obama's middle name at all, and kicked out a guy from a rally who did.' But they were all certain he had done so. How can intelligent professionals, whose business is broadcasting facts, believe stories that have no more truth than the Easter Bunny?

We have to ask why people who normally put stock in evidence-based reasoning, who believe in the scientific method, who believe that assertions must be backed by facts, so fervently believe utter and complete rubbish. It's not because they're stupid or because they're evil or like to go around smearing innocent people. Most folks who are passionate about politics believe that they're doing the right thing for their country, and would disagree with the notion that they're maliciously spreading rumours and gossip. The idea that progressives or conservatives are simply evil and therefore enjoy hurting the country and sabotaging its leaders is an unsatisfactory one. The answer is simpler. We believe all kinds of silly, false, less-than-factual things about political candidates because there are a lot of people who make a lot of money telling us this rubbish. There are many vested interests that have a financial stake in making sure we think the other party is scary, stupid, venal and not to be trusted with the reins of power. All of our beliefs are being manipulated by the absolute best communication strategies money can buy. We are under bombardment during a presidential campaign, for nearly two years, by the most sophisticated advertising techniques known to man, which skillfully stoke every anxiety we have to make sure that we not only vote, but donate to make sure that the advertising can continue. Remember, presidential elections are popularity contests, and each candidate will stop at nothing to get you to pull the lever for them. They will do whatever it takes, play on any fear you have, butter you up on any vanity you've got, to make sure you don't even consider voting for the other guy.

Another feature of American democracy is the amount of money it takes to run it. Because American elections are decided by majority vote, the campaigns need to reach the population either via door-to-door or phone campaigning, which is expensive, or through the media, which is even more expensive, to get us to vote their way. So these messages aren't just there to get us to vote, they're also designed to get us to donate. The constant bombardment of political advertisements – to make us anxious, to make us scared, to flatter us, to play to our anxieties, to pamper our vanity – is all designed to get us to donate. Voting is nice, but if we can be convinced to reach into our pocket and give $20 or $25 or, preferably, the yearly maximum of $30,800 to a national political party, then we've really proved our worth in the democratic process. So the campaigns, the parties, and the advocacy groups make sure the air is thick with all kinds of sophisticated messages calibrated perfectly to appeal to us to make sure that we are primed and ready to give because we're so afraid of our political enemies. It doesn't matter whether Michele Bachmann is crazy or not; there are lots of groups making sure you think she is and waiting for your call to donate to make sure that she stays out of the Oval Office. It's the same thing with media organisations – they know that it's a fight for advertising dollars, even with the bonanza that comes their way every four years, so they will tell you the most exciting yarns possible in the hope that your eyeballs will be fixed to the screen during advertisements and so they can shift papers off the shelf.

We'll be investigating the kinds of manipulations used to make sure we vote the right way and donate to the right organisations. Everything from our worries about status and class anxiety to our fears about sex and ageing, to our vanity about our intelligence to our money worries, are all fair game to make sure that we believe what we need to believe to open up our wallets. We'll find out how these kinds of manipulation work and why organisations pick these particular passion points to get us to behave the way we want us to.

I don't want you to think that this is a book with heroes and villains. I don't blame the media for wanting to tell an exciting story – content production is a business, after all, and most people don't have the appetite for serious political debate. They want fun, fluff and scandal; and since the media industry is in the business of selling eyes, ears or papers, they have to do what they have to do. But you shouldn't think that Jon Stewart is doing anything noble or civic-minded when he plays video of Republicans saying silly things, gurning all the while to the delight of his youthful audience. He's playing to his audience's anxieties to gain ratings and to enhance the bottom line of the corporation that owns his show. He will do anything to get your eyeballs to look at advertisements, so his show makes money, just like the Obama campaign will do and say anything to make sure American dollars contribute to the $1 billion total.

Brits, who can't directly participate in American elections, but are still interested in the process of electing the leader of the free world, will get exposed to these sophisticated advertising techniques that get Americans to donate money for political causes. If there's a juicy story about Michele Bachmann making a gaffe on the campaign trail or a lady making lurid claims about something Herman Cain did to her in a car over a decade ago, it's going to make it into the American press, and, thanks to the global reach of both the internet and social media platforms, it's going to go worldwide. More Brits probably saw Rick Perry forget the third branch of government he'd cut than knew what David Cameron was saying about the Euro crisis, because it's better television. And certainly no one covered presidential candidate Newt Gingrich's thoughts about the inflationary policies of the Federal Reserve when they could talk about the rumour that Perry is so dumb he can't remember his own policy positions. Obama's campaign wants Americans to think about Perry being dumb. The Democratic Party wants Americans to think about Perry being dumb. The Center for American Progress, a progressive 501(c)(3), wants you to think about Perry being dumb. Therefore, *The Guardian* and the *Telegraph* want Brits to think Perry is dumb, because if they've got the video of Perry making his gaffe, by making sure the video's disseminated on their website, it gets eyeballs to guardian.co.uk, appealing to advertisers. It doesn't matter whether or not Perry forgetting something on stage actually means he's dumb or not; it's a hilarious video, and brings in web traffic. Cha-ching!

So let's go into this 2012 election with our eyes open. Now is no time to be naïve. I'm going to tell you about some of the tricks that will be used on you to make sure that you think and behave in certain ways. Perhaps a more sophisticated understanding of how we're being manipulated could help create the impetus for real change to get us out of the rut America is stuck in. We'll all improve American civic life by understanding why so many of us are willing to accept rumours and smears as fact.

1

AMERICAN CLASS

Many people are beginning to acknowledge that Americans feel a powerful prejudice against those they perceive to be of a different class. This class prejudice informs a lot of our popular culture, particularly television; classic American TV shows like *Hee Haw*, *Green Acres* and *Mama's Family* poke fun at redneck life, but a show like the *Fresh Prince of Bel-Air* makes fun of upper-class manners and mores. Mark Twain's *Adventures of Huckleberry Finn* is stuffed with class anxiety, and Twain's feelings about it become quite clear when poor, orphaned, lower-class Huck is the only person to treat Jim with respect and affection.

In politics, however, because the field tends to be populated with class elites, you don't get a lot of humour going from lower class to upper class. In fact, it's just the opposite. There's no way to say this delicately, so let's just come straight out with it – it is not uncommon for rich people, who live in fashionable coastal neighbourhoods in the affluent, coastal states to think that they're smarter, cleaner, more civilised and just all-around better than poorer people who live in the South or Midwest. Upper-class and upper-middle-class Americans are deeply prejudiced against people who they believe bear the signs of a lower class: religious belief, large families, attendance of public schools, an insistence on living in unfashionable red states. You often hear these kinds of insults from television commentators; former CBS anchor Katie Couric described people who live in the American Midwest as the 'great unwashed'.[8] Writer David Carr said of the inhabitants of flyover country (so called by coastal residents because you fly over it while going to the other coast): 'Kansas, Missouri, no big deal. You know, that's the dance of the low-sloping foreheads. The middle places.'[9] Journalism professor and progressive media watchdog Eric Alterman called people who disagree with him 'f*cking NASCAR retards'.[10] There is a simple description for this kind of behaviour: old-fashioned bigotry. We don't often recognise this as class bigotry because we're not as good at recognising class prejudice as we are at recognising racial or sexual bigotry – but that's what it is. And what this bigotry is doing is turning political dialogue into an endless round of insults and gotcha moments, with facts and reason taking a back seat to self-righteousness and goofy hysteria.

The conventional wisdom is that prejudice comes from fear or anxiety. This was well expressed in then Senator Barack Obama's famous observation during a fundraiser that people who are concerned about their economic position and their financial future 'cling to guns or religion or antipathy to people who aren't like them or anti-immigrant sentiment'.[11] The middle and upper-middle classes' prejudice against the working classes, the rural, the religious and the Midwestern is fear and anxiety translated into anger and bigotry against people from their own country, who can be caricatured in a seemingly familiar way. The British philosopher Roger Scruton coined a phrase to describe this fear of one's own home or self: 'oikophobia'. It's the exact opposite of xenophobia, the fear of the unfamiliar; oikophobia is the fear of the familiar.[12]

The British term 'oik' doesn't have the same resonance of low-class, white-trash undesirability in the USA, but once we get past that transatlantic linguistic problem, you see it every day. Americans, particularly those who live on the coasts, who are in the professions, who consider themselves of a particular class and status, have no problem with insulting the beliefs, intelligence and preferences of those they consider lower class. Upper- and upper-middle-class people have a phobia of rednecks.

This visceral disgust and dislike, which masks deep-seated fear and worry, is what we mean when we say class anxiety. The bourgeoisie, who at the moment are controlling the levers of power in the United States, have two deep fears: 'exploitation from above, and overthrow from below.'[13] They don't much like the idea that a super-rich cabal of bankers are earning more than the rest of the country (though they do like the political donations to the Democratic Party the financial industry provides), but what they like even less is the notion that some upstart redneck hillbillies from someplace awful like South Carolina or Minnesota or even Alaska, with funny accents and public university degrees, could wrest the levers of power from their clearly more deserving hands. American politics has become a Marxist class struggle, where the bourgeoisie are so desperate to preserve the power they have from a proletarian revolution, they're clinging tooth and nail to everything they have. Marx writes:

> The modern bourgeois society that has sprouted from the ruins of feudal society has not done away with class antagonisms. It has but established new classes, new conditions of oppression, new forms of struggle in place of the old ones.[14]

The middle class in America, the modern bourgeoisie, are deeply suspicious of anyone who tries to move up the class ladder, invading what seems to be their rightful place. While the coastal American bourgeoisie parrot sympathetic refrains on class mobility, the fact remains that a lot of public discourse – and particularly political discourse – sounds like class warfare against the working class, particularly when it comes to people like Governor Palin, who represented the strongest threat to the middle-class elite that they'd faced in a while.

For example, former *Newsweek* writer Jon Meacham wrote,

'Do we want leaders who *are* everyday folks, or do we want leaders who *understand* everyday folks? … Do I think I am right in saying that Palin's populist view of high office … is dangerous? You betcha.'[15] The implication is clear – somebody like Sarah Palin, who is herself 'everyday folks', just isn't good enough to be president of the United States. Another example occurred when numerous bloggers and columnists gleefully quoted and analysed an anonymous John McCain staffer's characterisation of Palin and her family as 'Wasilla hillbillies from coast to coast'; *Daily Telegraph* blogger Iain Martin sniggered, '"Sarah Palin and Wasilla hillbillies" has a great ring; it sounds like a struggling country combo which plays numbers by Hank Williams and Bob Wills at a roadside bar outside Nashville.'[16] But it's not just Palin, and it continues to this day. Progressive blog Salon.com wrote an article called 'Rick Perry's Redneck Guide to Fixin' the Gov'mint',[17] featuring a picture of the Texas Governor shooting a gun in the air. Syndicated columnist Kathleen Parker, who parlayed her anxiety over electing someone as proletarian and uncouth as Sarah Palin into a brief television career for CNN (her show was cancelled for lack of ratings), said that Newt Gingrich's rise in the polls in late 2011 was due to 'an affirmation of the Republican base's preference for a good ol' boy from the South rather than an exotic from a vacation reef out in the middle of the ocean'.[18] Gingrich's surge couldn't be because a large number of Americans like his policies, according to bourgeois warrior Parker; it had to be because Gingrich is from the South and therefore familiar, whereas Obama is exotic and strange.

British journalists and television producers also enjoy getting in on the fun of insulting the American working class; they love to feature redneck freak shows for the delectation of their middle-class audiences. A particularly egregious example was *Jamie Oliver's American Road Trip*; when he wasn't mangling American history and patronising cowboys, he was busily finding the absolute poorest, most disadvantaged, vulnerable, and down-and-out people he could and goading them into saying racist things about President Obama. The television programme achieved its goal; no matter how bad things got for Oliver's viewers, they could still feel class superiority over an unemployed construction worker living in a trailer park, crying that he was unable to feed his family while trying desperately to warm himself at a fire in a discarded trash can.

But it's not just Democrats, progressives, and bien pensant Brits who are happy to exploit class anxiety for their own ends. *Wall Street Journal* editorial writer James Taranto lambasts former Democratic presidential candidate John Kerry by calling him 'the haughty, French-looking Massachusetts Democrat', again emphasising just how foreign and freaky the senator is to Taranto's audience. Note that writers like Meacham and Taranto don't discuss anything of substance about what the two politicians say or believe – it's their own class biases that colour their perceptions of Palin and Kerry. It doesn't take thought or intellectual heft to promote these kinds of stereotypes – but audiences find them comforting. It lets the columnist tell his readers: *It's OK. I'm one of you.* Since columnists make their money by getting people to read the paper in which they appear, it's in their interest to appeal to as devoted an audience as they can. As one writer put it, 'Newspapers are businesses like any other. And the function of a business is to give its customers what they want. And in many cases, what the customers want is not the "truth" but the comfort that they are right.'[19]

And that's where the Palin Effect begins to kick in. Because people don't really want truth that disturbs their already held beliefs, but instead to have the comfort that they're right, there's a cultural imperative to use class prejudice, our most deeply held and unverbalised prejudice, to create the impression that there's an impassable gulf between conservatives and progressives, that the other side is a redoubt of the most nefarious and despicable characters you can imagine. You may think that's overstating the case, but compare these two quotes and note the sense that the other side is impossibly evil, foreign and alien. For the progressives/liberals, here's former actress and radio personality Janeane Garofalo:

> The reason a person is a conservative republican is because something is wrong with them. Again, that's science – that's neuroscience. You cannot be well adjusted, open-minded, pluralistic, enlightened and be a Republican. It's counter-intuitive. And they revel in their anti-intellectualism. They revel in their cruelty … first you have to be an a**hole and then comes the conservatism. You gotta be a d*** to cleave onto their ideology.[20]

And on the other hand, here's the writer behind conservative blog 'The Daily Retard':

> I think what the REAL problem with these fucktards is that they are so totally insulated from any semblance of what normal Americans call reality they honestly have NO CLUE what they are doing to us. Look for a minute at the strongholds of so-called liberals in our society – the Hollywood elite, tenured college professors (and the education system in general), organised labor union leaders and the mainstream media … NO ONE in ANY of those groups has EVER had an actual job, any idea how to actually work for a living, no idea how to create anything, no experience whatsoever in the real world. And THESE are the people that are 'advising' the dumbass liberals who currently hold an overwhelming and likely unconstitutional majority in Washington. How the fuck can you blame them for their stupidity?? I mean, if dumbass liberals had any common sense, they wouldn't BE liberal.[21]

In these two quotes, you can read anger, suspicion, self-right-eousness and, above all, an overwhelming belief that not only are their beliefs better than the other side, but that the other side is so malevolent, so alien, so unalterably different, that they couldn't possibly find anything redeeming about the opposition in a million years. This is called 'football team' politics; just as Millwall fans think West Ham is the devil incarnate (and vice versa), and Washington Redskins supporters think Dallas Cowboys fans employ Satan himself for wake-up calls on Sundays, liberals and conservatives are convinced the other side is evil, unconvincible and unchangeable. It doesn't matter what my side does; my side is awesome and I never have to hold them accountable. It's just you lot over there who are so terrible and malicious; it's you who I have to oppose. One of the most disappointing things about the Obama administration is his supporters; policies that bothered them deeply when Bush was president are now hunky-dory since their man started working in the Oval Office, like the Patriot Act, extraordinary renditions and warrantless wiretapping. All these were worth denouncing at every opportunity when a Republican was President, but now that there's a Democrat in office, they're fine. Since Obama is 'one of us', for reasons that upper-middle-class progressives instinctively hold, it's somehow all right that policies that were utterly wicked from 2003 to 2008 became OK on 20 January 2009.

But why do the upper and middle classes feel such bigotry towards the working class? London-based writer Owen Jones explores middle-class intolerance against the people who have the bad taste to be poor and unfashionable in his book *Chavs*, again using a middle-class term of abuse towards the working class. The British are finally beginning to engage with the idea that perhaps it's just as distasteful to make fun of somebody for the fact that they're poor or from a naff part of town as it is to make fun of someone because of the colour of their skin or who they love. Certainly they have their own vocabulary of abuse for the working-class poor: oik, yob, yobbo, chav, pikey, hoodie, plus regional variations. All we've got in American English is redneck, hillbilly and trailer trash, although former Florida congressman Alan Grayson did rather creatively call Sarah Palin 'an Alaska chillbilly'.[22]

Jones begins his book provocatively, indicting his right-thinking, politically fashionable friends for their ignorance of this issue:

> I [was] at a friend's dinner in a gentrified part of East London one winter evening. The blackcurrant cheesecake was being carefully sliced and the conversation had drifted to the topic of the credit crunch. Suddenly, one of the hosts decided to raise the mood by throwing in a light-hearted joke. 'It's sad that Woolworths is closing, where will the chavs buy their Christmas presents?' Now, he was not someone who would ever consider himself to be a bigot. Neither would anyone else present: for, after all, they were all educated and open-minded professionals. All would have placed themselves left-of-centre politically… If a stranger had attended that evening and had disgraced him or herself by bandying around a word like 'Paki' or 'poof', they would have found themselves swiftly ejected from the flat. But no one flinched at a joke about chavs shopping at Woolies.[23]

This is a watershed moment in class analysis; finally, maybe we'll get to the heart of the reasons why the inhabitants of the salons of Islington are so ignorant of and unfair to the working poor! But, sadly, Jones chickened out; when it comes to the causes behind this particular form of middle-class prejudice, he predictably, and implausibly, connects it to things his right-thinking friends would find properly icky: Margaret Thatcher, the Conservative

Party and the *Daily Mail*. Clearly, blaming class bigotry on any of these factors is not going to be an adequate explanation. These nice, left-leaning professional people will always vote Labour or die, darling, and they certainly aren't reading the *Daily Mail*. Since they hate Margaret Thatcher with the heat of a thousand suns, and have done ever since they listened to latter-day punk bands at dingy clubs in the mid-1980s, it's unlikely they learnt their bigotry at her proverbial knee. In short, those explanations don't work. In the same vein, columnist Polly Toynbee in *The Guardian* sharply criticised a Liberal Democrat peer, Baroness Hussein-Ece, for using the word 'chav', but Toynbee also blames the Tory Party as well as income inequality for the Baroness' insensitive comment. Which, again, is an unsatisfying explanation; if progressive, Labour- (or Lib Dem-) voting, *Guardian*-reading people are opposed to the Conservative Party, wouldn't they reject any kind of prejudice and bigotry that issued forth from Tory belief? How can Liberal Democrats somehow be influenced by Conservatives to become bigots? It doesn't make sense.

No, it's Karl Marx and Friedrich Engels who have a better explanation of why nice middle-class people in leafy, fashionable neighbourhoods fear and abuse the working poor. In the *Communist Manifesto*, they envision the proletariat revolution as the inevitable product of class struggle, but in order for that revolution to happen, they note:

> The first step in the revolution by the working class is to raise the proletariat to the position of ruling class, to win the battle of democracy. The proletariat will use its political supremacy to wrest, by degrees, all capital from the bourgeoisie, to centralise all instruments of production in the hands of the State, i.e. of the proletariat organised as the ruling class; and to increase the total of productive forces as rapidly as possible.[24]

Now we can see why someone like Sarah Palin or Michele Bachmann or Rick Perry, who Marx would classify as coming from the proletariat, is so threatening to the political establishment – if they, or someone like them, were to wrest political power away from the nice, middle-class, professional, privately educated political elite, it would be the first step towards a true political revolution. A Palin-led revolution wouldn't be a Communist revolution as Marx predicted, but, nonetheless, it would in fact be a political victory for the working class, which would lead to a loss of power for the bourgeois elite.[25] It's classic Marxist dogma that if there were an actual revolution from the proletariat, the bourgeoisie would robustly defend their power structures before giving them up to the proletariat: 'before going under, they defend themselves to the death like savage, wounded beasts, until the up-and-coming system administers the coup-de-grace.'[26] No one ever asks the losers of a revolution how they feel about their defeat, but I think it's fair to say that being on the losing end of a power struggle isn't much fun. The bourgeoisie does not want to give up its power to the proles. That's why Palin, and people like her, are so deeply disturbing on a visceral level to the American elite; in Marxist terms, she threatens their stranglehold on political and economic power, and they don't like it one bit.

Republicans like Sarah Palin, Michele Bachmann, Rick Perry and Newt Gingrich are considered members of the proletariat, while someone like Katie Couric is part of the bourgeoisie. Life has moved on a bit since 1848, so the designations Marx gave economic classes aren't quite what they used to be (after all, there were no television anchors in the nineteenth century). And there's a paucity of good class analysis anyway in American political and historical thought, because of its mythology about equality and the irrelevance of socio-economic class. It sounds impossibly quaint to talk about national mythologies, but every country in the world likes to believe in and tell stories about itself. The cornerstone of the American mythology is that it is the land of the American Dream, where anybody can strike it rich and become famous and successful. You could be an immigrant fresh off the boat one day and twenty years later you could be richer than Croesus – it's the American way. This story has been an important part of the American mythology for over two centuries. Even before there was a United States of America, people came to its shores for economic opportunity and the chance for a better life for themselves and their families.

Because this myth was such an important part of American culture, it used to be thought that America was a classless society. Why obsess about class if your economic status could be defined by you, not the circumstances of your birth? All have an equal opportunity to succeed. The famous chronicler of the early American political system, Alexis de Tocqueville, noted in 1831 that while Americans appreciated freedom, what they really valued was equality:

> I think that democratic communities have a natural taste for freedom: left to themselves, they will seek it, cherish it, and view any privation of it with regret. But for equality, their passion is ardent, insatiable, incessant, invincible… They will endure poverty, servitude, barbarism – but they will not endure aristocracy.[27]

The concept is that we should all have equality of opportunity. Success, fame and fortune should be available to everyone, not just a few aristocratic toffs to the manor born. As the Declaration of Independence says, we are all entitled to certain inalienable rights and to deny anyone those rights because of the circumstances of their birth is not only un-American, but inhuman. The idea of equality, at least of a certain type, was coded into the early American DNA and, as de Tocqueville observed, Americans cherished it.

It sounds terrific, but the reality is, it's just not true. Americans have always had and always will have a complicated socio-economic class system. Not only are there the tragedies of slavery and the treatment of American Indians; in addition, the extraordinary size and variety of the American economy inevitably led to haves and have nots. From landed plantation owners to hard-bitten corn farmers, from New England burghers to frontiersmen in the Northwest Territories, there have always been socio-economic class markers that have put an indelible stamp on American society. We just don't like to admit it very much. Leonard Reismann, author of the 1959 book *Class in American Life*, noted drily:

> 'We don't have classes in our town' almost invariably is the first remark recorded by the investigator. Once that has been uttered and got out of the way, the class divisions in the town can be recorded with what seems to be an amazing degree of agreement among the good citizens of the community.[28]

One of the hallmarks of the American Dream is being able to give your children a future that will ensure that they are better off than you are. This deeply beloved narrative can be found in books, movies and political campaigns. You can be whoever you want to be – literally anyone can grow up to be president of the United States. It's part of the story Americans like to tell themselves. But we all know in our hearts that we live in a class structure, with markers and emblems that are as recognisable to us as they are inscrutable to outsiders. It's about the town you live in. The clothes you wear. The hairstyle you adopt. The way you speak. The school your kids go to. The kind of furniture you have in your house. The hobbies you have. The food you eat. This isn't any different from any other country – certainly not Britain – but there are few nations that felt quite as certain that the class system didn't matter as the USA. This isn't as true as it used to be; in the last twenty years, as we've been thinking further about economic inequality and worrying about what that means for class mobility, Americans have become less touchy about the fact there are classes in American society – they acknowledge it, and the raft of eulogies for the American Dream shows that Americans want to believe in the idea that anyone can become successful, but no longer believe it possible.

Here's a brief class taxonomy. Upper-class people in America live in places like Manhattan, NY or Malibu, CA or Middleburg, VA or Greenwich, CT. They are generally incredibly rich, but the money could be inherited as well as earned – and in fact if it was earned, it has the slight whiff of vulgarity about it. Place is an extremely important marker in American class strata – it's not only where you live that says something about you, but also where you spend your leisure time and what you do in it. If you play mini-golf in Myrtle Beach, South Carolina on your summer holiday, you are of a very different class than if you sail around St. Simon's Island, Georgia. It's expected that the upper class goes to Harvard or Yale or Dartmouth, and their children will have every intention of crossing their autumn leaf-strewn quadrangles as well. If you went to any university outside the Ivy League, and maybe Stanford or Duke, you are effectively barred from the upper class and mostly locked out of the upper-middle class. If you went to a state-funded school, forget it – you are hopelessly hick. You can find this kind of elite in the South or in certain areas of Chicagoland, but there's just a certain kind of cachet about the coasts that the Midwest and the South simply don't have. Writer and professor Paul Fussell believes that high-class status is inversely associated with convenient access to bowling, and notes that the most bowling friendly areas are 'regrettable places'. He also notes that if your locale is a site associated with religious fundamentalism, like Greenville, SC or Lynchburg, VA, then it's out for the upper crust; he says 'no high-class person can live in any place associated with religious prophecy or miracle'.[29]

Below is the upper-middle class, where you have your professionals – doctors, lawyers, consultants, politicos, college professors, media heavyweights and software entrepreneurs, among others. There's an ambiguity about whether those in the financial sector belong here or in the upper class; they make the same kind of money as people in the upper class, but they do still receive a pay cheque from an employer, which is slightly not done in the absolute upper echelon. These folks live in places like San Francisco, CA or Brooklyn, NY or Arlington, VA or Bethesda, MD; lovely places that are convenient for daily commutes and have lots of amenities designed to make life easier for busy working people. People here shop at Pottery Barn and Crate and Barrel for their furniture; they do their grocery shopping at Whole Foods and Trader Joe's; they worry about organic food for their kids, and are fond of telling other people how to have a healthy diet and achieve optimum nutrition; they read the *New York Times* and *New York Magazine* if they feel literary and aspirational. Upper-middle-class white people in their teens and early twenties are anxious to have the right opinions and the right consumer goods that display the stories about themselves they want to believe. They love Europe and claim to have a favourite 'football' team (by which they mean soccer, and it's invariably Arsenal). They usually studied abroad for a semester, some place like Spain or Italy, and claim it changed their lives forever and made them feel like citizens of the world. These are the people who nod sagely when Europeans lament that most Americans don't have a passport, secretly feeling glad their parents have the money to pay for expensive international plane tickets and live near a convenient international airport.

Below that you've got the middle class, which contains middle management, professions like accountancy, nursing, teaching, software development, public sector workers and, importantly, entrepreneurs. For whatever reason, entrepreneurs in fields like haulage and landscaping, even if they're quite wealthy and especially if they don't live in the best parts of the east coast, aren't considered part of the upper-middle class. Nobody is going to get to be part of the upper-middle, even if they make millions of dollars, from a landscaping or haulage business. These entrepreneurs might be wealthier than a lawyer, but their class standing is lower. People in the middle class can live in smaller, older houses, often in the older parts of the suburban ring. When politicians talk about the middle class struggling, this is who they mean – people pulling down a pay cheque that's not quite large enough to insulate them against outside economic pressures.

Then you have a group of people who in Britain are called the working class and in America are called the working poor, although they might not like to classify themselves this way. They work as waitresses in diners and cheap restaurants in small towns, at the checkout in supermarkets and convenience stores, as care assistants in hospitals or nursing homes, or are workers in construction, plumbers or electricians. They might be farmers. Their economic situation is precarious; small economic pressures like a hospital stay or a car breakdown could wipe them out. They have very little political power and voice. It was interesting to see, in the Wisconsin recall elections of 2011, a Republican candidate, Kim Simac, make one of her selling points the fact that she was poor. Her husband was a farmer, she stayed home and home-schooled her kids, and her campaign was built around the fact that she had a right to political office just like anybody else (she lost).

It would be very easy to define class status through profession and salary. But it's not that simple. Class status is defined by a loose matrix of what class you come from, where you are on the career ladder, where you live, the taste you display, the friends you have, and more. Consider two hypothetical Americans, Olivia Miller and Troy Maupin. Olivia is twenty-five, rents a two-bedroom apartment on the Upper East Side of Manhattan with three girls she went to Sarah Lawrence with, works as a gallery assistant making $25,000 a year, is a vegetarian (and only eats organic vegetables), and is from Greenwich, Connecticut. She does yoga and loves spending time with her friends in the local wine bar. Her father is a lawyer and her mother is a homemaker. Troy's got a mortgage in White Hall, Virginia, on a small ranch house built in the 1960s. He's twenty-five, has a wife, two kids, a pick-up truck, and a big shaggy dog, a mutt he got as a puppy from his neighbour. Troy got a vocational degree from the local community college and owns his own HVAC business, pulling down $60,000 a year. His dad's a farmer, and his mum works as a secretary in the local school. He loves hunting and fishing, and takes the family to church every Sunday. Olivia considers herself upper-middle class, Troy considers himself working/middle class. By any material standard, Troy is better off than Olivia. He owns a home and makes more money than Olivia does, but she lives in a more high-class location and has higher class hobbies and interests. Her family has higher class status. In terms of achieving the goals of middle-class life, Troy is better off. But Olivia thinks she's the one who's more successful. If Olivia were to meet Troy, she would consider him a dumb redneck, and he would consider her a city snob. They'd be like foreigners to each other.

Again, geography is incredibly important to the class strata, which is linked to the history of settlement in the United States. Farming communities will always have less cachet than port communities, and the coasts are higher up the class ladder than the middle. Desirable locales include New York, San Francisco,

Washington, DC, the New York suburbs of Connecticut and Martha's Vineyard. Other places are undesirable, like Detroit, Topeka, Cheyenne and, certainly, Wasilla, Alaska (dear me!). The elite American accent is as neutral as possible, although exceptions can be made for a patrician regional accent that sounds nice on NPR, like the honey-sweet drawl of Roy Blount, Jnr. Sarah Palin's strong regional accent grates on the ears of American cultural elites like the scrape of an expensive sailing boat on the dock. Elites live in apartments in New York and characterful homes, preferably old ones, in the suburbs; their houses have Mexican tiles in the kitchen and hardwood floors in the living areas. Inhabitants of flyover country carpet their ranch houses. One thing I've never intellectually understood is why a tiny, roach-filled apartment in an inner city has more class status than a spacious double-wide trailer in the countryside, but it does.

According to ABC News, 64 per cent of Americans identify themselves as either middle class or upper-middle class, and define the middle class as owning a home, feeling financially secure, being able to save for retirement and being able to take an annual vacation. Most definitions of middle class include working at some kind of professional office job and having a college degree – hence the classic American nomenclature of either having a 'white-collar' job, indicating you wear a shirt and tie to the office, or a 'blue-collar job', indicating you wear a uniform. But then things get a bit more complicated, as George Orwell pointed out:

> Economically, no doubt, there are only two classes, the rich and the poor, but socially there is a whole hierarchy of classes, and the manners and traditions learned by each class in childhood are not only very different but – this is the essential point – generally persist from birth to death… It is in fact very difficult to escape, culturally, from the class into which you have been born.[30]

This is why Olivia considers herself upper-middle class and why Troy thinks of himself as working class. Certain manners, mores and behaviours are observed particularly by each class, get passed on from parent to child, teacher to student, peer group to peer group. Class mobility really depends on being able to observe those behaviours correctly. If you can't, or won't, it can lead to hostility. So, for example, Olivia could engage in a little class tourism by renting a pick-up truck and driving all over Manhattan for a day, and she might think of herself as rebellious and ironic for doing so. But if she moved to Virginia to start a construction business, everyone would treat her like an ignorant city slicker, and she wouldn't have anything in common with her business colleagues. Similarly, Troy could move to New York, but he'd probably be considered an ignorant country bumpkin, and he would probably find his business colleagues banal and unduly focused on trying to find the best apartment and the hottest restaurants. This is why Democrats often fail miserably when they try to 'get in touch with the heartland', and why Republicans are so scornful of 'Beltway cocktail parties'; faking class is incredibly difficult.

The American population is now increasingly segregated by class, and so its politics are also becoming divided by class. This is why it's becoming harder and harder for the two parties to find any kind of common ground – they're both full of people who don't really know or understand each other. The party and class lines aren't falling in expected ways at all. The Democrats are now the party of rich people – bankers, professionals, public sector employees, as well as a coalition of special interest voters like African-Americans, women and LGBT people. The Republicans are the party of small business owners, middle management and white people without a college education.

The stereotype is that the Republicans were the party of the rich. Not anymore. These days, the more educated and affluent vote for – and financially support – Democrats. During the 2008 election, Barack Obama received more campaign donations from employees of hedge funds and investment banks than any other sector.[31] In 2007, Nielsen marketing did a study of political donations to primary candidates in each party. It discovered that in the top ten most affluent segments of the population, 64 per cent of donations went to Democrats and 36 per cent went to Republicans. Democrats were donated to by 69.9 per cent of urban voters in 2008, as opposed to 30.1 per cent given to Republicans.[32] In 2011, *USA Today* revealed that the five states that had the highest average income per person were all blue states in the 2008 election.[33] Further crunching the *USA Today* study numbers, the *American Spectator* noted: 'the highest per capita income states had an 80 per cent Democratic Senate ratio and 75 per cent Democratic House ratio; while the states with the lowest per capita income had a 70 per cent Republican Senate ratio and a 75 per cent Republican House ratio.'[34] The evidence is clear; the economic and cultural elites are Democrats. Voting Democratic is a culturally elite thing to do. The party of the common people, the proletariat, if you will, are the Republicans.

This plays out politically in all kinds of ways. Progressives in America, who tend to vote Democrat, like to think of themselves as concerned for the poor, oppressed or disadvantaged in whatever way. In fact, they often express their concern over why less knowledgeable people than themselves insist on voting Republican when that will only further their oppression. They see flyover country inhabitants as baby birds that need Democratic politicians to help them, but to no avail. This kind of thinking emerged after the 2004 elections, when authors came out with handwringing tomes like *What's the Matter With Kansas: How Conservatives Won the Heart of America*, which aimed to try and understand why people insisted on voting for Republicans even though the Democrats would have been so much better. In 2005, Democratic House Minority Leader Nancy Pelosi, concerned that Democrats were losing the interest of the religiously observant, conducted workshops for Democratic Congressional representatives to reach Americans of faith, as *The New Republic* described: 'Attendees saw presentations on getting out the "God vote" – reaching voters motivated by their religious affiliation – and met with mega-church pastors as well as leaders from the religious left. The aim was simple: to formulate a sincere expression of progressive faith.'[35] I remember some Democrats tried their new knowledge out on talk radio, and it just didn't come across as genuine; Democratic Congressmen sounded like kids who'd just learned some Bible verses at Sunday School.

The notion that the middle of the country was filled with alien beings who needed to be 'related to' reached a low-water point in the 2004 election. There's always good fun to be had when patrician Democrats try vainly to connect with heartland voters by doing redneck things city folk suppose rural bumpkins like, such as hunting and fishing. John Kerry wasn't the first Democrat who hamfistedly tried to pretend he was a common man who shared concerns with rural people, but he was one of the most hilarious. The junior senator from Massachusetts (after posing for bird-hunting photo ops in full camouflage) claimed that to hunt deer, he loved to 'go out with my trusty 12-gauge double-barrel, crawl around on my stomach... That's hunting.' Columnist Mark Steyn wrote, 'This caused huge hilarity among my New Hampshire neighbours, none of whom knew anybody who goes deer hunting by crawling around on his stomach, even in Massachusetts. The trick is to blend in with the woods … crawling around on your stomach is a lousy way to hunt deer.'[36] Also, anyone who knows anything about guns (and clearly Kerry and his political team didn't) knows you shoot deer with a rifle, not a shotgun – shotguns are for birds, not large mammals. Kerry also averred that he loved ploughing fields as a kid:

> When I was twelve years old, my passion was being allowed to go out and sit on the John Deere and drive it around the fields and plough. And I learned as a kid what it was like looking back and see those furrows, and see that pattern and feel a sense of accomplishment, and end up dusty and dirty and tired, but feeling great, looking back at that field that you'd ploughed.[37]

I suppose it's possible that you could have a passion for ploughing, but it's not something that most people who actually have to do it for a living often express. A quick look at Kerry's biography says he spent most of his summers as a youth on the family estate in Brittany, so it's difficult to know exactly when he did his ploughing, though again, it is possible. But when Kerry expressed his passion for ploughing in his distinctive Boston Brahmin lockjaw, it just didn't ring true somehow.

Because Senator Kerry didn't really know about hunting and farming or just didn't seem believable as a deer hunter or a farmer, any kind of mistake exposed him to ridicule. He'd have been better off saying, 'I don't hunt but I don't have a problem with people who do,' rather than pretending to be something he wasn't. But, as *New York Times* columnist Nicholas Kristof said in 2004, 'Nothing kills Democratic candidates' prospects more than guns… If it weren't for guns, President-elect Kerry might now be conferring with incoming Senate Majority Leader Daschle.'[38] But was it guns or was it class? Was the problem that Kerry was trying too hard to slum it with the less culturally elite, which made him seem like a buffoon? People in the salons of Islington like to laugh about how Republicans felt Bush passed 'the beer test' while Kerry failed, but if John Kerry wasn't smart enough to figure out that he couldn't win the heartland by faking some kind of rural machismo, how could he be smart enough to be president of the United States? One could argue that patrician George W. Bush was better at faking it than Kerry was, and … you'd be right, he was. Say what you will about Bush, he certainly had better diplomatic and acting skills than Kerry did.

In 2008, candidate Obama wisely never made gun control an issue, but his famous fundraiser comment – 'it's not surprising then that they [rural Pennsylvanians] get bitter, they cling to guns or religion or antipathy to people who aren't like them or anti-immigrant sentiment or anti-trade sentiment as a way to explain their frustrations'[39] – revealed quite a bit about how urban and suburban professional elite felt about gun ownership and religious belief, which are culturally undesirable to the American elite. Naturally, people who believed in God and owned guns disagreed quite vehemently with this notion that their deeply held beliefs came from bitterness or anger with their economic situation. Commentator John Podhoretz said,

> Obama's astonishing sentence offers a syllogistic string of super-ciliousness: Gun ownership is equated with religious fanaticism, which is said to accompany hatred of the other in the form of opposition to immigration and support for trade barriers. It drips with an attitude so important to the spiritual well-being of the American liberal – the paternalistic attitude that says, 'Oh, well, people only do thing [sic] differently from me because they are ignorant and superstitious and backward' – that it has survived and thrived despite the suicidal impact it has had on the achievement of liberal political goals and aims.[40]

Podhoretz objects to this caricature of gun owners and church-goers as bitter, angry, poor and xenophobic, only participating in these strange and alien activities because of the negativities in their lives. Indeed, he describes this caricature as a necessary belief for 'the spiritual well-being of the American liberal' – Obama's audience at the fundraiser – because that's literally the only reason they could understand that someone would want to do something as odd and awful and white-trash as shoot a gun at a target range or go hunting or voluntarily spend an hour of their Sundays at church.

Christian Lander, who writes the satirical website 'Stuff White People Like', says that young, urban elites love knowing what's best for poor people – how they should eat, dress, work and play— and believe that poor people make the choices they do (like shopping at Wal-Mart or voting Republican) because they just don't have the means to make the 'right' choices. But, Lander notes, 'it is ESSENTIAL that you assert that poor people do not make decisions based on free will. That news could crush white people and their hope for the future.'[41] Nice left-leaning, well-meaning urban coastal dwellers can't conceive that poor people might choose icky things like Wal-Mart and fast food because poor people might actually like them. They don't want to acknowledge that people in the working class might actually want to make their own decisions. So for these progressive individuals, if you can't relate to those who are different from you, or those who make different choices than you do, the next step is to demonise them.

Those 'weird' people that Obama talked about at his San Francisco fundraiser, who later came to be called 'bitter clingers', are people that San Franciscans never meet. They never get to know anyone who shoots a gun or hunts game for their supper or works the land for a living or is an observant Christian. But caricatures of these bizarre people exist in the media as straw men for progressive comedians and cultural commentators. In the absence of any real data about these putative inhabitants of rural America, they tell themselves stories about why they do such strange things. And the problem goes both ways, as blogger James Joyner points out:

> Urban elites tend to view rural America, especially Southerners, as a bunch of yahoos. Rural Americans, meanwhile, think big city types are elitist snobs who don't love America. There are similar resentments between rich and poor, educated and not, and even Ivy League/State College. In private gatherings, where people think they are among the like-minded, one hears shocking bigotry along those lines. There's a huge cultural divide that's been with us since well before (and, indeed, was a major factor in causing) the Civil War. Great national crises, like World War II and the 9/11 attacks, bridge those divides but only temporarily. And the permanent campaign that has characterised our politics in recent years continues to poke a stick at these wounds.[42]

Just as somebody like Olivia Miller, who could easily be in the audience at an Obama fundraiser (if Daddy bought a ticket), finds somebody like Troy Maupin strange and foreign, Troy finds Olivia equally strange and foreign. Their interests, hobbies, beliefs and values are totally different. They don't know each other, they don't understand each other, and they certainly don't like each other. Someone like Troy, in the 2008 election, believed that Obama was a socialist and was going to take away all the money he earned and distribute it to people on welfare, whereas people like Olivia believed that John McCain was a warmongering fascist and that Sarah Palin was going to criminalise abortion. When I was interviewing progressives about their feelings on the current crop of conservative candidates, one gentleman told me that he hated Sarah Palin because she 'believed humans walked the earth with dinosaurs and is a Dominionist'. I asked what a Dominionist was, and got no reply, but it turns out it's a fairly standard attack in progressive politics these days. A Dominionist is someone who wants to establish a Christian theocracy in the United States. Since Palin has never said anything about wanting to establish a Christian theocracy, one has to conclude that if you think she's the spearhead of some kind of secret conspiracy to turn America into a Christian version of Iran without telling anybody, you might want to adjust your tinfoil hat. Another woman told me 'all conservatives are selfish'. Still another said 'Republicans want to take us back 100 years'. I bet neither of these people have ever met a Republican, but they consume messages about the GOP from reassuring media they listen to, read and watch. They then spout back these canned opinons they've absorbed from people who are profiting by broadcasting them.

These days, class-based attacks against anybody who opposes President Obama have gotten stupider and more desperate, underscoring just how deeply rooted they are in fear and anxiety. For example, Scott Brown, a Republican from Massachusetts, ran a successful campaign in 2009 for the US Senate seat formerly occupied by Ted Kennedy; the centrepiece of his campaign was his state-wide tour in his five-year-old pick-up truck. In response to his surprising victory, commentator Howard Fineman said, 'in some places, there are codes, there are images, ah, you know, there are pickup trucks, uh, you could say there was a racial aspect to it one way or another'.[43] Owning a pick-up truck has a 'racial aspect'? At what point does ownership of a pick-up truck turn you into Bull Connor? This isn't considered political analysis, it's ridiculous hysteria. Here's another example: Ed Schultz, an anchor for cable news network MSNBC, accused Governor Rick Perry of racism because Perry said at a stump speech, 'Getting people back to work is the most important issue that faces this country, being able to pay off the 14 trillion – or 16 and a half trillion dollars' worth of debt.

That big black cloud that hangs over America.' Schultz said, 'That big black cloud he's talking about is President Barack Obama!' Well, reading the quote itself would lead the observer to conclude that Perry was talking about the debt NOT Obama, but just to be sure Schultz got to make his smear, MSNBC edited out the end of Perry's sentence, which was, 'that debt, which is so monstrous'. Schultz had to apologise for falsely calling Perry a racist.[44]

These are the rhetorical tricks that make you think thoughts like 'all Republicans are racist'. Confirmation bias is the tendency to believe things that confirm our already held beliefs, and the tendency to reject what makes us question our beliefs. Political strategists count on confirmation bias to make sure that we add our cash to the ever-rising fundraising totals, and they do this by making sure that 'everyone knows' certain things. But it's not serious and considered analysis, it's scaremongering. People who falsely accuse others of racism, people who have to invent their opposition research from thin air, people who see racism around every corner, who think that their opponents are using weird code language that can only be deciphered with some secret decoder ring, are not people who are secure in the intellectual underpinnings of their positions. These are the rhetorical tricks that you use when you're backed into a corner, scared and desperate. Somebody who makes up childish insults about a political opponent isn't doing so because they believe their arguments are right, they do it because they're frightened and anxious. Any time somebody talks about a 'racial aspect', it's a guarantee they're too scared or too ignorant to talk about actual policy, so they just have to pull some nasty sounding epithets out of thin air, which, of course, suits the political fundraising establishment just fine.

It's no secret that presidential elections are getting ever more expensive. In the 2008 election, Barack Obama raised $770 million for his campaign. More people gave to his campaign than any other presidential campaign in history. John McCain, who chose to have his campaign funded through the public purse, unlike his opponent (who wanted unlimited funds), raised $238 million, a princely sum, but one which was obliterated by Obama's total. Because of campaign finance reform laws in the United States, political donations are now divided into two categories – hard money and soft money. Hard money is what's donated to the candidates themselves, the party committees, and the Congressional and Senate campaign committees. These donations are regulated by the Federal Election Commission (FEC) and there are limits on how much and who can donate. Hard money raised by the Democratic Party, the Democratic Congressional Campaign Committee and the Democratic Senate Campaign Committee, was just over $763 million. That's in addition to the Obama for President campaign, so, altogether, the Democrats raised over $1.4 billion of regulated money. The Republican hard money total was over $792 million, not including what was raised by McCain.[45] So the Republicans raised just about a billion dollars themselves. Again, that's just FEC regulated money.

Then there's unregulated money, called 'soft money'. Because Congress can enact no law which restricts the freedom of speech (thank you, First Amendment of the United States Constitution), various courts have interpreted political donations to be a form of speech. This caused some consternation in 2010 when the Supreme Court of the United States said that, as concentrations of persons, corporations have the right to speak about elections, which means they can donate to advocacy groups or make their own ads. In any case, soft money organisations generally are non-profit advocacy groups which are named after the tax code that governs them; they are called 501(c)(3) organisations or 527 organisations. The most famous of the 527s is the Swift Boat Veterans for Truth, which casts doubt on Senator John Kerry's account of his time serving in the Vietnam War in the 2004 election; but there are plenty on both sides of the political spectrum, and they generally advocate for political causes and raise money for their advocacy. Soft money receipts totalled over $400 million in 2008.[46] Because soft money organisations aren't regulated by the FEC, there's no upper limit on donations they can receive, as long as they don't endorse a political candidate, and there's no regulatory body that makes sure that their political messaging is true. Taken together, various political groups raised nearly $3 billion for one presidential election. That's larger than the GDP of forty-one countries. And that money came from all of us – well, all my American readers, anyway. Alas, Brits can't donate money to an American election; if you aren't American, and you did donate to Obama, like Eddie Izzard bragged he did, you broke federal election law. Sorry Eddie.

It's important to remember how much money is needed for an election and how it's raised when thinking about the class anxieties political communication exploits. When you consider how many donations are needed for a presidential campaign, it's no wonder that the tools political consultants use cut to our very hearts. The broadcasting industry is expecting a spend of $3 billion in 2012 for television and radio ads. President Obama has pledged to raise $1 billion for his presidential campaign, and if his approval ratings still stay in the doldrums, he'll need every greenback of it to counter the message that he hasn't done a good job. It's also important to remember that political speech is unregulated. Freedom of speech is precious; however, unregulated speech means that it's incumbent upon us to figure out what's true and what isn't, what is a real matter of importance to the affairs of the United States and what's simply psychological manipulation designed to whip up our tribalism and our class anxieties.

There's another force at work behind garden-variety class anxiety in the elites' extreme and irrational dislike of politicians who they perceive as being lower class. I've mentioned the founding myth of America, that there is ultimate freedom of opportunity; anyone, literally anyone, can succeed and rise to the top if they're willing to put in the hard work. This is the idea behind the American Dream, a dream that reached its apex after the Second World War. Post-1945, the middle class expanded dramatically because the economy grew enough to allow many more people to acquire the trappings of middle-class life – houses, cars, vacations, appliances etc. The sky was the limit; if you worked hard and applied yourself, why wouldn't you be able to buy yourself a nice house and take the kids to the lake in the summer? This is not to say that this period in American history was socially or culturally idyllic – there was a great deal of injustice in American society as well as societal upheaval. But from an economic standpoint, in terms of being able to achieve middle-class status, the task was easiest from about 1945 to 1973. Many economists call this the 'golden age' of the American middle class. Incomes were more equal during this period than at any other in American history. American production reached its zenith as, in the years following the Second World War, Europe was spent as an economic force. The space race led to extraordinary advances in science and technology, which built up the American university system, as well as scientific and technological communities in places like the IBM campus in Malibu, California. It did seem as though a decent American life was available to everyone.

Things began to change in the 1970s. Since 1979, growth of American wages of the bottom 90 per cent of earners has increased at a smaller percentage than the top 10 per cent. Cheaper goods, thanks to globalisation and retail distribution models pioneered by big-box stores, have offset the pain somewhat, but according to the *Financial Times*, economists now seem to think that this is a structural problem, immune to the business cycle, and that in today's United States, you have a smaller chance of swapping your lower income bracket for a higher one than in almost any other developed economy – even Britain on some measures.[47] The Brookings Institution, an American think tank, had a slightly rosier take on economic mobility in the United States, expressed in a research project entitled Economic Mobility in America. The report found:

> The American Dream is alive if somewhat frayed. Most people are better off than their parents, but slower and less broadly shared economic growth has made the economy more of a zero-sum game than it used to be, with very high stakes for the winners. Some subgroups, such as immigrants, are doing especially well. Others, such as African Americans, are losing ground.[48]

And what about the vast majority of working Americans? Brookings found that in the last thirty years, male income has declined by 12 per cent. However, family income has gone up since 1974, due largely to the entrance of women into the workplace. Average family income has only gone up by 9 per cent. The authors of the report say, 'Unless the rate of economic growth increases, Americans will experience an improvement in its standard of living that is only one-third as large as the historical average for earlier generations.'[49]

People in the middle class have a bleak view of their future. Here are a few statistics from the Pew Research Center about how the middle class feels about its own economic prospects:

A majority of survey respondents say that, in the past five years, they either haven't moved forward in life or have fallen backwards. This is the most downbeat short-term assessment of personal progress in nearly half a century of polling by the Pew Research Center and the Gallup organisation.

Nearly eight in ten (79 per cent) respondents in the Pew

Research Center survey say it is more difficult now than five years ago for people in the middle class to maintain their standard of living.

The median debt-to-income ratio for middle-income adults increased from 0.45 in 1983 to 1.19 in 2004.

A new single family house is about 50 per cent larger and nearly twice as expensive now as it was in the mid-1980s.[50]

Americans are working harder and harder to try and retain the standard of living that they grew up with or grew accustomed to, while costs keep rising and wages are stagnant. Cost increases in housing, health care and education are all outpacing the rate of inflation. One of the people profiled in the *Financial Times* piece about the crisis in the middle class said, 'We need four jobs to keep our heads above water.'[51] With unemployment very high, economic growth stagnating, public spending cuts looming and general economic malaise in the air, the vaunted confidence that Americans have always felt is quite tarnished at the moment. We all feel insecure about our financial futures.

That said, Americans feel quite strongly that anyone should be able to achieve economic success, because, as the Brookings report pointed out, 'most believe that opportunities to get ahead are abundant and that hard work and skill are well rewarded'.[52] But as the Occupy Wall Street protests show, there's a serious anxiety, among young people in particular, that they will ever have the opportunities to get ahead, and they're anxious to find a scapegoat. But when the story that we tell ourselves turns out to be untrue, what happens to our belief in ourselves? What happens to how we feel about other Americans?

As the golden age of the American middle class recedes further and further into the past, and the demands of a globalised economy puts further pressure on twentieth-century economic models, politicians are going to want to soothe the woes of what is a very large voter bloc. And it's going to be very difficult because there are no easy answers to how to fix what's wrong with the American economic engine that's worked pretty well since the Second World War. Difficult discussions aren't a natural part of political discussion; blame, finger-pointing and scapegoating are. So we can expect a great deal of class anxiety rhetoric from politicians as voters begin to demand answers on where the jobs are and where the money has gone. What we need, of course, is an intelligent, reasoned discussion about where the American fits in the twenty-first-century global economy. But thanks to the financial needs of a presidential race, that isn't likely to happen.

2

WHO ARE YOU CALLING STUPID?

Without question, the most common accusation levelled at Republicans is that they're stupid. Michele Bachmann, Sarah Palin, Rick Perry and even history professor Newt Gingrich all get this insult, but it's been applied to just about every Republican under the sun, including George W. Bush, Ronald Reagan, George H. W. Bush, and Gerald Ford (I guess nobody called Dick Cheney stupid because he was considered the 'evil mastermind' of the Bush administration). With Palin, it was particularly vicious. Fox affiliate reporters in Northern California were recorded saying, '[her] dumbness doesn't come from sound bites'. MSNBC anchor Chris Matthews wondered if 'not knowing things she ought to know' should stop her from running for president (to which his guest, blogger Andrew Sullivan, replied, 'No! Her not knowing things in her view is qualification for being president.'). Radio and TV presenter Cenk Ugyur says that if you think Palin is smart enough to be president, 'then there is no sense in talking to one another anymore because we are not operating in the same reality, or planet'.

Well, get ready to blast off to Mars, because I'm going to say something really controversial: I don't think Sarah Palin is dumb. I don't think that Republicans in general are dumb. I don't think there's any evidence that any of them are stupider than President Obama, who has said some really stupid things in the past four years, and certainly none of them are any dumber than Vice President Joe Biden, who says something stupid more or less every time he opens his mouth. Republicans' opponents would like them to be dumb, because that means they don't have to intellectually engage with their arguments. It's much easier to say, 'Simplification of the tax code? Geez, what an idiot!' as opposed to actually thinking about how a flat tax would affect the economy. In addition, people from upper-middle-class backgrounds who have an expensive university education, which they've taken out massive loans to pay for, are deeply anxious that some yokel from Alaska or Minnesota or Texas or Georgia with a degree from a public land-grant university (horrors!) might be in a position of prominence and power while they're slaving away at their desks in some office job. But that doesn't mean Republicans are dumb, just that their opponents wish they were.

Satirist Stephen Colbert, in one of his cleverer moments, called this kind of belief that just feels true, but doesn't have any evidence behind it, 'truthiness'. When asked to define 'truthiness', Colbert said, 'Truthiness is what you want the facts to be as opposed to what the facts are. What feels like the right answer as opposed to what reality will support.' We again return to the notion of a 'reality-based community' of facts rather than 'faith-based' beliefs – we ought to believe what we believe because we've got the evidence to back it up, not just because it feels good or right. We shouldn't abandon this rather sensible view of the world now that President Bush is out of office. We should still base our assertions on facts, things that are provably accurate, as opposed to beliefs that just feel right despite evidence to the contrary. So, I'm going to present the illustrative case that Sarah Palin isn't actually stupid, and that to assert that she is shows a need to believe something is true despite facts and evidence to the contrary.

The stupidity charge is a powerful one to keep you from considering voting for another candidate. Nobody likes to think of themselves as stupid and they certainly don't like associating with stupid people either. If one political party can convince you that their opponent is an idiot, you're much more likely to open up your wallet to keep the idiot as far away from the levers of power as possible. That's why Democrats like to get out front of the stupidity sweepstakes and make sure that they let their core voters know just how dim their opponents are. And they can do it very easily because Republicans don't tend to have the class markers (an expensive education, lots of degrees, the right kind of professional training) that middle-class urbanites recognise as 'smart'. So when they say, 'Rick Perry is stupid because he graduated from Texas A & M', since we know that Texas A & M is a state school without a particular intellectual pedigree, it's a code Americans recognise for being 'not so bright'.

To be honest, when you call someone stupid, it says much more about you than it does that person. Here's an example. Suppose you're watching TV and a public figure is doing an interview and pronounces Massachusetts as 'Massatoosetts'. Would you think that this person was the dumbest person ever? That they didn't know how to pronounce the name of the Bay State? Or perhaps you might think that they were only human and made a mistake that anybody could make? It would probably depend on who the person was. So, in our hypothetical example, let's say it was Sarah Palin who mispronounced Massachusetts. That would be yet another example of how dumb she is, right? But what if I told you that Barack Obama was the one who mispronounced Massachusetts? Is he dumb for doing so? Or did he just make a careless mistake?

Our perception of the person making the mistake colours how we judge the mistake. If we perceive them as stupid, then we think the mistake is an example of stupidity. If we perceive them as smart, then the mistake becomes human error. So Barack Obama, with his Harvard degree and silky speaking voice (who did mispronounce Massachusetts in an interview) will be excused for his silly mistake, whereas Sarah Palin (who did say squirmish when she meant skirmish) will be followed around by that mistake for the rest of her life.

A great example of this can be found in an *Independent Magazine* article on Michele Bachmann. Its author, David Usborne, interviewing some of Bachmann's fans – and finding himself deeply amused by the red-state America freak show – suggests to the Bachmann supporters that Palin 'might not be too bright'. The supporters retort, 'Well, at least Palin doesn't think there are fifty-seven states.' Here's his reaction:

> Who does? 'Obama does,' all three reply in unison. (Subsequent research yields a moment in the 2008 campaign when a worn-out Obama at a town hall indeed misspoke to this effect. He was quick to correct himself, of course.)[53]

Usborne is wrong. It's not true that Obama corrected himself quickly; in fact, he didn't correct himself at all. For all we know, the evidence of this incident indicates that Obama really does believe that there are fifty-seven states. But Usborne, who clearly is of the opinion that Obama is clever, excuses Obama's gaffe. Because he believes certain things about Obama, he attributes the mis-step to the candidate being 'worn-out', not dumb, and then states the untrue assertion that Obama corrected himself, when in fact Obama did not. Would Michele Bachmann have received this kind of credit? Of course not; Usborne believes she is stupid, and stupid she will for ever be, no matter what kind of facts insert themselves into the situation. 'Intelligence' or 'stupidity' rests on the person judging the gaffe, not the gaffe itself.

In fact, it is quite fascinating to hear people who believe that Republicans are stupid try to justify their beliefs; generally the evidence they produce to prove this stupidity is spurious. Here are a few examples regarding Palin:

'I can see Russia from my house.' Sarah Palin never actually said that; Tina Fey, an actress on *Saturday Night Live*, did while satirising Palin. Not that it matters to the BBC; they're still reporting this as a Palin quote. Palin's actual quote was, 'You can actually see Russia from land here in Alaska, from an island in Alaska… I'm giving you that perspective of how small our world is and how important it is that we work with our allies to keep good relations with all of these countries, especially Russia.' It is factually true that islands in Russia and Alaska are as little as 2 miles apart.

'Africa is a country.' This turned out to be a complicated political hoax that duped reporters at MSNBC and the *LA Times*. It has been debunked by McCain campaign staffers.

'We need to be supportive of our North Korean allies.' Yes, she did say this on Glenn Beck's radio show. But we have to ask ourselves, is this a 'Massatoosetts' moment or does she actually believe that the USA is allied with North Korea? The evidence suggests the former; when she's corrected, she agrees and repeats 'South Korea', and then later in the interview, she refers to North Korea as an enemy.

In fact, sometimes when media commentators try to prove people like Palin are stupid, they end up looking pretty idiotic themselves. *Slate* magazine runs a series called 'Palinisms', in which the author, Jacob Weisberg, giggles about various dumb things Palin is supposed to have said. Here's an example: 'During the flight here, between our countries, it did not escape me that Japan lies about halfway between my Alaskan home and India.'[54] What's dumb about that? Japan *does* lie halfway between India and Alaska. And actually, if you look at the context of her remarks, given at a speech to the *India Today* Conclave in New Delhi, her mentioning Japan seems even less stupid:

During the flight here, between our countries, it did not escape me that Japan lies about halfway between my Alaskan home and India. I trust you will join me in expressing solidarity with the Japanese people as they recover from such tragic events. Their determination & resiliency won't fail them. The world community stands united to offer help to them in the 'Land of the Rising Sun'. Thoughts and prayers are with you, Japan. Life is fragile – precious – we're in this together; may Japan know our caring heart at this time.[55]

I'm not sure why it's thick-headed to express sympathy and solidarity with Japan, which had just experienced a devastating tsunami (the earthquake and tsunami occurred on 11 March 2011; this speech was given on 18 March 2011). Maybe Jacob Weisberg needs to spend a little time with a world map.

The events that did the most to cement Sarah Palin's reputation as an enormous thicko were the two major television interviews she gave during the 2008 presidential election; the first with Charlie Gibson for *ABC World News Tonight*, and the second with Katie Couric for *CBS Evening News*. The ABC interview came first, on 11 September 2008. There was a bit of an international crisis going on at the time, as Russia had made some military incursions into Georgia. So, naturally, that was going to be addressed as part of the interview.

I received a press release from ABC World News the afternoon before the interview was to air. The headline was, 'SARAH PALIN WANTS TO DECLARE WAR AGAINST RUSSIA!' The copy in the press release was, 'Sarah Palin thinks the response to Russia is to declare war. See more in the interview with Charlie Gibson tonight.' There was also a promo trailer for the interview that I saw that afternoon, and the clip broadcast went as follows:

GIBSON: Wouldn't we then have to go to war if Russia invaded Georgia?
PALIN: Perhaps so.

At the time, I thought, 'Gosh, she's really aggressive.' However, when I watched the interview, I saw the full question and answer:

GIBSON: And under the NATO treaty, wouldn't we then have to go to war if Russia invaded Georgia?
PALIN: Perhaps so. I mean, that is the agreement when you are a NATO ally, is if another country is attacked, you're going to be expected to be called upon and help.

That is an extremely uncontroversial point; if you're a NATO member and another NATO member state is attacked, under Article V of the NATO treaty you have to provide military aid. I thought it was awfully unfair of ABC News to make Sarah Palin look more bellicose than she was through the promo material for the interview.

It turns out that I didn't know the half of it. Conservative media watchdog Newsbusters has alleged, and years later ABC News has yet to deny, that the Charlie Gibson interview was edited to make Sarah Palin look stupider than she actually is. In fact, ABC News released full unedited transcripts of the interview so viewers could see the edits that had been made for broadcast. Let's take a look at the full question about NATO. The quote you see above is what actually made it to air. But in the unedited transcripts that ABC News released, Palin went into some detail about international diplomacy (unaired parts are in bold):

GIBSON: And under the NATO treaty, wouldn't we then have to go to war if Russia went into Georgia?

PALIN: Perhaps so. I mean, that is the agreement when you are a NATO ally, is if another country is attacked, you're going to be expected to be called upon and help.

But NATO, I think, should include Ukraine, definitely, at this point and I think that we need to – especially with new leadership coming in on January 20, being sworn on, on either ticket, we have got to make sure that we strengthen our allies, our ties with each one of those NATO members.

We have got to make sure that that is the group that can be counted upon to defend one another in a very dangerous world today.

GIBSON: And you think it would be worth it to the United States, Georgia is worth it to the United States to go to war if Russia were to invade?

PALIN: What I think is that smaller democratic countries that are invaded by a larger power is something for us to be vigilant against. We have got to be cognisant of what the consequences are if a larger power is able to take over smaller democratic countries.

And we have got to be vigilant. We have got to show the support, in this case, for Georgia. The support that we can show is economic sanctions perhaps against Russia, if this is what it leads to.

It doesn't have to lead to war and it doesn't have to lead, as I said, to a Cold War, but economic sanctions, diplomatic pressure, again, counting on our allies to help us do that in this mission of keeping our eye on Russia and Putin and some of his desire to control and to control much more than smaller democratic countries.

His mission, if it is to control energy supplies, also, coming from and through Russia, that's a dangerous position for our world to be in, if we were to allow that to happen.

Interviews always have to be edited for time, but what's interesting about this particular edit is that all of Palin's endorsements of diplomacy and economic sanctions have been completely edited out. All that remains is her endorsement of force.

There was another case in which Palin was edited to make her seem hungry for war. Gibson turned the question to what should be done about Iran (unaired portions are in bold):

GIBSON: So what should we do about a nuclear Iran? John McCain said the only thing worse than a war with Iran would be a nuclear Iran. John Abizaid said we may have to live with a nuclear Iran. Who's right?

PALIN: No, no. I agree with John McCain that nuclear weapons in the hands of those who would seek to destroy our allies, in this case, we're talking about Israel, we're talking about Ahmadinejad's comment about Israel being the 'stinking corpse, should be wiped off the face of the earth', that's atrocious. That's unacceptable.

GIBSON: So what do you do about a nuclear Iran?

PALIN: We have got to make sure that these weapons of mass destruction, that nuclear weapons are not given to those hands of Ahmadinejad, not that he would use them, but that he would allow terrorists to be able to use them. So we have got to put the pressure on Iran **and we have got to count on our allies to help us, diplomatic pressure.**

Again, it's telling that Palin's words about diplomatic pressure are completely edited out, so much so they have to cut her off in the middle of a sentence. Everything she says about diplomacy and international cooperation is just gone; in its place is a dim, dizzy warmonger, a female George W. Bush. To be fair, for ABC, it's a much more exciting story to have Warmonger McCain and Lady

Bush fighting for the soul of the nation against Saint Obama and Holy Joe; in the presidential election soap opera, it's a lot more exciting to have two diametrically opposed sides, rather than two sides who more or less agreed with each other, as Palin did with Obama.[56]

The ABC example is particularly instructive for the future of US political coverage because it shows you that you really can't trust what you see and hear. We are being manipulated at all times by political advertising, but usually we're able to make a choice to open our minds to new ideas or allow our biases to remain intact. But in this case, we weren't even given the choice – we were lied to in order to create a picture of Palin that didn't exist. Whether we were lied to because ABC wanted to create a better story, or because it was in the tank for Obama and needed to present Palin as a warmongering idiot to make sure Obama won, we'll never know. ABC News has set the precedent; it's OK to edit out entire portions of interviews to make the subject espouse completely different beliefs than what is actually said. Now, when you watch an interview, particularly with a Republican candidate, we all have to ask: am I being lied to? Is what I am watching really the truth or is it simply a manipulation? Because of Palin's shameful treatment by ABC, in this electoral cycle most Republicans are deeply suspicious of 'legacy media' (so called because they existed pre-internet) outlets like the three broadcast networks, CNN and the major newspapers. In fact, one candidate, former Utah Governor Jon Huntsman, killed his primary candidacy because he did interviews with *Vogue* and the *New York Times*, which disgusted primary voters to no end.

It's a negative feature of modern political debate that the default position we take regarding our opposition is that they're stupid. It brings an unnecessary hostility to the proceedings and it makes negotiation very difficult. If both sides feel the other is irredeemably dumb, then both sides come to the table unwilling to find common ground or at least understand the other's position. This is one of the reasons political debate is as heated as it is today. If it were up to me, I'd like to remove the word 'stupid' from politics because it's become meaningless. Stupid is not the same as wrong. Stupid is not the same as mistaken. Stupid is not even the same thing as erroneous. But if you want to dismiss your opponent's thoughts out of hand, or make sure your opponent is seen as less than credible, the concept is a useful tool, which is why the notion has been part of the political vocabulary for decades. Blogger Don Surber points out that the last four Republican presidents have been subjected to the same attacks that Palin underwent and the current crop of candidates, particularly Newt Gingrich, are undergoing:

- Dumb as a rock (Ford, Reagan, George W. Bush)
- Inarticulate (Ford, George H. W. Bush, George W. Bush)
- Crazy (Reagan, George W. Bush in 2004)
- Out of touch (Reagan, George H. W. Bush, George W. Bush)
- Lousy parent (Ford, Reagan)

Again, the attack works because it doesn't require intellectual engagement. Any ignoramus can call someone stupid, but it takes much more intellectual effort to explain why a policy position is wrong or misguided. Also, among a peer or class group, it becomes an easy way to delineate 'us vs them'. If you don't have any ideological or intellectual reasons to dislike Gerald Ford, but you know he's a Republican and therefore bad, 'stupid' becomes a great way to disassociate yourself from him.

The same thing goes on with Republicans against Democrats; they are also guilty of not engaging intellectually with liberal or progressive ideas, calling them 'stupid' or 'crazy' and so on. But since a liberal/progressive point of view is so much more prevalent in the media and political establishment, it's easier for labels on Republicans to stick. If you ask any resident of San Francisco whether or not George W. Bush is stupid, they will most likely tell you that he is. You'll see jokes about how stupid George W. Bush is on *Saturday Night Live* and late night talk shows, in *The Onion*, in the movies – hell, even if you go down to an average comedy club in London on a week night, the lazier comics are *still* telling jokes about Bush, the American idiot.

It turns out the 'stupid' jibe has an awful lot of class anxiety about it, and is yet another way for the upper-middle class to sublimate their anxiety about losing power to the American proletariat, by making fun of and marginalising the educational choices the poor and rural make. College education has vastly expanded in the United States; these days, in order to live a middle-class life you have to have at least a bachelor's degree and preferably a professional degree (a law or medicine degree, for example) as well. Nobody disputes that the percentage of Americans with a college degree has increased exponentially in the last sixty years. In 1950, US census data shows that 6.2 per cent of Americans had a college degree. In 2008, 27.4 per cent of Americans had a bachelor's degree or higher. University education has, for the last several decades, been seen as the ticket to the American Dream, and at least as far as wages are concerned, the figures bear it out. In 2000, a college graduate could expect a wage premium of 50 per cent compared to someone who didn't graduate from college.[57] Most middle-class or upper-middle-class jobs in the USA require a college degree.

But, more importantly, going to college – and indeed, which college you go to – confers middle or upper-middle-class status. But like all things class-related in America, the delineation of which university signifies which class isn't easy. Undisputedly, at the very top of the university class strata is the Ivy League; these are all historic, privately funded, expensive institutions in the north-east of the United States. The children of the nation's elite go here, as do people who wish to be part of the nation's elite. An Ivy League degree, particularly from the three most elite members within it (Harvard, Yale, Princeton) is the golden ticket to future fame, fortune and success. But that is where the clear lines end, because even though there are seven members of the Ivy League, what a degree from any of the others 'means' in terms of class status is considerably foggier. Is a degree from Brown somehow more or less worthy than a degree from Penn? Why will parents fight tooth and nail to get their child into Dartmouth but feel crushed if the kid gets into Cornell?

And if you think the Ivy League is foggy in terms of class status, it gets even worse as you go outwards. There are 4,352 institutions of higher learning in the United States, and they have a ranking in terms of the status and class standing that they confer. There are 'Ivy League equivalents', like Stanford and Duke. There are extraordinary science institutions, MIT and Cal Tech, which provide a world-class education but are just a bit too nerdy to confer the same class status as Harvard. There are the elite state-funded schools: Berkeley, the University of Virginia, the University of North Carolina-Chapel Hill and the University of Michigan, which are 'better' in terms of status than the average state college, but still have the unmistakable proletarian whiff of public education (disclosure: your author went to UVa). There is the universe of private colleges, some of which confer status and some of which don't, depending on the fashion of the day. The absolute bottom of the barrel are state universities like the University of Massachusetts, Ohio State, and Governor Sarah Palin's alma mater, the University of Idaho.

Caitlin Flanagan, a former prep school counsellor in LA, wrote about trying to navigate the extremely thorny issue of college admissions and class status. She describes the 'unstoppable tears' of teenage college applicants, families falling apart, and counselling being prescribed. She writes:

> I could have understood the forceful nature of the families' emotions if the stakes had been higher. If the child had a single shot at a scholarship and a college education, and a letter of rejection meant that he or she would lead a fundamentally different life – that was a situation I could imagine being rife with heartache and regret. But when the sting of a Bowdoin rejection was lessened (the same day) by the salve of a Colby acceptance, when a rejection from Dartmouth meant the student would be off to Penn – where was the horror?
>
> Each of the hot hundred colleges held a certain position in a vast and inscrutable cosmology that only the students and their parents seemed to understand. The very names of schools I had always considered excellent made many students shudder – Kenyon, for example. They would snap briskly to attention if I said 'Williams' or 'Amherst'. So why not Kenyon?

As fascinating and welcome as the article is, I believe she's being a bit creatively naïve when she wonders why students smile at Williams and weep at Kenyon. This is a class distinction that my British readers will wonder at and my American readers will understand instinctively. For Americans, what college you went to 'says' everything about you, your class, your intelligence level, your personality type etc. Like all class distinctions, this kind of thing is totally arbitrary; there's no reason why Amherst should be more desirable than Kenyon, but people instinctively feel that a person who went to Amherst is somehow smarter, more successful and more special than a Kenyon graduate. Also, Amherst is located in fashionable Massachusetts, while Kenyon is located in rural Ohio. Americans instinctively feel that a Duke graduate is further up the ladder of the American Dream than a Vanderbilt graduate. A Berkeley grad. is better than a UC-Irvine grad. And so forth.

In terms of class status, all these private and 'public Ivy' institutions rank above most state-funded schools. The reason is a class wrinkle of American history. Many state colleges, particularly if they have 'State' or 'Tech' in their name, are classified as 'land-grant' universities. These were created by the Morill Act of 1862 to provide publicly funded institutions of higher learning for agricultural and technical vocations. Michigan State, Virginia Tech and Iowa State are all examples of these. The idea was to provide higher education for the working classes, as opposed to the classical education provided by traditional universities. They were formed in response to the Industrial Revolution, and were designed to spur innovation in agriculture, technology and engineering. Note that the fields in which they specialise are useful and practical, as opposed to the more abstract fields taught by their older counterparts. Much has been written about why elites value knowledge that you can't use more than knowledge that has practical applications. But in the ineffable class structure of American universities, a geography-anthropology degree from private Vassar, located in New York State, is more valuable to people with similar class status than a degree from Virginia Tech in forestry, despite the forestry degree being more 'useful'. Equally, the Virginia Tech student's friends and family would probably think that getting a geology-anthropology degree from Vassar is an expensive waste of time and money, and something impossibly rarefied.

People who hold positions of political power are much more likely to have gone to a traditional university, and particularly a private institution. Since 1980, all but one US president has attended an Ivy League university (and the last president to have forgone higher education completely was Harry S. Truman). Of the 111th Congress, which took office in 2009, numbering 533 people, only thirty-four did not have a bachelor's degree. Harvard had the highest number of graduates in that Congress, followed by Stanford.[58] And none of the justices in the US Supreme Court went to either public universities or law schools.

In an article called 'The Failure of Meritocracy', writer Megan McCardle quotes a corporate recruiter who hired the best of the best for the financial services industry. It's becoming an increasingly rarefied world which only denizens of the Ivy League can penetrate – even students from Ivy League equivalents are somewhat suspect. Students who go to the Ivy League tend to come from very similar backgrounds and have very similar life experiences, and don't engage with different and challenging ideas. So isn't it terribly surprising that elite professions like finance and law seem to inhabit an ivory tower that seems disconnected from the real world? Isn't it interesting that the derivative market, which played such an important part in the credit crisis, sprang from the brains of Ivy League graduates? If there had been class and ideological diversity at those financial institutions, might someone not have said, 'hey, this isn't a good idea'? We'll never know. President Obama has been criticised for being out of touch, but look at his roster of economic advisors; it's full of professors from Harvard and the University of Chicago, and Ivy League-trained bankers. And yet unemployment still stubbornly stays around 9 per cent and people feel bleaker about the economy than at any time since the 1970s. Is it time to re-evaluate the pre-eminent status that Harvard holds in American intellectual circles? How well has Harvard actually done in training competent leaders for the future?

Social scientist Charles Murray gave a talk at the American Enterprise Institute on 'The State of White America', in which he discussed demographic trends among non-Hispanic white people. He noted that there were two classes emerging from within the traditional socio-economic class system – a new lower class and a new upper class. The new upper class consisted of people who went to a nexus of elite universities and had leadership positions in the nation's entertainment, tech, financial and government industries. And, he noted, this new upper class is becoming increasingly isolated from, ignorant of, and hostile towards the working class. As an example, he said he tracked where 14,000 graduates of Harvard, Yale and Princeton moved to after graduation. The highest concentration of these graduates were in Cambridge, MA (where Harvard is located), and the second highest concentration of these graduates was in Princeton, NJ (where Princeton University is located). So much for the vaunted 'intellectual curiosity' of these intellectual elites – they never leave their college towns after they've graduated! More worryingly, because these people tend to cluster together in college and afterwards, they never get to know how Americans in places like Buffalo or Akron live, which results in isolation and hostility. An Ivy League graduate who lives in Cambridge occupies a different planet from a Texas A & M graduate in Houston, and each is extremely suspicious of the other's life experience. If you are a person in this new upper-middle class, enjoying a professional life in a wealthy suburb of Washington, DC, and you have been untroubled thus far in your life by interactions with the working class, encountering someone like Sarah Palin is like having ice-cold water poured over your head. You may have never met someone who looked like that, talked like that, had interests and beliefs like that. For our hypothetical upper-middle-class person, who's never met a farmer, a factory worker or a tradesman he or she wasn't paying for a service, it becomes easy to demonise and then stereotype Palin as an idiot rube and a dumb hick, because they can't conceive of her in any other way.

But there's more to the intellectual snobbery against Sarah Palin and members of the Tea Party than mere unfamiliarity. I want to return to the 'vast cosmology' of the university system in the United States. Ranking class status by the university one attends is something Americans instinctively understand. They learn it by hearing about it from their friends and family, they learn it by going through the admissions process and they learn it by actually being part of the university system itself. When I went to the University of Virginia, a traditional liberal arts university, we were encouraged to think of ourselves as smarter than those yokels at Virginia Tech down the road. We were spending our time thinking about Thucydides and the Foucauldian master-slave relationship, which is clearly much more important and valuable than whatever agricultural science they were learning in Blacksburg. This isn't true at all, of course, but in terms of finding our place in the American class hierarchy, we needed to believe it about ourselves. And that is the nomenclature of the cosmology of American higher education. The institutions of higher education that we attend help us create the story we tell ourselves about where we fit in the American class system.

To illustrate this further, I'd like to introduce you to Nicole T., a 28-year-old who lives outside Boston and is a PR manager for a security software company. Nicole considers herself a member of the middle class; her father is a machinist and her mother is a day care provider. She told me that 'not going to college was not an option' for herself and her two sisters – her parents 'demanded' their kids go to college. So Nicole put herself through school by taking out loans, which her parents co-signed, and taking several jobs at a time to pay for her books and living expenses. To cut down on costs she went to Salem State University, which is a publicly funded institution in Massachusetts. It was necessary for her to go to a public institution, she told me, because it was important to 'keep well within our means'. She pointed out that she had many friends who went to more expensive colleges, but when they all graduated, they had the same employment opportunities. She does think that there's a 'status thing' about different colleges, but her attending a publicly funded university hasn't stopped her becoming successful in any way – in fact, she is under the impression that it's helped her make a positive impression on managers throughout her career. She said, 'The message I most want to convey is to be proud of what you do, whatever school you attend.'

The affordability of a state university like Salem State is becoming ever more important as the cost of tuition spirals ever upwards. According to the College Board, in 2009 the average tuition fee alone at a public four-year institution for in-state students was $6,591 per year, whereas for a private four-year institution it was $25,177. The latter means a six-figure investment for tuition alone – it doesn't include housing, food, books, entertainment and other sundry expenses. And the costs continue to go up, far outpacing inflation and wages. Nicole told me she graduated with $20,000 worth of debt, which requires payments of about $200 a month. She said that considering her friends who went to schools like Syracuse graduated with $60,000 of debt, she never had any shame in going to a state university – it was a good economic decision. And when looked at in terms of dollars and cents, a six-figure investment seems like an awfully high price tag to cement your place in the upper-middle class of American society.

Indeed, the amount of student loan debt is worrying. The total amount of unsecured student loan debt in the United States has now exceeded $1 trillion. And thanks to bankruptcy legislation passed by Congress in 2005 (championed by then-Senator Joe Biden), student loan debt cannot be discharged through bankruptcy. You are responsible for paying it until you die and can be collected by garnering wages, social security payments and unemployment benefits.[59] The average student graduating from university in 2009 graduated with $24,000 in debt, which, as Nicole demonstrates with her $200 a month payment, isn't insurmountable, although it will take her ten years to pay it off. But what about someone with $60,000 worth of debt or more, who's got to keep paying for thirty years? That degree from Amherst, nice though it is, starts to weigh a bit more on you, particularly if you're trying to make it in New York or Washington, DC in a field like journalism or advertising, where you start on $25,000 a year.

Is it really so surprising that people who are struggling with the debt incurred just to enter the middle class, people who are trying to make ends meet, buy a house, save for retirement – in essence, do all the things that they were promised they could do if they went to university – feel the gorge rising in their throat watching this woman who went to a 'lower-class' institution succeed and thrive, transcending her traditional class boundaries? As one blogger writes, 'I can tell you, being privy to the endless, incendiary rants, coming from hordes of liberal women – age demo twenty-five to forty-five – they rip her to pieces, they blame her for everything, and the jealousy/resentment factor is so clear and primal.' It is very easy to see that the hatred of Sarah Palin might well be displaced anger at their situation. They're stuck in an office, paying off loans endlessly, living with room-mates, unable to get ahead. It's not hard to understand the resentment of urban 25–45-year-olds; they're desperately trying to pay off their student loans (if they can can get a job at all) while trying to achieve the upper-middle-class lifestyle promised by getting a bachelor's degree from a 'good' institution. How dare Sarah Palin, some rube from God knows where, who paid for her education through beauty pageants rather than taking out loans like nice people, leapfrog them? How dare Sarah Palin, majoring in broadcast communication from the deeply provincial and unfashionable University of Idaho, get to have a voice on the national stage? And this, after collecting credits from four other universities! In the ineffable universe where class and education are conflated, Sarah Palin has committed just about every gaucherie there is – and has succeeded despite it all. And deep inside, for many people in the middle class who are trying desperately to make ends meet, that hurts.

Twenty years ago, it was easier to achieve the trappings of the middle class. But that simply isn't true anymore, and is particularly untrue for people living in places like San Francisco, New York City and Washington, DC. It simply costs too much for most young college-educated professionals who live and work there to buy a house and save for retirement. So what differentiates them from the yokels who live in places like Des Moines and Dallas, who aren't one rent payment away from homelessness, who can afford to buy a house without rats and a kitchen two people can be in at once? Blue state denizens believe they're smarter. They've read *Paradise Lost*. They know all about bell hooks and the male gaze. And that helps them feel superior to people like George W. Bush, who says his favourite philosopher is Jesus, or Sarah Palin, who didn't name a newspaper she read on a regular basis. They may not be able to eat tonight, but at least they're clever.

The isolated upper-middle class and the struggling middle class and young upper-middle class need something to differentiate themselves. They need to distinguish themselves from the work-ing classes. They need to tell themselves a story to find their place within the American class system. A university education isn't enough; going to the 'right' university isn't enough; money isn't enough; even living in the right place isn't enough. They need to establish themselves as superior to others. This is why the notion of 'stupidity' doesn't mean anything except 'you are different from me'.

3

THE SEGREGATION OF AMERICA

A classic theme in literary analysis, historical analysis and psychological understanding is Fear of the Other. As humans, we band together in tribes that are familiar to us; the notion goes all the way back to hunter-gatherer days, where the tribe had to stick together for warmth and survival. Because our brains haven't evolved to handle the reality of the modern world, goes the thinking, we still have a tribal mentality – we stick together in our little hunter-gatherer bands, just as we did millennia ago. We cling to things that seem familiar and reject those that are unfamiliar. We band together with those who are like us and shut out those who are against us. This Fear of the Other can lead to prejudice, violence, war and hatred; we see it in discussions of slavery, the Civil War and religious strife. Shylock is a villain in *The Merchant of Venice* because of Fear of the Other. Kurtz's downfall in *Heart of Darkness* comes from Fear of the Other. The most influential film in early American cinema, *Birth of a Nation*, which President Woodrow Wilson supposedly described as 'like writing history with lightning', is about good Americans triumphing over the Fear of the Other. It appears everywhere in our cultural history. Because Fear of the Other is such a powerful cultural trope, it can be exploited by leaders for their own ends. We've seen this happen in Nazi Germany, fifteenth-century Catholic Spain, the Congo; tribal prejudices and fear of outsiders lead people to acts of great hatred and violence. Terrible things have been justified because of Fear of the Other. But it's a powerful tool for psychological manipulation and it works to get people to behave in the ways their leader wants them to.

In American politics, violence isn't the way to achieve electoral power – power belongs to whoever is better at shaping public opinion. And the best and most efficient way to do that is to use the Fear of the Other to make political opponents seem bizarre and strange. People's natural tribal prejudices can be manipulated to create fear and anxiety about the strange, the different, the foreign, in order to scare them into voting for a particular candidate or other; this prevents having to get into the messy weeds of policy analysis and keeps political campaigns on a visceral, emotional level, which is handy for the current fundraising model.

Jedediah Bila, a conservative woman living in deep blue Manhattan, tells lots of scary stories about what happens to a person who dares to disagree verbally with the progressive orthodoxy, but perhaps the most frightening is the one where she meets an elderly woman who was assaulted for wearing a pro-Sarah Palin pin. The woman handed Bila back her own Palin pin, which Bila had dropped, and cautioned:

> 'Please be careful… I nearly got knocked to the ground because of one of those a few weeks ago. It's just not worth the fight, you know?' As I watched her exit the deli, I stood wondering what in heaven's name had possessed someone to nearly knock down a barely five-foot, eighty-something-year-old woman because of a pin. Where in the hell am I living?[60]

It's a short journey from demonisation to dehumanisation. The kind of person who feels free to hurt a grandmotherly old woman because of her political beliefs is going through the same mental process that allows the justification of slavery or the justification of murdering another human being because of their religion or tribe. The attacker no longer sees his or her victim as human. They've been demonised to the point that the attacker doesn't recognise the victim as part of the human family anymore; they're foreign, different, Other – and must be removed. A lot of political rhetoric springs from the same impulse as racial, religious or sexual prejudice; political strategists are using the tools of bigotry to make people behave in a way that suits their needs. So, when current House Minority Leader Nancy Pelosi announces that Republicans 'are saying that women can die on the floor' or when Vice President Joe Biden warns that more rapes and murders will happen in American cities if the American Jobs Act isn't passed, or when the Republican National Committee depicts Nancy Pelosi and Senate Majority Leader Harry Reid as Cruella de Vil and Scooby Doo, respectively, it invites you to no longer see them, and by extension their political parties, as human, but as weird, alien beings who must be destroyed.

There's no question that the technique of portraying your political enemy as a bizarre alien has a long tradition in modern politics. Much ink has been spilled about the late Republican strategist Lee Atwater's 'Southern strategy' to pick up disaffected Dixiecrats for the Republican Party who were upset about African-American civil rights. Preying on the fear of others has certainly been used in Republican political campaigns; there have definitely been Republican political messages preying on white voters' fear of African-Americans: famous examples are Jesse Helms's 1984 ads decrying affirmative action or George H. W. Bush's 'Willie Horton' ad in the 1988 election, which, accompanied by Horton's menacing mug shot, recounted the crimes committed by convicted murderer Willie Horton while he was on furlough. During the 2008 election, a rumour spread, mostly by far right online magazines, that Barack Obama is a Muslim. But the Democratic Party is equally as guilty of manipulating its supporters to hate and fear the other political party: when African-American Republican candidate for Senate Michael Steele went to a Baltimore debate,

Oreo cookies (black on the outside, white on the inside) were thrown at him[61] and his credit report was illegally obtained by the Democratic Senate campaign committee for opposition research.[62] Virginia Democratic Congressman Jim Moran accused Jews of driving the support for the war in Iraq, saying 'If it were not for the strong support of the Jewish community for this war with Iraq, we would not be doing this.'[63] Democratic Candidate for Senate from Virginia Jim Webb constantly made fun of his opponent George Allen's middle name, two years before making fun of candidates' middle names mysteriously became frowned upon. The middle name, Felix, was considered a good line of attack because it was unusual for a good ol' Virginia boy and, as it was discovered during the campaign, came from Allen's Jewish heritage.[64] And often Democrats aren't as subtle as just making fun of a candidate's race or heritage when trying to portray them as the Other; some of them just come right out and say it, as when Vice President Joe Biden likened Republicans to terrorists,[65] or when Congressman Steve Cohen compared Republicans to Nazis,[66] or when talk show host Joy Behar announced Republicans are 'evil, immoral, unethical and also stupid'.[67] Really? Is it possible that all the millions of Americans who identify as Republicans are all evil, immoral and stupid? Are they really all Nazis? Are they all racists? Of course not, but it's easier to demonise a group that way if you don't know any and aren't prepared to say such things to the faces of people who live in your neighbourhood, who take their kids to your kids' school, who visit your bank and grocery stores. My friends and family would say to me, once they knew I didn't think Sarah Palin was the most evil person ever in human history, that they were worried I'd joined 'the other side'.

Salon Magazine ran an illuminating article by a blogger named Taffy Brodesser-Anker called 'I Can't Believe My Best Friend is a Republican'. In it she describes how her best friend Janet, a conservative Republican living in a sea of liberal Democrats, drives her crazy with weird political beliefs. Much to the consternation of the author, Janet seems to inexplicably and wholeheartedly subscribe to these beliefs. But Brodesser-Anker finds that rather than being evil or stupid, Janet has actually thought through her beliefs, and has rational reasons for holding them. It turns out that discussing opposing political points of view solidifies the intellectual underpinnings of Brodesser-Anker's opinions. She writes:

> We need friends who differ from us. It's easy to watch Republican extremism and think, 'Wow, they're crazy.' But when someone is sitting face to face with us, when someone we admire and respect is telling us they believe differently, it is at this fine point that we find nuance, and we begin to understand exactly how we got to this point in history. We lose something critical when we surround ourselves with people who agree with us all the time.[68]

Being able to think through why you believe what you believe, to be able to test your opinion in real-world situations in which you come face to face with someone who is as intelligent and human as you are, actually does your mind and your understanding of the world so much good.

City dwellers love to say that urban diversity makes for more tolerant communities. The idea they champion is that getting used to living with people of different ethnicities and nationalities makes us all more understanding and tolerant of those different from us, but the idea works better in theory than in practice. For example, Joe Klein from *Time* magazine imagines a hick rube like Sarah Palin frightening redneck, racist heartland voters with a vision of America 'changing for the worse, overrun by furriners [sic] of all sorts: Latinos, South Asians, East Asians, homosexuals ... to say nothing of liberated, uppity blacks.' However, the actual

America that Joe Klein lives in, ritzy Pelham, New York, is more lily-white than the America Sarah Palin lives in, Wasilla, Alaska (87.33 per cent white to 85.46 per cent).[69] If Mr Klein wished to experience true diversity, ideological diversity works the same way as physical diversity; exposure to lots of different ideas makes us tolerant, understanding and, at the end of the day, more intellectual than walling ourselves off in some ideological – or indeed actual – ghetto. Perhaps Mr Klein should try it where he lives.

But this hardly ever happens any more – and that's the problem. People don't often have friends or acquaintances from other political persuasions. It's not that a person isn't vulnerable to Fear of the Other manipulation if they have friends, neighbours and colleagues who are the Other, but it's harder to do and harder to make it stick. In the United States in 2011, most people don't know anybody from the other political party. We are the most politically segregated that we have ever been in our nation's history. There was a time when Republicans and Democrats lived in the same neighbourhoods, socialised at each other's houses, even had friendly debates with each other at the Elk Club. Those days are almost extinct. This is due to a number of factors: the decline of public intellectual life, increasing economic mobility, the decline of the manufacturing sector and income inequality. But the result is clear: political beliefs have become a lifestyle choice that one selects when moving to a place like good schools, leafy streets, coffee shops and farmers' markets – and opposing political beliefs become as alien as little green men from Mars. Which leaves us all vulnerable to attacks demonising the Other, exactly the situation that the political economy needs to fund a multi-billion dollar election.

Because of this, people who are minorities in a sea of political majority opinion and who have differing political views from their friends and colleagues, particularly if they're conservative, feel the need to keep quiet to avoid ridicule and ostracism. It's not only physical assault they have to worry about, like Jedediah Bila's elderly friend in New York City. Author Harry Stein, who wrote a book on the phenomenon, quoted a gay friend of his in San Francisco, who said, 'it's a lot easier to be gay in San Francisco than a Republican', adding that when he came out as a Republican 'friends abandoned me. I got called a fascist, traitor, crazy, insane, a racist.'[70] Jonathan Haidt, the psychology professor who described political beliefs as creating a 'tribal-moral' community, said he had corresponded with conservative graduate students 'whose experiences reminded him of closeted gay students in the 1980s'.[71] We're so separated from those who have different political beliefs that when we find a representative of the demonised Other, we seem more than happy to demonise former friends and relatives as well. This hardly seems right or just. How did this come to be? Was America always this politically segregated?

In 1953, sociologist C. Wright Mills wrote, Americans were not 'radical, not liberal, not conservative, not reactionary ... they are inactionary; they are out of it'. From the late 1940s to the mid-1970s, political partisanship just didn't seem to matter to most Americans. Faith in public institutions began dropping throughout the 1960s, reaching its nadir after the Watergate scandal in 1973. And then, after the 1976 election, something began to happen. That post-Watergate election was a closely contested one between Republican Gerald Ford and Democrat Jimmy Carter, with the very future of the presidency hanging in the balance. Carter won, but, most interestingly for our purposes, only 26.8 per cent of voters lived in counties that voted for one candidate over another at rates higher than 50 per cent. These kind of major results gave these localities the nickname 'landslide counties'. In subsequent elections we started seeing a big uptick in the numbers of people who lived in these so-called 'landslide counties', to the point where in the 2008 election, 47.6 per cent – nearly half of the American population – lived in a county where 50 per cent or more of the people voted for one candidate or another. This is why people don't know very many adherents to different political beliefs; they don't live near one another any more. If you're American, you have a one in two chance of living in an area where you probably won't get to meet somebody who votes for the opposite political party.

In the 1990s, up to 100 million Americans relocated across a county border. The phenomenon was particularly pronounced among young people: in 1990, twenty to thirty-four year olds were evenly distributed among America's 320 largest cities; in 2000, 80 per cent of them were concentrated in twenty-one cities. Almost half of them had a college degree. Those twenty-one cities also saw increased wages, perhaps unsurprisingly, since highly educated young professionals were clustering together; wages in Austin, Texas, for example, increased by 7.1 per cent per year, in the same period but only by 1.8 per cent per year in Wheeling, West Virginia. The American economy, which looked like a flat plateau in the golden years of 1945–75, now had great peaks and troughs around its urban areas. And as we've seen, urban, wealthy, highly educated places almost always vote Democrat; rural, poorer areas without concentrations of college-educated people vote Republican.

Prior to the 1970s, people obviously had political leanings and different political cultures, but they tended to be more mixed up in suburban neighbourhoods. Political partisanship just wasn't particularly important to them. But since the societal upheaval of the late 1960s, the hysterical reaction both for and against über-conservative Barry Goldwater, and the arrival of powerful, donation-led advocacy groups in the late 1980s and early 1990s, political partisanship seems really important to a person's self-image. People are now acting on the knowledge that just as you can move to a neighbourhood to be around leafy streets, coffee shops, museums or wide open spaces, lots of trees, and a small-town feel, people are now moving to be with those who are more politically like themselves, for the comfort and security of ideological sameness. Writer Bill Bishop, who's studied the phenomenon, says:

> An Episcopal priest told me he had moved from the reliably Republican Louisville, Kentucky suburbs to an older city neighbourhood so that he could be within walking distance of produce stands, restaurants, and coffee shops – and to be among other Democrats. A journalism professor at the University of North Carolina told me that when he retired, he moved to a more urban part of Chapel Hill to escape Republican neighbours. A new resident of a Dallas exurb told a *New York Times* reporter that she stayed away from liberal Austin when considering a move, choosing the Dallas suburb of Frisco instead. 'Politically, I feel a lot more at home here,' she explained. People don't need to check voting records to know the political flavour of a community. They can smell it.[72]

What's fascinating about what's happening in America now is that while we know different people have different tastes – some people like to have loads of coffee shops and chichi restaurants around, while others like to live by the local church and have lots of fields to play sports in – those kinds of things have political value as well. If you want to have coffee shops where you live, you're most likely a Democrat. If you want to have churches where you live, you're most likely a Republican. Political beliefs are becoming as much of a lifestyle – and class – choice as a car or a pet or one's clothes. And as such, Democrats and Republicans don't really want to interact with each other. Bishop quotes a man on his neighbourhood email list who, after receiving emails from a conservative living in the neighbourhood, wrote: 'I'm really not interested [in] being surprised by right-wing emails in my in box, no matter what its guise. It makes me feel bad, and I don't like it.'[73]

Political debate can be exhausting, but it seems like people don't even want to have a whiff of political disagreement in case an impromptu episode of *Hannity and Colmes* breaks out. But Americans used to love arguing over politics and had long-time friendships despite (or perhaps because of) ideological differences. Witness the friendship between political enemies John Adams and Thomas Jefferson, who despite profound partisan differences had a deep and enduring relationship in which their correspondence bristled with intellectual argument, no doubt echoing many lively nights of conversation and debate when they saw each other in person. Adams wrote to Jefferson, 'You and I ought not to die, before we have explained ourselves to each other.' The early chronicler of American democracy and culture Alexis de Tocqueville remarked wryly:

> The cares of politics engross a prominent place in the occupations of a citizen of the United States; and almost the only pleasure an American knows is to take a part in the government and discuss its measures. This feeling pervades the most trifling habits of life: even the women frequently attend public meetings and listen to political harangues as a recreation from their household labours … an American cannot converse, but he can discuss: and his talk falls into a dissertation. He speaks to you as if he were addressing a meeting; and if he should chance to become warm in the discussion, he will say 'Gentlemen' to the person with whom he is conversing.

Perhaps his point about discussing rather than conversing is still true. But there was a time when Americans were happy to discuss and debate political disagreements. But perhaps, after 200 years of democracy, with civil war and political chicanery and Watergate to contend with, Americans these days would rather seek out reassurance than debate. Susan Jacoby, a writer who studies the decline of American intellectual life, says that when she was put up in a student dorm after a university lecture, her experience was disturbing: 'Gone were the "high level of noise and laughter", the "late-night and all-night" conversations she remembered from her own undergraduate years.'[74] Or perhaps the problem is that people just don't like encountering ideas they disagree with any more. As Bishop says, 'Opposites don't attract. Psychologists know that people seek out others like themselves for marriage and friendship. That the same phenomenon could be taking place between people and communities isn't all that surprising.'[75] For a number of reasons, people aren't seeking to broaden their intellectual horizons any more; they're retreating back into cocoons of safety, where no new ideas will disturb them.

Robert Putnam, the social scientist who tracked the decline in civic participation in his book *Bowling Alone*, found that the more high-tech and highly educated a city was, the less likely the inhabitants were to participate in civic and public activities. In high-tech cities like New York, San Francisco, San Jose and Atlanta, the inhabitants were more interested in politics and less interested in attending church, not surprisingly, but were also more likely to engage in individualistic activities like skiing or yoga, and less likely to participate in clubs, community projects or to volunteer than those in low-tech cities.[76] And that, I think, is a major cause of the decline of rational civil discourse in American public life. We used to spend time with people from different backgrounds because we were involved in the life of our communities. Now we go through our days just spending time with the friends we made in high school or in college. Since American life is now so segregated by income and education, two generations have sprung up without many opportunities to meet people who are considerably different from themselves. And since we aren't involved in projects in the community, we've lost the skills of engaging with others who might disagree with us or persuading our fellow city residents to accept our side of the argument. Instead, we just go camping for the weekend or out to the bars with our friends from school.

The political segregation of America is reflected in our gerry-mandered political districts. Political scholars Joseph Bafumi and Michael C. Herron have noted that since the 2006 mid-term elections, members of Congress are actually more ideologically extreme than their voters.[77] This leads, political observers theo-rise, to a great deal of our problems. Ideological extremism may be a symptom, but the disease is gerrymandered Congressional districts which are drawn to provide safe districts for one party or another. In the 2010 Congressional elections, two-thirds of the 435 House seats were won with victory margins of twenty points or more. Seven states had nothing but landslide victories. And two out of three Americans didn't even bother to vote in that election. Interestingly, the proportion of landslide victories was about the same as the last 'throw the bums out' mid-term election in 1994, but in all the intervening elections, the proportion of landslide elections didn't drop below 72.9 per cent.

There are a number of reasons why safe Congressional seats actually hurt American democracy. Safe seats reduce minority representation in statewide and national office; if you've ever wondered why there are so few African-American senators in the United States Senate, it's because most African-Americans get political experience in the House of Representatives, which is carved into majority-minority districts to provide guaranteed Democratic and Republican victories. So most African-American politicians have no experience running for statewide office, they're not used to calibrating their message for a large, diverse audience, and therefore don't often get recruited for Senate elections. In addition, too many safe seats encourage corruption and a lack of accountability; since constituents will keep on pulling the lever for the Democrat or the Republican, the member of Congress has no incentive to cooperate with the other party or even do a good job serving his constituents. You end up with incredibly corrupt members of Congress, like Republican Duke Cunningham of California, who went to jail after pleading guilty to accepting more than $2 million in bribes, or Democrat William Jefferson of Louisiana who collected cash bribes which he stored in casserole dishes in the freezer (feel free to insert your own 'cold cash' joke). Safe seats also encourage ideological extremism; if you represent a majority from one party, your constituents aren't going to be interested in how well you get along with the other party. They want red meat, raw and bloody – they want to see how you beat up the leader from the party or gave a fiery floor speech. Since there's no incentive to compromise, Congress just won't do it, and that's why the debt ceiling negotiations were such a debacle and the super-committee tasked with cutting the budget failed utterly.

The slow strangulation of American democracy is truly sad to see. The system depends on people being willing to participate in it from a local level on up, and if the people abdicate that responsibility it leads to political corruption and mob rule. De Tocqueville says that 'the townships, municipal bodies and counties form so many concealed breakwaters which check or part the tide of popular determination'. [78] But if we decline to participate in government at its local level, and instead retreat into ideological fortresses where we obsess over silly issues like middle names, then we get the government we deserve – a corrupt banana republic where we have little influence and even less say over what occurs.

And the very absence of politics from Americans' daily lives, except for the soap opera that plays out in newspapers and on cable channels, must seem deeply mystifying, because people only know one set of actors. Bishop says that because of political segregation, 'Americans' political lives are baffling … the facts we see on television – a nearly fifty-fifty Congress, a teetering Electoral College and presidential elections decided by teaspoons of votes – simply don't square with the overwhelming majorities we experience in our neighbourhoods.' He quotes University of Nebraska social scientist Elizabeth Theiss-Morse on this subject, who reveals from her research:

> People said many times, 'Eighty per cent of us agree… We all want the same thing. It's those 20 per cent who are just a bunch of extremists out there.' It didn't matter what their political views were. They really saw it as us against this fringe. The American people versus them, the fringe.[79]

With increasing political segregation, increasing geographic segregation and the decreasing likelihood Americans will ever meet someone who disagrees with them, it's not surprising that a caricature of the opposing party rose up in most people's heads, and it's not surprising that there's so much anger and distrust between the two parties. Movie critic Pauline Kael supposedly said indignantly after Nixon's election in 1972 that she didn't know anybody who voted for him, so she didn't see how he could have won, and that's exactly the experience most Americans have when thinking about politics; the people that vote for the opposite side are strange, weird, bizarre and alien. They are deeply disturbing and not to be trusted. Trader Jeff Carter wrote that someone once said to him at a progressive Chicago party, 'Wouldn't it be better if only people like us could vote?'[80] Despite the remark's resemblance to something that wouldn't have been out of place at a White Citizen's Council in 1950s Mississippi, the sentiment must seem appealing

to everyone who thinks that the rest of the country must be populated with bizarre people who are too stupid, crazy or out of touch
to be trusted with the tools of democracy.

The funny thing is that if we could spend a little time talking
with people who were different from us, we might feel a bit more
sympathetic to their beliefs. Europeans love to criticise Americans
for not having passports and visiting other countries, but most
Americans hardly ever visit the vastly diverse landscapes and populations in their own country. Joe Klein, the *Time* magazine writer
who likes to talk about racial diversity but chooses to live in a
largely white, undiverse enclave, decided to do just that; he extri-
cated himself from ritzy suburban New York and decided to spend
some time with Tea Party supporters in Texarkana, where the
Texas-Arkansas state line runs right through the centre of town.
And he discovered something rather extraordinary, particularly to
Time's readers – the Tea Partiers might just have a point. Instead
of being Bible-thumping Christian extremists that want to outlaw
abortion and the teaching of evolution in public schools, what
they're worried about is the federal government getting in the way
of making a livelihood. Klein found out that local builders can no
longer get quick 'character loans' from the bank that they need for
construction projects, thanks to the Dodd-Frank financial reform
Bill. Even the bankers were complaining how difficult the new
regulations made doing business – they told the writer that they'd
love to make more loans, but the law made it nearly impossible to
do so. After these interviews, Klein wrote:

> It seemed to me that the closer the Tea Party folks got to home,
> the more legitimate their beefs were. On the most basic, local
> level, their concern about waste and corruption seemed a good
> thing, a valuable revival of citizen concern after a long period of
> apathy. And the federal government does tend to impose layer

upon layer of new regulations without keeping track of how they're working.

It's interesting that as soon as Klein got out of the New York bubble and met Americans on whom federal legislation had a concerted impact, he suddenly learned that their concerns weren't so unfounded. In fact, he came away thinking that they're not entirely insane, except when someone calls President Obama a socialist, after which he notes, 'When they're talking about character loans, I'm all ears. When they're fantasising about socialism, I'm not.' [81] Is calling Obama a socialist an attempt to demonise him, to make him scary and threatening? Absolutely it is; it's a political rhetorical device to make the speaker's cause seem more sympathetic and the President's less familiar, less American, less caring about the constituents he's pledged to serve. But they've got the same problem Klein does; they don't spend time with people who see things from Obama's perspective – all they get is their own point of view. They therefore assume that Obama means to hurt them because he's a socialist and anti-American – why else would he and the other Democrats in government be trying to take their livelihoods away? They ascribe the trouble to malice rather than being a result of good intentions gone wrong.

The practical result of political segregation is that the two sides have grown so far apart that they can't even agree on the meanings of what we all say anymore. A total inability to listen to and understand each other means that major problems facing the Unied States literally can't be solved because there's no interest or incentive to do so. Immigration, for example, is one of the most controversial topics in American politics today; it's impossible to talk about it without either side calling the other either a racist or a criminal. I can tell you from personal experience that the immigration system in the United States is horribly dysfunctional; trying to immigrate legally to the USA is an expensive, drawn-out nightmare that forcibly separates families, whereas immigrating illegally subjects innocent people to all sorts of exploitation and cruelty. There is nothing good about the American immigration system, but we are so mired in anger and suspicion on both sides that it'll probably never be fixed.

The state of Arizona has been a frontier in the worsening Mexican drug war and crime in major Arizona cities has been getting steadily worse since 2009. As a result, in 2010 the Republican legislature of Arizona passed, and the Republican Governor Jan Brewer signed, Senate Bill 1070, which allows law enforcement officials to enquire about the immigration status of people they pull over if there is a 'reasonable suspicion' that they might be in the country illegally. The rest of the law essentially makes what had already been federal immigration crime a state crime in Arizona (employing undocumented immigrants, smuggling human beings etc.). It must be noted that the law states, rather clearly on the first page, that race, colour or national origin can't be the sole determinant of 'reasonable suspicion'.[82]

Nonetheless, Brewer, the Arizona legislature and the state itself were immediately subject to a firestorm of criticism and boycotts because they were accused of racial profiling and being prejudiced against Hispanics. The state tourism industry suffered the loss of up to forty conventions. Pop star Shakira criticised the law; her spokesperson said, 'Shakira is deeply concerned about the impact of this law on hard-working Latino families... She is coming to Arizona to try to learn more about ... how we can ensure that people in the state of Arizona are not being targeted because of the colour of their skin.'[83] There were so many comparisons of Arizona to Nazi Germany that the Simon Wiesenthal Center had to tell people to knock it off, saying 'there was no need to demonise opponents, even when they are mistaken, to those whose actions led to history's most notorious crime'.[84]

People are smart and they can develop their own ideas about immigration or whether they feel that Senate Bill 1070 is right or wrong. Perhaps it was too heavy-handed an approach to dealing with Mexican drug war-related crime. Perhaps it did place too heavy a burden on immigrants who were already in the state, who would be severely hampered in their movements. There's no doubt that many border communities are frustrated by the influx of undocumented immigrants. When I've asked Californians, Arizonans and Texans about what they object to regarding illegal immigrants, they tell me they dislike signs everywhere in Spanish, they don't appreciate their hospitals being shut down because hospitals can't treat so many people unable to pay their emergency room bills, and they don't like the increased crime rate from gangs making their incursions into the USA. They never say, 'I hate Mexicans'; in fact, they often are Mexican. But many progressives look at the list of concerns above and say that no matter what people who object to immigration say about schools or hospitals or crime, these are just masking the real problem – they hate Hispanics. End of. I suppose it's possible that they do – they might in fact not like the demographic changes happening to the community. But I've never heard any first-hand evidence of that, and I don't think it's helpful to assume prejudice exists when, in fact, there are other valid concerns being raised. It doesn't make the crime situation any better to demonise people who are concerned about severe drug trafficking problems and a surge in kidnapping cases in Phoenix as racists and Nazis. Drug-related crime hurts everybody in Arizona – Hispanic, Anglo, African-American, American Indian. In July 2010, twenty-one people were killed in a gun battle just 12 miles south of the Arizona border. Two of their heads were found stuffed in between the bars of a cemetery fence.[85] Will insulting Arizonans bring them back? If we can't even talk about the reality of a serious problem without descending into *ad hominem* attacks, how are we ever going to solve the really serious problems facing us? Political segregation is not only making public discourse uglier, it's making it dysfunctional. We're so segregated from one another, and there's so much political gain to be had from making sure we don't agree, we're frankly unable to solve any of our rather severe problems.

Another example of political segregation getting in the way of doing actual good work for the country was the fight over raising the debt ceiling. This turned into a philosophical debate and mud-slinging match, with Republicans using the issue to force debates over cutting spending, entitlement reform and deficit reduction. The Democrats' riposte was that if the debt ceiling wasn't raised, economic havoc would break loose. It wasn't a new fight; debates over the debt ceiling have been an annual controversy for many years. I remember fights over the debt ceiling when I started working in political journalism and no doubt there will continue to be debt ceiling arguments until the end of time. Notably, in 2006, the junior senator from Illinois, one Barack Obama, said while voting against raising the debt ceiling:

> Increasing America's debt weakens us domestically and inter-
> nationally. Leadership means that the buck stops here. Instead,
> Washington is shifting the burden of bad choices today onto
> the backs of our children and grandchildren. America has a debt
> problem and a failure of leadership. Americans deserve better.[86]

These were the days when the Democratic Party was campaigning on the same fiscal responsibility platform the Republicans have now, but their dreams of balancing the federal budget, as has happened time and time again, foundered on the rocky shores of entitlement spending and public service employees' pensions.

Since the heady days of the 2006 mid-term election campaign, though, Democrats have embraced public spending as a way not only to create Keynesian economic stimulus, but also to end the ills that income inequality creates. In an interview with the *Wall Street Journal* during the debt ceiling debacle, House Majority Leader Eric Cantor (R-VA), said that there was a fundamental philosophical difference between the Republicans and the Democrats on the issue of taxing the rich:

> The debate always returned to the status of the top marginal rate for individuals earning over $200,000 and $250,000 for couples... Mr Cantor argued that some large portion of the income that flows through the top bracket comes from 'pass-through entities' – that is, businesses – and 'to me, that strikes at the core of what I believe should be the policy, and that is to provide incentives for entrepreneurs to grow'... By contrast, he says, 'Never was there ever an underlying economic argument' from Democrats. 'It was all about social justice. Honestly, one of them said to me, "Some people just make too much money."'[87]

The major political battle over the economy, the single most pressing issue for the 2012 election is going to come down to the following philosophical question: how should tax policy be used to stimulate economic growth? Should our taxes be used to redistribute income from the rich to the middle class and the poor as well as to provide government jobs for the unemployed or should tax rates be cut for business owners so that they can create the engine of growth through the private sector? There are lots of complex economic issues behind this philosophical conundrum, and it's an unemotional argument anyway because there are merits to both sides and lots of unknown variables that decrease certainty. So, for the purposes of the election, it's much easier and more effective to call the Republicans 'selfish' and 'cruel' and the Democrats 'socialist' and 'anti-American'. Unfortunately, when we do this, we end up in a situation where people refuse to talk to each other, because no one likes to be insulted. In addition, Americans who are whipped into a frenzy by manipulative political advertising aren't in a mood to reward compromisers, particularly since most of Congress is so polarised by party. So Congressional representatives, coming from segregated local districts, refuse to talk with one another, they refuse to negotiate, their ideological positions become entrenched, and America's credit rating gets slashed for the first time in its history. Congratulations all round.

We know all too well that demagoguery and demonisation are effective political tools. Researchers Ken Goldstein and Paul Friedman discovered that not only does negative advertising raise interest in elections, it can also raise the perception of the election's importance, which increases turn-out.[88] This is why it's so important to make sure your version of events is the one that captures the public's attention first, and why, whenever any kind of political event occurs, there's such an army of people available to chatter away on television, radio, in print and online to tell you how to feel about it.

A great example is the meme that the Tea Party is racist. Since its explosion onto the public scene, politicians, media commentators and bloggers have been accusing Tea Partiers of being prejudiced against minorities. Part of the accusation comes because they oppose an African-American president, and part of it is because that's the worst epithet their opponents can think to hurl at them. For a while, the front-runner for the Republican nomination, thanks largely to Tea Party support, was Herman Cain, who is African-American. The development tied progressives up in knots, because it's not exactly straightforward to accuse someone of being a racist when there's a popular groundswell to elect an African-

American. This hasn't stopped people from trying, though; commentator Janeane Garofalo hypothesised, 'People like Karl Rove liked to keep the racism very covert. And so Herman Cain provides this great opportunity so you can say "Look, this is not a racist, anti-immigrant, anti-female, anti-gay movement. Look we have a black man… Look he's polling well and won a straw poll!"'[89] That's pretty darn covert prejudice, if a party is trying to hide their racism and their beliefs that African-Americans are inferior to everyone else by, uh, popularly supporting an African-American man for president. Karl Rove sure is wily!

Cain's candidacy foundered due to his response to a number of women accusing him of sexual harassment. The accusation of white women being sexually harassed by a black man has very strong cultural currency in the United States because of the ugly history of white men hurting and killing black men because they 'looked' at white women or insulted them in some way. Emmett Till's murder, one of the flashpoints of the civil rights era, occurred because two white men were insulted that Till whistled at a white woman. The most influential film of the 1920s, *Birth of a Nation*, was a celebration of the Ku Klux Klan, which pledged to protect the honour of white women from marauding African-Americans. So it's quite interesting that progressives championed the white women making unspecified allegations against a black man. Facts on the ground about these accusations were awfully thin; even after he suspended his candidacy we still don't know what Cain did or didn't do, and the story from the one woman who named specifics is unverifiable because she made her accusation after the criminal statute of limitations had expired, and therefore it can't be tried in court. Equally, when a woman piled on and accused him of having an affair, there was still no attempt to get any kind of verifiable detail; he was considered a philanderer, and because there was so much controversy about his purported relationships with women, it overwhelmed his campaign. We will never know what the truth is about what he did or did not do with these women. Because Cain's response was muddled, and because he had no interest in foreign policy, which made primary voters unwilling to defend him, his candidacy was doomed.

A more sophisticated reporter, Dave Weigel, actually gets to the heart of the Tea Party racism charge – but what he discovers is that the two sides can't agree on what racism actually is. Weigel points out that even though Cain was in fact a Tea Party darling, and Tea Partiers do support African-Americans in their movement and encourage them to run for political office, they still hold what he describes as 'negative views of blacks and Hispanics'. To support his point, he quotes Christopher Parker from the University of Washington, who did a study on the Tea Party and race. The study consisted of asking white people, both Tea Party supporters and non-supporters, to tell him whether they agreed with certain state-ments about black people. Here's one of the statements: 'Irish, Italians, Jewish and many other minorities overcame prejudice and worked their way up. Blacks should do the same without special favours.' Seventy per cent of white people agreed with this, and 88 per cent of Tea Partiers also agreed. Do you agree with this statement? If you do, then you hold a 'negative view' of African-Americans.

Is that really racism? What the study seems to be testing is people's feelings about affirmative action, not African-Americans. There's not necessarily a logical connection between supporting affirmative action and being a racist, but to Parker and Weigel, it's enough to say that rank-and-file Tea Partiers are only supporting Cain because he's a token who supports their racial views. The gulf between the two sides is so wide there will never be any kind of consensus on the topic; to Weigel and Parker, if you don't support affirmative action, then you're irredeemably racist, and to the average Tea Partier, supporting affirmative action has nothing to do with your feelings about the capabilities of African-Americans or any other ethnic minority. Both sides are walled off, they're not talking, they won't come to an agreement, so they hurl *ad hominem* attacks from parapet to parapet.

There's another factor to Democratic politicians insisting that Republicans and Tea Partiers are and forever will be horribly racist. Ninety-five per cent of African-Americans voted for Obama in 2008, 88 per cent of African-Americans turned out for Kerry in 2004, and 90 per cent pulled the lever for Gore in 2000. Particularly in close elections, Democrats desperately need African-Americans to stay as a solid voting bloc or else their election hopes will be seriously doomed. Cain promised to deliver one-third of the African-American vote if he was the nominee for president; if he did, Obama's re-election would be extraordinarily difficult, if not impossible. Political observers have to wonder whether the extraordinary barrage of sexual harassment, assault, and infidelity claims – without specifics – were designed to neutralise Cain before he could peel off any African-American votes. Democrats have to do everything they can to make sure African-Americans aren't tempted by Republicans, which is why they shout 'Racist!' at every opportunity, whether it's warranted or not.

But the accusation can stick, because most people in the media – and indeed most people who consume the legacy media – don't know anybody who would ever support the Tea Party. They don't do as Joe Klein did and travel to Arkansas to find out more about these people and their beliefs – that would be icky and boring. In my interviews with Tea Party members, I found them to be very normal and not terribly different from myself, but most people living in the UK or in blue neighbourhoods in the USA would never get to speak with a Tea Partier, let alone get to know their concerns. Too many people, therefore, happily live with the misconception that the Tea Party is horribly bigoted; they enjoy the stereotypes presented for our delectation on the evening news and never bother to find out the truth. Interestingly, the Tea Party has also demonised the Occupy Wall Street protestors, who gained prominence in the autumn of 2011; they dismiss them as 'smelly hippies' or 'over-entitled kids', which, while true in some cases, doesn't reflect the true nature of the movement, nor does it recognise the common ground that they share. So a true political partnership that could possibly solve the major problem of the buying of influence in American politics is destroyed thanks to Fear of the Other.

This desperate need to demonise the Other for political gain has resulted in the ultimate expression of political segregation: truly repulsive 'dog-whistle' politics. The idea behind dog-whistle politics is that in a world where overt racism is frowned upon, certain things can be said by political candidates to their supporters that let them know their true feelings about ethnic minorities, women etc. There is no question that there are certain racial epithets, like 'Oreo', that have cultural currency and which are offensive. The trouble comes when the dog whistles become absurd. MSNBC anchor Ed Schultz explained that South Carolina GOP ('Grand Old Party' a traditional nickname for the Republican Party with its abbreviation – GOP – a commonly used designation) Senator Jim Demint used an 'old Southern racist term' when Demint said, 'If we are able to stop Obama on this [health care law], it will be his Waterloo. It will break him.' Schultz clarified that the racist term was 'It will break him.' The television presenter invited Dr James Peterson, a professor of Africana studies at Lehigh University, to explain why this was racist:, '"Break" is a racist verb, a term that was used to destroy, mentally and physically, slaves… [Demint's] comment shows how dark some of these racial discourses can be in presidential politics.'[90] Really? The word 'break' is some sort of racial pejorative? Huh. Another example came when Newt Gingrich said:

If you look at the collapse of Detroit and the rise of Texas, would you rather live in the state that's had the most job creation in the last ten years or a city that's collapsed? I know, and Governor Rick Perry knows, how to get the whole country to resemble Texas. President Obama knows how to get the whole country to resemble Detroit.

MSNBC anchor Chris Matthews called this the 'worst' example of race-based language he'd heard 'since Reagan talked about welfare queens'. Apparently, because Gingrich mentioned Detroit, – a majority black city – it's, as one of his guests said, 'race-baiting language'.[91] So don't talk about the economic problems of Detroit, because that's racist!

The notion of 'dog-whistle' politics strangles rational discussion and becomes more about thought control and getting your opponent to shut up, rather than having an open exchange of ideas. Calling someone a racist is what people say when they don't want to take policy seriously, when they don't want an audience to engage with new ideas; it forces the speaker to defend him or herself against the charge of racism rather than debate the merits of the idea itself. Any time someone calls a political opponent a racist, it's a sign they don't want to engage in intellectual civic discussion.

It's funny that even though Americans are polarised by political party, when it comes to actual beliefs on issues, they're not terribly far apart from one another. Morris Fiorina, a professor at Stanford, examined this phenomenon, and concluded that it was politicians, political consultants and the media who were stoking the blue state-red state war, because it certainly wasn't actual Americans doing it. He wrote:

Publicly available databases show that the culture war script embraced by journalists and politicos lies somewhere between simple exaggeration and sheer nonsense. There is no culture war in the United States; no battle for the soul of America rages, at least none that most Americans are aware of… If swing voters have disappeared, how did the six blue states in which George Bush ran most poorly in 2000 all elect Republican governors in 2002 (and how did Arnold Schwarzenegger run away with the 2003 recall in blue California)? If almost all voters have already made up their minds about their 2004 votes, then why did John Kerry surge to a 14-point trial-heat lead when polls offered voters the prospect of a Kerry-McCain ticket? If voter partisanship has hardened into concrete, why do virtually identical majorities in both red and blue states favour divided control of the presidency and Congress, rather than unified control by their party?[92]

Fiorina pointed out that while political activists, lobbyists and employees of cause groups feel as though they're soldiers in a constant war, most Americans are much more moderate in their beliefs. He quotes the example that most self-identified Republicans are in favour of gay marriage, much to the chagrin of social conservative activists. It's so disappointing that because of the influence of money on politics, organisations are desperate to exploit our anxieties and prejudices to make us vote or donate. Studies indicate Americans are moderate, tolerant people who are more than happy to live and let live, who don't want to impose their beliefs on anyone else. But because we need to be roused into the electoral booth every two years, we're fed all sorts of attacks that prey on our worst impulses to get us to donate and vote the right way. And it's a chimera.

Every time I go to a pub in London and say that I'm writing a book about the 2012 election, I immediately get asked by a grinning Brit whether or not Michele Bachmann is going to win the Republican nomination (the answer, by the way, is no, because she flamed out in a September 2011 Republican debate by stating that vaccines can cause mental retardation. So much for the GOP not believing in science!). British media organs like the BBC and *The Guardian* like to prop up politicians like Bachmann because it reinforces the Brits' own sense of tribalism – whatever our problems are, at least we don't have idiot politicians like that! – and because it's a terrifically exciting story, that insane Christianist Americans are poised for a theocratic takeover because of the incredible prejudice, craziness and stupidity of the great unwashed redneck, fat inhabitants of middle America. It is a great story, but it's one that's too good to be true. Writer Walter Russell Mead notes that the American population, in the last fifty years, has become more open, more tolerant, more thoughtful and more just than ever before. He recalls a time when people were beaten for interracial relationships, when divorced people couldn't get married in mainline Protestant churches, when *Time* magazine called gay people 'deviates', when *Ulysses* was banned. They say the past is a foreign country, and it is almost impossible to imagine an America like that today – anyone who holds such beliefs is rightly held up for mockery. But this was the tenor of mainstream discussion! Mead explains what caused the change:

On a whole variety of issues ... the United States has moved steadily and inexorably to a more permissive and open stance ... the country continues by and large to move culturally toward tolerance and acceptance of diversity ... what we are seeing is the continued triumph of individualism in American life ... the right must accept that individuals in our society can only be compelled by their own consciences on an ever growing list of cultural and social issues.[93]

The increasing individualism in American political thought is the positive flipside of the paucity of civic participation in the twenty-first century; because the majority of Americans believe that so many social questions should be left up to the individual, rather than decided by the state, it's made us all much more open and tolerant of how people want to live their lives. That's an unambiguously positive trend. It also means that the Christianist nightmare of fevered BBC imaginings – the horror of a President Bachmann – won't ever come true. Most people just don't see the point of hating others because of their lifestyle choices. A Christianist theocracy just isn't possible in the USA – not enough people are bothered about how others live their lives.

That doesn't mean that tribalism can't be employed for political purposes; it just can't be used for something that the American people have already rejected. Gerald Ford's divorce was an issue in the 1976 presidential campaign, for example, but now it seems almost impossible to believe that anyone would care. But demonising people because of their political beliefs? Thanks to the political segregation of America, political consultants have landed on a tribalism that can work in their favour.

But it doesn't have to be this way – you don't have to participate in this kind of psychological manipulation for the benefit of some lobbyist on K Street or an advocacy group seeing you as their own personal ATM. When you hear a political commentator paint 'all conservatives' or 'all liberals' a certain way, or when you hear a politician say that 'all Democrats do this' or 'all Republicans do that', recognise they're exploiting one of our most human weaknesses: our tendency to band together against outsiders. Know this manipulation for what it is, and use reason and analysis to judge whether the critique is warranted.

4

CIVILITY FOR ME BUT NOT FOR THEE

On 8 January 2011, a young man opened fire at a Tucson supermarket where Gabrielle Giffords, the local Congressional representative, was holding a public event. It was a horrific scene. Nineteen people were shot, six of them fatally, including a nine-year-old child, Christina Taylor-Green. Rep. Giffords was herself shot in the head, but miraculously survived. The event horrified the world.

But in the midst of all the public expressions of grief and shock, one man saw a fantastic political opportunity. He was Markos Moulitsas, the founder and editor of the progressive 'Daily Kos' blog, who tweeted the following later that day: 'Mission accomplished, Sarah Palin.' He linked to an article from the progressive blog 'FireDogLake', showing a map from the SarahPAC website (the website for Palin's political fundraising operation) in which Congressional seats that would receive campaign funds in the 2010 election were demarcated with targets – one of them being Giffords' seat. Because of this map, according to Moulitsas, Palin was responsible for the shooter gunning down Giffords and eighteen other people. Bear in mind that we knew nothing about the shooter except his name – and even that was spelled wrong in a lot of news reports – it didn't matter that he was the one who actually pulled the trigger. The event was Sarah Palin's fault.

If you believed the evidence that Moulitsas and other progressive bloggers were offering, it could seem like there was an epidemic of violent rhetoric coming from the American right wing. A tweet that Palin had put out in March 2010, saying 'Commonsense

Conservatives & lovers of America: "Don't Retreat, Instead – RELOAD!" Pls see my Facebook page' became a portent of deadly violence. People quoted Sharron Angle, the Republican candidate for Senate in 2010, saying:

> I feel that the Second Amendment is the right to keep and bear arms for our citizenry. This not for someone who's in the military. This not for law enforcement. This is for us. And in fact when you read that Constitution and the founding fathers, they intended this to stop tyranny. This is for us when our government becomes tyrannical... I'm hoping that we're not getting to Second Amendment remedies.[94]

They tried very hard to pin the violent rhetoric on Michele Bachmann saying she wanted Minnesotans to be 'armed and dangerous on the issue of the energy tax', but when it emerged from the context of her remarks that she actually meant them to be 'armed and dangerous' with informational fliers that she'd brought to an event, the accusation fell down somewhat.[95]

The sudden plethora of examples of violent rhetoric, as progressives saw it, caused sympathetic bloggers to leap on the meme with delighted enthusiasm. One blogger at 'Daily Kos', writing under the pseudonym 'Thunder Road', scolded:

> The social context in which this horrific event took place was one of hatred and intolerance, promulgated by Sarah Palin, Glenn Beck, Rush Limbaugh, Sharon [sic] Angle and so many supposed leaders who irresponsibly and subtly (sometimes, not so subtly) fanned the flames of violence, hatred and intolerance ... all of those who promoted, with a wink and a nod, target maps and 'second amendment remedies', you have blood on your hands.[96]

'Thunder Road' wrote this one day after the shooting, when we still didn't know anything about the shooter other than his name, and yet he or she thought it not only logical to blame the shooting on some purported social context, but also to use the deaths of eight people and Giffords fighting for her life as a launching pad for a kind of political gamesmanship. Then the claim that Palin was somehow responsible for the shooting began to be repeated in the legacy media, not just the blogosphere; the majority whip in the Senate, Dick Durbin (Democrat; Illinois), intoned on CNN: 'The phrase "don't retreat, reload", putting crosshairs on congressional districts as targets – these sorts of things, I think, invite the kind of toxic rhetoric that can lead unstable people to believe this is an acceptable response.'[97] Then the floodgates opened and it became rather fashionable to wonder whether the country's overheated political rhetoric was creating a toxic environment that could somehow spawn murders:

> 'Shooting Throws Spotlight on State of U.S. Political Rhetoric,' reports CNN. 'Bloodshed Puts New Focus on Vitriol in Politics,' states the *New York Times*. Keith Olbermann clocked overtime on Saturday to deliver a commentary subtitled 'The political rhetoric of the country must be changed to prevent acts of domestic terrorism.' The home page of the *Washington Post* offered this headline to its story about the shooting: 'Rampage Casts Grim Light on U.S. Political Discord.'[98]

The best crystallisation of the argument that tough political talk could somehow drive people to murder was realised in an infamous *New York Times* editorial that all but said Republicans were inciting violence by opposing government policies. The editorial board of the paper of record said:

101

It is facile and mistaken to attribute this particular madman's act directly to Republicans or Tea Party members. But it is legitimate to hold Republicans and particularly their most virulent supporters in the media responsible for the gale of anger that has produced the vast majority of these threats, setting the nation on edge. Many on the right have exploited the arguments of division, reaping political power by demonising immigrants, or welfare recipients, or bureaucrats. They seem to have persuaded many Americans that the government is not just misguided, but the enemy of the people.[99]

Many in the progressive blogosphere, Democrats, members of the media, nice people on the Upper West Side of Manhattan, equally nice people in the San Francisco Bay area, and right-thinking people in the salons of Islington believe this argument wholeheartedly, and espouse it with great fervour, but it's got one major problem: it is utter and complete codswallop from beginning to end.[100] There was no particular upswing of violent rhetoric from the right that wasn't matched by the left; Palin hadn't said anything more objectionable than, for example, what President Obama had said during the campaign. Martial campaign rhetoric is standard for both parties; a few days after Democrats, progressives and their fellow travellers promised to tone down the rhetoric, they immediately went back to calling Republicans and Tea Party members idiots, racists and Nazis, while continuing to make violent threats and in some cases actually do violence against them.

The whole notion of 'a new civility' in political rhetoric or a 'new tone' has been so thoroughly discredited at this point that even *New York Times* columnist Paul Krugman, who popularised the felicitous phrase 'eliminationist rhetoric', isn't banging the drum for it anymore. But for a time in 2011, the idea that there ought to be prescribed ways to discuss political issues, particularly when Republicans or conservatives were doing the speaking, did actually gain some traction. It'll no doubt be brought up again when Democrats feel incensed about the intense campaign that the Republican nominee will run in 2012. But let's be clear: the behaviour of Democrats and progressives both before the Giffords shooting and in the weeks and months afterwards revealed that calling for 'a new civility' was just a fancier way of saying 'Shut up, I don't know how to respond to your argument.' We'll see lots of people talking about the 'violence of Republicans' and the 'inchoate rage of the Tea Party' and such in 2012, and none of it's true – but it serves a handy purpose, like the racism charge. The charge of incivility stops candidates from persuading voters about issues and forces them to defend themselves, effectively killing any kind of political debate.

It's easy to think of the civility battles as an old fight – after all, the resentments that they exposed were the raw wounds that partisans were feeling after the two previous elections. Conservatives were angry at the way their ideas, and Palin in particular, had been treated in 2008 and progressives were incensed about the way they'd been treated in 2010. But what does this have to do with the future? The notion of 'a new civility' is dead; why should we resurrect it? In their 2004 book, *The Way to Win: Taking The White House 2008*, Mark Halperin (a progressive journalist who lost his job at MSNBC for calling Obama 'a dick' on air – three cheers for civility) and John Harris called this process 'freak-show politics':

[Freak-show politics] is promoted by the erosion of basic habits of decorum and self-restraint, in politics and media alike. In an earlier generation, these habits meant that people more often refrained from fully expressing how much they loathed one another. In the current generation, self-restraint is commonly regarded as a weakness and rarely is rewarded economically or politically. The result is that the extreme and eccentric voices who always populated the margins of politics now reside, with money and fame as the rewards, at the center. Michael Moore, please say hello to Ann Coulter. The collapse of filters and the collapse of civility together have changed the purpose of politics. The goal now is not simply to win, but to persuade voters (and donors and viewers and readers) that an opponent lacks the character and credibility even to deserve a place in the contest.[101]

There's nothing particularly helpful or illuminating for political understanding in the kind of freak-show politics that exists now in the papers, on cable TV channels and radio shows, and in the blogosphere, but it makes people feel good, it's fun to produce and in the end it provides ratings. Freak-show politics came about because of the human preference to learn about things in a narrative format; to tell a story in a way the audience can understand, the media needs to present it as linear narrative with a beginning, middle and an end. And of course, any media outlet needs to present its stories in the most compelling way possible, which is why most stories that appear about politics are soap operas, filled with conflict, anger, chest-thumping and betrayal. The media relies on conflict to tell its stories – it needs you, the audience, to identify with one side or another so you feel like you have some skin in the game and so you'll come back to your preferred media outlet to keep getting the latest on the ongoing political storyline.

In the end, that's what a presidential election is – a soap opera with the express intention of delivering audience and ratings. Election coverage is not cheap; you've got to pay for reporters to follow the candidates around from pillar to post, pay for their lodging, petrol and food, and sometimes even pay for space on the plane the candidates travel in. The early primaries are even more expensive, with phalanxes of reporters descending on the state capitals of Des Moines and Manchester to report on the dramatic proceedings therein. Local businesses have cottoned on to the quadrennial economic boom and adjust their prices accordingly. There was a snowstorm during the 2004 Democratic New Hampshire primary, which I was covering, and the Manchester Motel 8 I was staying at, which usually charged $35 a night, was charging stranded reporters $250. During election coverage, news networks, which always undertake an enormously expensive live broadcast with multiple satellite hook-ups and technologically tricky connections between reporters in remote locations, often use the opportunity to unveil all the latest technological toys, because a presidential election is the best way to showcase how cutting edge and serious your news organisation is. In 2008, ABC News promised to 'transform Times Square' with a live outdoor broadcast and results displayed on three huge digital signs, one 23 feet high. CBS News promised the anchors would be using 'interactive touch screens to bring viewers the most updated results and information in real-time. … [Analysis will use] state-of-the-art technology to display vote counting and demographic data.' Fox News promised to broadcast its election coverage on two enormous jumbo screens, one at Times Square and one at its HQ.

The coolest technological toy to come out of the 2008 election was used by CNN, which described it this way:

> CNN will enhance interviews with remote correspondents and guests using hologram projection. The network has built sets powered by hologram technology at both campaign headquarters making it possible to project three-dimensional images into the Election Center. From the New York set, anchors will exhibit more natural conversations with newsmakers and CNN correspondents in the field by interacting in real time with their 3-D virtual images.

So instead of having the anchor, Wolf Blitzer, talk with correspondent Jessica Yellin over a screen in Grant Park, Chicago, twenty different cameras filming Yellin at once beamed a 3-D image of her into the New York studio, looking for all the world like the image of Princess Leia that came out of R2D2's memory bank in *Star Wars*. They used the technique just twice, once for Yellin and once for Black Eyed Pea will.i.am. Of course, CBC had to ruin the fun, pointing out that this technology wasn't really a hologram, but in fact something called a tomogram.

Holographic (or indeed, tomographic) projectors don't come cheap, and if CNN was going to go all *Star Wars* and project Jessica Yellin into the studio from 2,000 miles away one night a year, they had to get some pretty lavish advertising spend, meaning they had to pull in serious eyeballs. You don't get ratings by having a reasoned, comprehensive discussion of the economic costs of resetting payments for crop insurance or the travails of the municipal bond market. You get ratings by airing a lot of gubbins about which side is more racist, which First Lady connects better with the public (and which one is more of a lady than the other), which candidate you'd rather have a beer with, which has more 'fire in the belly' etc. During the 2008 election I worked as a producer on a financial radio programme for Fox News Radio in which the bread and butter issues were social security reform, pensions reform and the crisis in the housing market. But on the day that Governor Palin released the news that her daughter was pregnant, just a few days after she'd gotten the vice presidential nomination, we got so many calls about whether she was or wasn't a suitable candidate we actually exceeded the number of calls our phone system could take and literally blew the processor, which made a popping noise as it died. Most people don't want to talk about unfunded pension liabilities; they want to talk about pregnancy out of wedlock and the 'morality of abstinence education'. Sex, anger, betrayal and soap opera – these are the building blocks of modern political discourse because the networks and newspapers need to keep the money and advertisements rolling in to buy the toys to show off how big, important and necessary they are in an age where they're under constant financial pressure. And to call political coverage a soap opera isn't even a metaphor any more; the casting company behind reality juggernaut and deeply educational television programme *Jersey Shore* has put out a cast notice for 'Strong-willed, well-informed, great-looking, outspoken partici- pant in the American political system, with something to believe in and a hell of a lot to say about it… [for] a *major* cable network.'[102] Hey, arguing about politics, particularly if you're hot, is big-time money. Do we think this soap opera is going to be a high-minded discussion of important political principles? Or is it going to be a high-risk speed contest of who calls somebody 'Adolf Hitler' first?

Guy Debord, a Marxist thinker who was the most influential member of the Situationist International, an intellectual collective that flourished in the 1950s and 1960s, noted that what we think of reality is actually a spectacle, designed to keep us productive and entertained. He wrote:

> The society which rests on modern industry is not accidentally or superficially spectacular, it is fundamentally spectaclist … as the indispensable decoration of the objects produced today, as the general exposé of the rationality of the system, as the advanced economic sector which directly shapes a growing multitude of image-objects, the spectacle is the main production of present- day society … the spectacle subjugates living men to itself to the extent that the economy has totally subjugated them.[103]

In order for us to exist in our modern industrial society, in which all of us are increasingly engaged in labouring to make things that are increasingly alienated from our own needs and wants, we have to have some sort of rationale to keep going on with our lives, because otherwise we would be overcome with despair at the office-bound worker drones we've become. The 'spectacle' is Debord's way of describing it; 'the culture industry' is how Adorno and Horkheimer described a similar phenomenon, but the results are the same – we are fed exciting stuff to keep us entertained and quiet in the hope that we won't actually try to create some real social change. So don't expect actual coverage of issues that will make a difference when it comes to presidential politics. The media will give the teeming masses what they want – sex and lies and videotape – because that's what brings in the eyeballs, which in turn attract the advertisers. As neo-Situationist linguist Noam Chomsky put it:

> The real mass media are basically trying to divert people. Let them do something else, but don't bother us (us being the people who run the show). Let them get interested in professional sports, for example. Let everybody be crazed about professional sports or sex scandals or the personalities and their problems or something like that. Anything, as long as it isn't serious.[104]

Unlike Chomsky and his fellow travellers, I don't think that the focus on the soap opera of presidential politics comes from malice on the media's part – they really do need to pay for expertly coiffured anchorpersons and shiny studios and, more importantly, the actual reporters and producers who are going out and finding good stories and reporting on them in interesting ways. And you're not going to get that without getting advertisers. But what this means is that we, as the audience of a media which is part of the spectacle, have to be really careful to think critically about what we see and hear – because so much of it is designed to manipulate us to think in certain ways for business reasons, not because it's, you know, true.

This is why the notion of the 'new civility' is a particularly brazen load of rubbish. It's a common sentiment that we're living in the most partisan and polarised period in American history. Massachusetts Governor and presidential candidate Mitt Romney said President Obama was 'one of the most divisive [presidents] in American history',[105] whereas his Vermont counterpart, Howard Dean, claimed that President Bush was.[106] Anyone who thinks this has either a short memory or a limited knowledge of American history, because there have been much more partisan and polarised periods than this one. In 1856, US Senator Preston Brooks walked into the Senate chamber and beat Senator Charles Sumner with a walking cane until he was unconscious. In 1850, Senator Henry Foote of Mississippi pulled a gun and aimed at fellow Senator Thomas Hart Benton of Missouri. It didn't get any better after the Civil War was over. Imagine what those years must have been like: Americans had been fighting against each other in living memory; people who had, decades previously, met each other on the battlefield were now passing each other in the halls of the US Capitol. The memories were certainly bitter and those memories were used to great partisan advantage, particularly from the victorious North, the Republicans, over the losing South, largely Democrats. In those days, you could re-enact the Civil war every time you cast a vote. Here's a campaign speech delivered by ex-Union Colonel Robert Ingersoll for Republican Rutherford B. Hayes in 1876:

> Every man that shot Union soldiers was a Democrat... Every man that loved slavery better than liberty was a Democrat. The man who assassinated Abraham Lincoln was a Democrat... Every man that wanted the privilege of whipping another man to make him work for nothing and pay him with lashes on his naked back was a Democrat... Every man that clutched from shrieking,

shuddering, crouching, mothers, babes from their breasts, and sold them into slavery, was a Democrat. Soldiers, every scar you have on your heroic bodies was a Democrat. Every arm that is lacking, every limb that is gone, is a souvenir of a Democrat. I want you to recollect it.[107]

This kind of speech was called 'waving the bloody shirt', by which they meant a uniform splattered with the blood of your martyred comrades. The remarkable thing about this speech is how personal it is – he used the anger he felt over the Civil War to whip the Republican convention into a partisan frenzy – and had you been in that hall that day, could you really say you could have resisted? You'd have been shouting and cheering for Democrats' blood like everybody else. It's an extraordinary example of political rhetoric – and it worked, too; no presidents were elected from former Confederate states until Harry Truman in 1946 (and he'd already been president because of FDR's death).

Even in more modern times, the rosy glow of history masks political rancour. President Obama wrote in an editorial longing for more civil political discourse, 'We are all patriots who put the welfare of our fellow citizens above all else. It was a philosophy that President Reagan took to heart – famously saying that he and Democratic Speaker Tip O'Neill, with whom he sparred constantly, could be friends after 6 o'clock.'[108] That wasn't the reality, though. Rep. O'Neill often used to attack Reagan personally: 'The evil is in the White House at the present time. And that evil is a man who has no care and no concern for the working class of America and the future generations of America, and who likes to ride a horse. He's cold. He's mean. He's got ice water for blood.' Reagan speechwriter Peggy Noonan recalled White House Chief of Staff Don Regan's characterisation of the men's relationship: 'Sometimes they'd have a meeting and Tip would be there and they're laughing and getting along and it's very warm. And then Regan made a fist and punched it into his palm, "Tip would leave, go up to the Hill and turn on him just like a snake! It was treachery!"'[109] So when you hear that this is the most partisan period ever in American history, it may be an exciting story to sell papers – but it isn't actually true. There's no more violent political rhetoric now than there's ever been, and the violent rhetoric that is used isn't concentrated on one side or the other.

Political rhetoric by its nature is violent – it's just a convention in American political language to equate it with war. Palin got criticised for using martial words like 'targeting' in her campaign literature, but using martial rhetoric is standard practice in political media coverage. Even the word 'campaign' comes from military etymology. The bloggers behind conservative political blog 'Verum Serum' pointed out that the media often uses martial and firearms-related metaphors to describe political events:

- Dems Fire Opening Salvo in Budget War – *Huffington Post*
- First Salvo of 2012? – FactCheck.org
- Democrats Bid Begins with a Salvo – *Washington Post*
- Obama's Salvo at McCain – MSNBC
- Obama Takes Aim at Health Insurance Companies – NPR
- Obama Targets Insurers, Sells Health Plan – Reuters
- Obama Takes Aim at School Dropout Rate – *New York Times*
- Obama Takes Aim at Liberal Critics of Health Care Bill – CBS[110]

Clearly 'violent' metaphors were a pretty standard part of political vocabulary anyway. Most of these are from long before the Giffords shooting, so if someone were to make the case that violent language in the media sent Mr Loughner over the edge, it must have taken three or four years for the military terminology to really make him snap. And how would we be able to know which source of military terminology inspired him to do a personal re-enactment of *Rambo 2*? Was it the *Washington Post*, *Huffington Post* or MSNBC? Which media outlet will have to stop broadcasting to make sure future nutburgers don't decide to open fire?

And what about that map that Palin put on her campaign fundraising website in 2010? Despite the fact that there's no evidence Loughner ever looked at it, was it beyond the pale to represent an election campaign that way? To be fair, it had been causing concern since Palin's political action committee put it up on the website in early 2010. Even Gabrielle Giffords expressed her worries about it, as she said on MSNBC:

> GIFFORDS: Community leaders, figures in our community need to say 'look, we can't stand for this'. This is a situation where – people don't – they really need to realise that the rhetoric and firing people up and, you know, even things, for example, we're on Sarah Palin's targeted list. But the thing is that the way that she has it depicted has the crosshairs of a gunsight over our district. And when people do that, they've gotta realise there's consequences to that action.
>
> TODD: But in fairness, campaign rhetoric and war rhetoric have been interchangeable for years. And so that's – is there not, is there a line here? I understand that in the moment it may look bad, but do you really think that's what she intended?
>
> GIFFORDS: You know, I can't say, I'm not Sarah Palin. But I can say that in the years that some of my colleagues have served – twenty, thirty years – they've never seen it like this.

Fair enough, but one does wonder why, if the map on the SarahPAC website bothered her so much, she didn't also object to a map placed on the website of the Democratic Congressional Campaign Committee (DCCC; the Congressional committee in charge of electing more Democrats to Congress) at the same time as the Palin map, which marked targeted Congressional seats with bull's-eyes on potential pick-ups. It even says 'Targeting Republicans' on it and lists specific Congressional representatives, just as Palin's does.[111] Interestingly, unlike Sarah Palin, who is a private citizen, the DCCC is an arm of the Democratic Party, so it was the official Democratic Party that was 'targeting' Republicans, not just one person on her own. One also has to wonder why Rep. Giffords didn't object to a 'Daily Kos' blogger – remember, those were the guys who said Palin had 'blood on her hands' because of the target map – saying in 2008 that Giffords had 'sold out the Constitution' and that her vote put a 'bull's-eye' on her district.[112] Clearly, both sides were producing political maps with targets on them, both sides were targeting Giffords herself, and it would be impossible to say definitively which side's 'scary maps' were the ones which sent the madman over the edge (even if that were a logical argument to start with).

But there must have been something to the claims that there was an epidemic of violent rhetoric among right wingers like Palin, Michele Bachmann and the Tea Party, right? Wrong. Was it Sarah Palin who said during the 2008 presidential campaign, 'If they bring a knife to the fight, we'll bring a gun'? No, that was one Senator Barack Obama.[113] Was it Newt Gingrich who, in 2009, wished publicly that President Obama 'would go missing'? No, that was Senator John Kerry channelling Henry II about Governor Palin.[114] There's more: New Hampshire Democratic state representative Nick Lavasseur, when he wasn't saying he wanted to 'nuke the Japanese' for giving us anime, said that one of his favourite pastimes was 'the hunting of neo-conservative Reaganites'.[115] Rep. Alan Grayson said he wanted to 'get rid of Republicans entirely'.[116] Democratic Congressman Michael Capuano said at a campaign rally that attendees should 'get out on the streets and get a little bloody when necessary'.[117] Former Congressman Paul Kanjorski (D-PA) said of Rick Scott, the current Republican Governor of Florida, 'Instead of running for governor of Florida, they ought to have him [sic] and shoot him. Put him against the wall and shoot him.'[118]

When Palin dared to defend herself against the unjust accusations that she, rather than the shooter, was responsible for the Tucson attack, she used the phrase 'blood libel', which generally refers to the false accusation that Jews used Christian blood for religious rituals. She said, 'Journalists and pundits should not manufacture a blood libel that serves only to incite the very hatred and violence they purport to condemn.'[119] Since she had been falsely accused of murder, the phrase 'blood libel' didn't entirely seem unreasonable. But even this came under severe criticism. Abraham Foxman, president of the Anti-Defamation League, commented

> We wish that Palin had not invoked the phrase 'blood-libel' in reference to the actions of journalists and pundits in placing blame for the shooting in Tucson on others… While the term 'blood-libel' has become part of the English parlance to refer to someone being falsely accused, we wish that Palin had used another phrase, instead of one so fraught with pain in Jewish history.[120]

Media columnist Howard Kurtz tweeted, 'There was some sympathy for Palin over being tied to shooting – she chose to go inflammatory. Blood libel has special resonance for Jews.'[121] But, as *National Review* writer Jim Geraghty pointed out, politicians and commentators were often using the phrase 'blood libel' without receiving any criticism at all. Columnist Andrew Sullivan used it to describe anti-gay rhetoric. Eugene Robinson, another columnist, used it to describe the fear that African-American men would deflower white women. And Congressman Peter Deutsch (D-FL) used it to describe a statement he didn't like in the 2000 Florida recount.[122] It seems odd that people like Howard Kurtz did not rise up in righteous indignation against Sullivan, Robinson and Deutsch for using the term in situations that also did not expressly involve Jews

As the furore around the shooting died down, it became quite clear that the people calling for civility had no interest in making sure they lived up to their own standards. In February 2011, the Republican Governor of Wisconsin, Scott Walker, and the Republican-dominated state legislature created new legislation that limited public employees' unions' power in the state, as well as some forms of collective bargaining. And the unions showed up to protest, which is their right. But the violence that took place in Wisconsin only a month after the Giffords shooting, both in terms of rhetoric and action, showed just how empty the calls for civility were. Republican officials received numerous death threats – the State Assembly speaker even had to adjourn the session at one point because he couldn't guarantee members' safety. A note was slid under a Republican state senator's door that said, 'The Only Good Republican is a Dead Republican.' Signs were carried with the face of the Republican governor, Scott Walker, in crosshairs. Videos were posted of mobs attacking elderly Republican state officials. A journalist was assaulted and her video camera knocked out of her hands while the camera was still rolling.

The way the media characterised what happened in Wisconsin is very different from the way the media characterised Sarah Palin's rhetoric. As Yahoo! political contributor Mark Whittington wrote:

> Political observers remember the controversy surrounding a map put out by Sarah Palin's political action committee showing crosshairs over various states, representing Democratic politicians who had been targeted for defeat in 2010. The map has been the subject of heated arguments over the civility of political discourse following the shooting in Tucson, Ariz., that killed six and

severely wounded Congresswoman Gabrielle Giffords, one of the politicians so targeted. However the same people who excoriated Sarah Palin seem to have become oddly silent when similar graphics are used against a sitting governor. What was considered horrible for Palin and the Tea Party seems to be acceptable for union activists.[123]

And writer Lee Stranahan also pointed out the deafening silence of the media and the progressive blogosphere about what was happening in Wisconsin:

> Ignoring the story of these threats is deeply, fundamentally wrong. It's bad, biased journalism that will lead to no possible good outcome and progressives should be leading the charge against it. Just before writing this article, I did a Google search and it's stunning to find out that the right-wing media really isn't exaggerating – proven death threats against politicians are being ignored by the supposedly honest media. If you've never agreed with a single thing that Limbaugh, Bill O'Reilly et al have said about anything, you can't in any good conscience say that they don't have a point here. Death threats are wrong and if a story like Wisconsin is national news for days, then so are death threats.[124]

Since the Palin furore, the escalation of rhetoric from both sides has continued apace, and will continue to do so throughout the 2012 election. Comedian Roseanne Barr said that she thought rich people ought to be beheaded. State lawmakers in New York received letters saying that it was 'time to kill the wealthy' if they didn't renew the state's tax surcharge on millionaires, elaborating that 'if you don't, I'm going to pay a visit with my carbine to one of those tech companies you are so proud of and shoot every spoiled Ivy League [expletive] I can find'. Union leader Jimmy Hoffa said of

Republicans, 'Let's take these sons of bitches out and give America back to an America where we belong.' This kind of 'civility for thee but not for me' act is not really about elevating public discourse or making the political rhetoric more about policy and less about soap opera. If it were, you would see the standards being applied equally. But since they're only being applied to one side, one has to conclude that people calling for political 'civility' would really just like the people they believe to be uncivil – the ones they disagree with – to stop talking altogether. And this drama plays right into the hands of a media that needs conflict and drama to keep the ratings high; if you want attention, all you need to do is escalate your commentary about your political opponents and, hey presto, you get all the media coverage you want. It's a win for you, it's a win for the ratings and paper sales – but the American people lose.

Even before the Tucson shooting, people had been claiming that violent Republican rhetoric would end up doing harm to the country. Dana Milbank, a political reporter for the *Washington Post*, wrote in 2008:

> Unless the Republicans explicitly call on their supporters to reject the use of violence regardless of the election outcome, and unless they moderate their rhetoric so that an electoral loss is not seen as the end of the world by their most zealous supporters, then the possibility of an assassination attempt on Barack Obama cannot be discounted. More than any US political figure of the last two decades, he is the one who has most inflamed desperate (as well as hopeful) passions, and he is consequently the most likely to be targeted.[125]

One wonders where he was during 2000 to 2008, when death threats against President George W. Bush were commonplace and unremarked upon, when Senator John Kerry fantasised on television in 2006 about killing the President[126], when films came out depicting his assassination – and it didn't seem to bother anyone. In August 2009, numerous media sources reported that death threats against President Obama were 400 per cent higher than against President Bush, but the head of the Secret Service, Mark Sullivan, said that figure was a canard, and that the number of threats against Obama 'are the same level as it has been [against] the last two presidents'.[127] These facts show pretty clearly that violent rhetoric by itself isn't enough to drive people to commit violent acts; if the rate of violent threats against previous presidents is the same as against the current one, and those guys weren't assassinated, the change agent has to be something other than people making threats and engaging in violent speech. Based on this evidence, the case that violent language leads to assassinations isn't strong enough to stand up under the simplest of cross-examinations.

But neither is it helpful to say, 'Well, the other side does it, so I can do it too.' This point is really important to bear in mind – it's very easy in political rhetoric to excuse actions that your side does because 'the other side did it first'. It's called the *tu quoque* ('you too') fallacy: if my side does something that your side finds objectionable, but my side can prove that your side does it too, then my side can claim that your side has no right to object. This line of argument didn't work very well even when we were five (Mum: 'Stop hitting your brother.' Kid: 'But he started it!' Mum: 'Then you're both wrong.'), but that doesn't stop partisan activists from trying it anyway. While this kind of partisan bickering makes for terrific political theatre, and even better ratings, it reduces policy debate to the level of two school kids shouting taunts at each other and running away. Entertaining, sure. Enlightening? Not so much.

Adorno and Horkheimer, in their seminal essay 'The Culture Industry: Enlightenment as Mass Deception', are a bit more particular in their target than Debord was when talking about the complicity of the mass media in confusing and misleading the public both for their own profit and to make sure that the public keeps spending. They wrote:

> Amusement under late capitalism is the prolongation of work. It is sought after as an escape from the mechanised work process, and to recruit strength in order to be able to cope with it again. But at the same time mechanisation has such power over a man's leisure and happiness, and so profoundly determines the manufacture of amusement goods, that his experiences are inevitably after-images of the work process itself. The ostensible content is merely a faded foreground; what sinks in is the automatic succession of standardised operations. What happens at work, in the factory, or in the office can only be escaped from by approximation to it in one's leisure time. All amusement suffers from this incurable malady. Pleasure hardens into boredom because, if it is to remain pleasure, it must not demand any effort and therefore moves rigorously in the worn grooves of association.[128]

There are two points being made here. The first is that the entertainment industry, in which the news media must now be included, is designed to act as a type of refreshment in which we forget about the pains and tribulations of the working day and restore our minds and bodies for the next day's work. But also, for pleasure to remain pleasure, we can't really be challenged too much, otherwise thinking about whatever is 'entertaining' becomes another form of work. So entertainment must be deeply familiar or it won't please us – it won't have the refreshing qualities required for us to get out of bed every morning. This is why deeply familiar television show formats like *The X Factor* and *American Idol* are so popular, and why sitcom jokes don't change much from year to year. We need the familiarity so that the things that entertain us don't strain our brains too hard.

But it also means that our own thoughts are influenced by the news picking up familiar storylines and presenting them back to us as familiar archetypes which amuse and entertain us. That's why, no matter how hard anyone tries to change the initial impression, George Bush and Sarah Palin will be stupid, Dick Cheney will be evil, John Kerry will be spoiled, Barack Obama will be aloof, Mitt Romney will be a robot, Michele Bachmann will be crazy, Republicans will be racist, Democrats will be snotty, Congress will be fractious etc. etc. ad nauseum. None of these things are actually true (OK, Congress is actually fractious), but in the quotidian soap opera of politics that populates our papers and screens, the characters are portraying their predetermined storylines in as well-rehearsed and unvarying a show as a Christmas panto. The constant insults and threats and ridiculous airing of grievances are yet another part of the political soap opera which must be reported on, to create more excitement and drama, but that's all it is – just the longest television reality show on record.

Should we be angry at the *New York Times* for trafficking in the stereotype that political dissent means violence? Should we be disgusted by Fox News for engaging in television bear baiting – pitting one loud person against another loud person and yelling 'Fight!' Should we be disheartened by MSNBC for smearing its political opponents as racists and Nazis every night without asking for comment or clarification, or having the graciousness to ensure that its attacks are accurate? Jim Lehrer, the anchor of the *Lehrer News Hour* on PBS, says that he is 'not in the entertainment business' – and, as a result, the ratings of his show are crushed by not only all the major networks, but by both Fox News and MSNBC. People like the drama of the uncivil political reality show. They enjoy the insults and the fireworks. I think it would be unfair to ask us, the audience, to give up the pleasure we have in the narrative arc of a presidential campaign. Enjoying bickering and scandal *is* fun, and the professionals who provide it to us are at the top of their game. But it behooves us to understand that the storylines are just that, storylines, and to think critically about the narrative that's presented to us. It is so important to make sure that an examination of the facts at hand lead you to the conclusion your media source arrives at, and that you examine more than one interpretation of the facts to make sure you're not missing anything. In the age of news as entertainment, we've all had to become critical thinkers as well as news customers. And that's not a bad development.

5

BREAKING THE LAST GLASS CEILING

In all of American history, there have been three women who have made credible inroads into presidential politics. The first was Geraldine Ferraro, Walter Mondale's running mate in 1984, who was forty-nine when she was selected for the position. Then there was Hillary Clinton, who was sixty-one when she ran for president. And finally, there was Sarah Palin, the first woman on a Republican national ticket. She was forty-four years old, had a family with young children and a blossoming career as a very successful governor in Alaska. It was a combination that had never been seen before in national politics: an attractive, successful woman with young children trying to break through the very thickest glass ceiling and become the vice president of the United States. Palin running for a national office was one of the ultimate expressions of women having it all. It seemed like the ultimate repudiation of the 'Mommy Wars' of the 1980s; yes, you can have a family and be a national political figure as well. One would think that this would be a victory for working mums and for all those who believe that nothing should stand in a woman's way to achieve whatever she's capable of. But thanks to a heady combination of latent sexism from men and virulent jealousy from women, bien pensant progressives, who would ordinarily say that they believed wholeheartedly in women's equality, hated every moment of it.

We're used to seeing greying, avuncular figures running for president, although these days they're now more thrusting CEO types than grandfatherly Ronald Reagan. And we feel like we understand the personal lives of these men very well. So it makes sense to us, for example, that then-Senator Barack Obama was joined by his wife and two daughters on stage after he gave his speech at the Democratic convention in Denver in 2008. *People* magazine reported, 'When the speech was over, vice presidential nominee Joe Biden and his wife Jill joined Obama, Michelle, Malia, 10, and Sasha, 7, on stage as fireworks went off and streamers poured down ... the little girls in pink dresses played with confetti and waved to the roaring crowd.'[129] It also didn't cause much of a fuss when Senator John Edwards, when he ran for vice president in 2004 and for the top job in 2008, was joined on the campaign trail by his cancer-stricken wife and his two young kids.

But when Governor Palin stepped out onto the podium at the Republican national convention in St Paul, Minnesota, in 2008, the complaints about being both a vice presidential candidate and a mum began. John R. MacArthur sniffed in *Harper's Magazine*: 'Why should I cast a ballot for a candidate who is so desperate for my support that she's willing to exploit her unlucky offspring as a campaign prop?'[130] So what was the difference between Obama having his kids on stage at the convention and Palin having hers on stage? Ah, Sarah Palin is a woman. So according to Mr MacArthur, we have somehow travelled back in time to 1954 when ladies with small children weren't supposed to have successful careers. We heard this same retrograde philosophy from CNN anchor John Roberts, who wondered aloud after the convention,

There's also this issue that on April 18th, she gave birth to a baby with Down's syndrome... Children with Down's syndrome require an awful lot of attention. The role of Vice President, it seems to me, would take up an awful lot of her time, and it raises the issue of how much time will she have to dedicate to her newborn child?[131]

Again, I didn't realise that Palin's appearing on TV activated some kind of depressing TARDIS, magically taking us back to an era when women, especially ones with developmentally disabled babies, weren't allowed to work because they had to take care of the children.

There also was the notion that Sarah Palin was, well, just too good-looking to be vice president (never mind president) of the United States. Social scientists Nathan Heflick and Jamie Goldenberg published a study suggesting that voters, confronted with Palin's good looks, perceived her as less competent and less human than her male counterparts.[132] 'Less human' might seem a little extreme, but as feminist blogger Megan Carpentier pointed out, 'How many times did *you* call her "Caribou Barbie"?'[133] Also, and I'm going to be frank about this, Sarah Palin is a virile woman. She's not a dried-up husk, she literally is holding the evidence that she is in the prime of her life and still child-bearing. This means that she is a woman who is obviously still having conjugal relations with her husband. And the notion that a woman could be both sexually and politically powerful was just too much for some commentators. This could explain why people desperately wanted to believe the sad rumour, despite overwhelming evidence to the contrary, that Trig, Sarah Palin's youngest child, was actually Palin's daughter Bristol's son. The knowledge that the vice president of the United States was a sexually active woman was just too much for misogynist bloggers like Andrew Sullivan, who did the most to arouse suspicions regarding Trig's parentage.

These viciously sexist attacks didn't stop when McCain and Palin lost the election; in the eyes of some commentators, someone like Michele Bachmann, who's young (for a presidential candidate) and good-looking, just doesn't give off presidential vibes. *Washington Post* columnist Richard Cohen, for example, normally very progressive and pro-feminist and in favour of women's equality, says, 'Perry, who actually looks like a president ... will raise far more money and breeze by [Bachmann].'[134] What does Perry have that Bachmann doesn't that allows him to look like a President? It's easy to surmise that the issue, for Cohen, is that Rick Perry is a good looking man, whereas Bachmann is a good looking woman. Palin's and Bachmann's looks allowed many people to treat them less like capable people running for office and more like punching bags on which they could rain numerous rhetorical blows.

Everybody knows perfectly well that female candidates have to go through sexist garbage in the midst of a campaign. I remember seeing a T-shirt during the 2008 Democratic primaries featuring pictures of Obama and Clinton with the caption 'Bros Before Hos'. Hillary Clinton also had to endure troglodytes like Rep. Steve Cohen, D-TN, who compared then-Senator Clinton to Glenn Close re-emerging from the bath after being shot in *Fatal Attraction* because Clinton didn't withdraw from the primaries fast enough for his liking. Cohen said, 'Glenn Close should have stayed in that tub, and Sen. Clinton has had a remarkable career and needs to move to the next step, which is helping elect the Democratic nominee.'[135] (It was this comment, and then-Senator Obama's total lack of response to it, that lost him your humble author.)

But in the post-Palin universe, we now know that every conservative woman candidate in modern politics has to go through attacks about her womanhood. On the one hand, every conservative woman entering national politics is going to have to deal with concerned commentators and advocates worrying about the way she lives her personal life, bringing back the retro Mommy Wars calculus of 'you can have a family or a career, but not both' and using the progressive caricature of family values language ('But has she thought of her *children?*'). On the other, she's going to have to deal with sexist men and jealous women tearing her down for the sheer pleasure in expressing ugly vitriol. And she's going to have to deal with actual violent threats against her person by coastal political elites for daring to contradict what a woman ought to think.

This is the ultimate threat to the people who currently hold the levers of political power. The energy and excitement in politics right now is coming from women in their thirties and forties. Many of the young women I spoke to in the Tea Party are in leadership positions, and they are totally unconcerned about the lifestyle issues that most progressive feminists obsess over – they honestly couldn't give a rip about abortion, diversity or gay marriage. They are worried about the national debt and the size of the federal government. As economic issues become more and more important to many Americans, women whose political speciality is economic issues are going to find more electoral success than their left-leaning sisters wittering on about the primacy of the uterus. That's why the current Republican bench of potential political leaders includes women governors like Nikki Haley and Susana Martinez, whose signature issues are economic ones, not social ones. And this may also be the reason why Republicans, who lost the women's vote by 13 per cent in 2008, were able to close the gender gap altogether in 2010.[136] More GOP women than ever ran for Congressional office in the 2010 mid-term elections; there were 145 women GOP candidates.[137] While the actual proportion of women's representation in Congress didn't change much in the 2010 election, the willingness of women to enter politics – as Republicans – is growing by leaps and bounds. What's interesting is that this is happening on a local level as well as a national one. In Middletown, Connecticut (which is a very blue state), eight Republican women are running for local office – the largest number ever. All of them said that they cared deeply about their community, the reasons they were running were to create change in the local schools and the local town's economy. Abortion didn't come up.[138]

The Tea Party has a majority female membership; a 2010

Quinnipiac poll revealed that of self-identified members of the Tea Party, 55 per cent were women and 45 per cent were men.[139] Of the eight board members of the Tea Party Patriots who serve as national coordinators for the movement, six are women. Fifteen of the twenty-five state coordinators are women.[140] Women are an integral part of and in some ways are the driving force behind this energetic, grassroots movement. As conservative commentator Tammy Bruce says:

> The Tea Party represents stakeholders in the American system; people who were never involved in politics or thought they had to be, yet realised that political corruption and incompetence threatened not only their families, but the future of the nation itself. Economic collapse, the shocking spending by an Obama administration that most analysts agree is in over its head, combined with remarkable contempt shown citizens during the debacle of the healthcare debate and legislation, have mobilised those stakeholders – including women and their families – to take action.[141]

Time and again, when I interviewed members of the Tea Party they kept telling me they were tired of their voices and their points of view being ignored by the government. What the Tea Party represents are women who aren't going to take it any more – women who have a voice, who want to be heard and who are getting involved in politics because they can't see any other way for change. I was told many times that Sarah Palin wasn't a leader of the movement, but rather a representative of it; it had grown beyond Palin but looked to her success in forging her own path and creating powerful messages to develop political leadership for the future.

It does seem like the Republican national political candidates of the future will come from Tea Party roots. While Democrats are more successful in recruiting women to become legislators,

Republicans are more successful in recruiting women to become governors. Since the 2010 elections, there are twice as many Republican women governors as there are Democrats and more than twice as many Republican women lieutenant governors as Democrats. The path to the presidency from a state governor's office is easier than a legislative one, as the executive experience is already there. The Republicans are building a strong female bench that they can draw on to win more of the female vote in 2016, and 2020 should Obama win a second term. The Democrats have nowhere to go after Obama leaves office. It's not surprising conservatives are taking it for granted that Palin and Michele Bachmann are (or could be) serious presidential candidates; conservatives aren't fretting over whether the ladies are spending enough time with their children or insulting their looks – they're treating Bachmann the same way they treat Gingrich or Romney, and simply taking it for granted that she's a credible candidate, not a token woman who mouths feminine platitudes.

To Democratic politicians, all of these developments are worrisome. Keeping the women's vote is key to their ability to win future elections. In forthcoming elections, Democrats will have to keep women ideologically in line and negate the appeal of female economic conservatives spouting a populist message, like a Nikki Haley or a Susana Martinez. Susana Martinez is already on the shortlist for a vice presidential nomination, so Democrats are going to have to worry again about losing some of the women's vote to an intelligent, charismatic governor – and they're going to do everything they can to neutralise Governor Martinez the same way they did Governor Palin.

The first thing they'll say is that conservative women are stupid and crazy. Progressives need to frighten voters with the spectre of a woman president who somehow wants to destroy not only feminism, but the lives of her fellow women as well. This is why it was so important to spread the rumour that not only was Palin pro-life, but that she was personally interested in tracking down and jailing troubled teens who had had abortions. Gloria Steinem said in a 2010 interview that Palin can't call herself a feminist because she seeks 'to prevent other women from having abortions, to criminalise abortion',[142] even though Palin has in fact said quite the opposite. But it's important for feminist advocacy organisations and the Democratic Party for women, particularly young women, to think that pro-life politicians like Palin want to wrench control of their own bodies away from them and put it in the hands of the State, regardless of whether or not it's actually true.

This kind of thinking reached its apex in American politics in a poorly conceived and researched column by University of Chicago Professor Wendy Doniger, who wrote of Palin: 'Her greatest hypocrisy is in her pretense that she is a woman... She does not speak for women; she has no sympathy for the problems of other women, particularly working-class women.'[143] This isn't anything particularly new; Margaret Thatcher had to face attacks that she acted more like a male than a female. It was ridiculous then and it's ridiculous now. Not only does it imply that Doniger lifted Palin's skirt and took a look at what the former Governor of Alaska keeps under there, but it espouses the notion that since Palin disagrees with Doniger on issues like abortion and global warming it means that somehow the governor no longer has the right to call herself a woman. This is nonsensical hysteria in the extreme. Women are human beings. They have different opinions on things. It doesn't make you less of a human or less of a woman to disagree with someone. It's almost as though Doniger is espousing the belief that women should be *Stepford Wives* who agree with their progressive husbands, which is incredibly anti-feminist! It should go without saying that women have the right to express their opinions, despite the objections of sexist authoritarians like Wendy Doniger. It didn't help Doniger's case that she claimed Palin wanted to criminalise abortion and said that the Iraq war was God's plan, neither of which are true. It was also pretty funny that Doniger tried to paint Sarah Palin as an out of touch elitist, oblivious to the problems of the working class, when everyone else in the media was painting her as a stupid, redneck, hick chillbilly.

But this line of attack worked, at least for a while; women who might have been interested in giving Palin at least a fair shake, were scared away by the bogeyman of a stupid, calculating, anti-abortionist, Christianist mum who was somehow hell-bent on turning the United States into a theocracy in which every teen who had an abortion would be thrown into jail and all citizens would be required by law to shoot wolves from helicopters. We now see similar attacks used against Bachmann – MSNBC's Chris Matthews, for example, loves calling her names like 'balloon head' and 'nut case',[144] again creating the spectre of a dumb, crazy woman who despite her mental limitations has her hands very nearly on the levers of power. In fact, bloggers adore finding quotes from Bachmann and holding them up as 'evidence' of the fact that she is not only stupid, but tremendously horrifying and crazy. As always, though, the evidence given for stupidity, craziness and the ability to terrify doesn't hang together that well under scrutiny. There's a blog called 'Moronwatch' that, despite its anonymous author having a tenuous hold on the rules of standard English spelling and grammar, purports to keep an eye on the stupidity in American politics. He (or she) has made a speciality of pointing out what are considered, by the blog, 'moronic' Bachmann quotes; for example:

There is a movement afoot that's occurring and part of that is whole philosophical idea of multi-cultural diversity, which on the face sounds wonderful. Let's appreciate and value everyone's cultures. But guess what? Not all cultures are equal. Not all values are equal.

Mr (or Ms) Moronwatch sarcastically calls this a 'reasoned, well-thought out argument'.[145] Actually, it isn't a moronic argument at all; it's a problem that aid workers, human and women's rights groups and NGOs across the globe struggle with daily. When dealing with Somali cases of female genital mutilation or Yemeni cases of child brides as young as seven being raped by their forty-year-old husbands, anyone's assumptions about multiculturalism are going to be pretty seriously shaken. Bachmann might be wrong, and reasonable people can disagree, but in a world where little girls are given away in marriage against their will by their parents to men decades older than they are, and are then raped, impregnated and have to have the birds and the bees explained to them in hospital moments before they give birth,[146] it seems that there's at least a bit of evidence lending support to Bachmann's point of view. But to bloggers like Moronwatch it doesn't matter if Bachmann's argument has any merit in it – she's wrong, she's stupid, she's crazy – and we'd better not think about why, but rather just accept that she is.

The media and the blogosphere are quite good at creating bogeymen, the bogeyman of a stupid, crazy, religiously obsessed woman who wants to take your rights away. It's extraordinary that so many progressive women believe that the only way that a woman from the opposite side of the aisle can reach a position of power is through taking away other women's rights – it's as though they think women's rights are some kind of zero-sum game, as though there were a limited amount to go around. But yet again, in order to keep the donations rolling in, it's really important that women's groups make Republican women seem terrifying. The spectre of the marauding anti-feminist woman has, in the past, been a very effective one, even though the 2010 election shows it may be losing its efficacy.

Another line of attack is publicly fretting about whether a 'family values' conservative woman can be both a good politician and a good mum. Could there be anything more old-fashioned than the hoary battles over whether women can have successful careers as well as be capable mothers? If I seem frustrated that we're still nitpicking about whether a woman can 'have it all', it's because Susan Faludi in *Backlash* did an excellent job of debunking this junk back in 1992, and here we are in 2011, still fretting about the 'Mommy Wars' in public commentary. These kinds of issues are discussed in the most retro, sexist, conformist, straight-out-of-*Ozzie and Harriet* language. Sally Quinn of the *Washington Post* intoned with great concern and furrowed brow, and no doubt with clutched pearls, 'But I do still have grave doubts about whether a mother of five, soon to be six, with a special needs child and a child who is pregnant, is going to be able to put her country first.'[147] Stick the little lady back in the kitchen barefoot and pregnant, says Sally, because a capable adult woman with a successful career isn't able to distinguish between spit-up and Spitfire missiles! Never mind that Todd, a stay-at-home dad, takes care of the Palin kids. Kate Michaelman, the former head of the National Abortion Rights Action League, got it right when she said, 'It's absolutely sexist… It's these old, deeply held attitudes surfacing again about prescribed roles for women.'[148] Quinn's attitude is as regressive towards women's progress and gender as men who, when women entered the workforce, refused to pay them equal salaries because they 'only need pin-money'. Quinn seems to think Sarah Palin shouldn't work and Todd Palin shouldn't take care of the kids because men and women are different! This is straight-up old-fashioned chauvinism and should have no place in serious political discussion in the twenty-first century.

In 1972, then Senator-elect Joe Biden's wife Neilia and their three children went to collect a Christmas tree one week before Christmas. On the way home, a truck driver hit the car, killing Neilia and their thirteen-month-old daughter Naomi, and critically injuring Biden's sons, then three and four. Biden considered resigning from the Senate to care for his two little boys, who were thought to have profound injuries, but then-Senate Majority Leader Mike Mansfield convinced Biden to serve anyway. Biden's family moved in to help the newly single father take care of his children, but Biden still commuted home to Wilmington, Delaware, every night to tuck his children into bed.[149] Why didn't Sally Quinn criticise Joe Biden for the undue focus on his career at a time when his children needed him? Why didn't anyone tell Joe Biden in 1972 that he should focus on his family, not his political career? Men don't give up their political careers for family reasons; according to sexists like Sally Quinn, women should.

It's disgusting, and deeply prejudiced, seriously to propose that a woman can't be president of the United States and take care of her children. But it was an incredibly common accusation against Palin and will be for any conservative woman running for president. Bachmann's kids were a little old for news anchors and media commentators to fret about, but Nikki Haley, the Governor of South Carolina, has two young children, and she too is on the vice presidential shortlist. Women will never break through the ultimate glass ceiling unless ancient crones like Sally Quinn and John Roberts stop holding women back.

Commentators also accuse conservative women of using their children as a 'prop' to appeal to religious voters. There is not a politician in the country who doesn't use their kids as part of their campaign. When I produced live radio shows for the New Hampshire Democratic primary in 2004, I met Howard Dean's kids and Joe Lieberman's kids (and, for good measure, Lieberman brought along his mother, who was a lovely lady). As we've seen, Obama brought his young children on the campaign trail and they even did an interview for *Access Hollywood*.[150] Bringing your family on the campaign trail is a unique feature of US political culture; in the UK it's not common at all – you hardly ever saw media coverage of the issues facing the Blair, Brown or Cameron kids. Given that in American presidential elections bringing your family with you is standard political practice, why was Palin constantly accused of using her children, particularly her young son Trig, as a 'prop' on the campaign trail and even afterwards? It wasn't just the fact that he was so young, every press mention of Palin 'exploiting her kids' was accompanied by the fact that Trig has Down's syndrome. A few examples: *Washington Post* writer Kathleen Parker wrote in 2010, 'each time [Palin] sallies forth as Mama Bear to America's special-needs citizenry, invoking Trig's name amid demands for her children's privacy, a bit of uneasiness slithers between text and subtext. At what point do Palin's noble intentions become Trig's exploitation?'[151] Feminist writer Malia Littman griped, 'Mommy Dearest parades her Down's syndrome baby to national political conventions like a prop.'[152] Blogger 'feministymama' wrote:

> [Palin] decided to use baby Trig to get some lusty applause out of the audience, because, let's face it, there's nothing evangelical Christians love more than a developmentally disabled baby they can use to their own end… As a mother, it makes me sick to see this woman exploit her own sweet child … as a feminist, it just makes me want to grab this bitch by the beehive, take her out back, and beat the sh*t out of her!'[153]

Three cheers for civility!

What's really going on here? Is it the fact Palin has her baby (now toddler) on the campaign trail with her that's bothering these people or is it the fact that he's a Down's syndrome child out in the world for everyone to see? *Daily Caller* writer Jim Treacher says, 'I've never understood the charge that Palin "exploits" Trig. … What was she supposed to do, leave him in the car? If she hid him away with a nanny somewhere and refused to talk about him, do you really think [her critics] would have no problem with it?'[154] Palin herself has talked about her doubts about raising a developmentally disabled child, and told an audience in Indiana that she considered having an abortion.[155] Instead, she chose differently and proudly brings Trig everywhere with her in public. People often wonder what pro-life politicians would choose to do if they themselves were faced with a difficult childbirth situation; Palin chose and is living the consequences of her choice every day. Ninety per cent of people who find out they are pregnant with babies who have Down's syndrome choose to abort;[156] Palin did not, and is happy to have her very cute toddler with her as she makes speeches and greets her fans.

Progressive men often feel free to indulge their latent sexism by insulting a conservative woman using sexual vulgarities. For men, expressing their hatred of Sarah Palin allows them to release misogynist impulses while still being socially acceptable. It allows them to express their irrational misgivings about a woman president – men don't want to give up political power any more than the bourgeoisie do – without being accused of being sexist. It's a relief, in a way, so their feelings achieve a, shall we say, fully throated expression. Every single political candidate since the dawn of time has been insulted and casting aspersions on presidential candidates' sex lives dates back to 1802, when pamphleteer James Callender published allegations that President Jefferson had a relationship with his slave, Sally Hemings. But what's different about the attacks on conservative women is not only that they're incredibly vulgar, but that they're so crude and downright nasty.

It's also that nice progressive men, who ordinarily profess their support for women's equality and claim to abhor violence against women, are happy to indulge in a little misogyny on national television or radio. The language is about to get a bit salty, but you'll see what I mean.

Here's what James Callender wrote about Jefferson's relationship with Sally Hemings in 1802:

> It is well known that the man, whom it delighteth the people to honor, keeps, and for many years past has kept, as his concubine, one of his own slaves. Her name is SALLY. The name of her eldest son is TOM. His features are said to bear a striking although sable resemblance to those of the president himself … the AFRICAN VENUS is said to officiate as housekeeper at Monticello.[157]

This is just about the ultimate indictment of Jefferson that Callender could muster. The charge was explosive. He used indelicate language to describe Sally Hemings. He called her a concubine. For 1802, this was serious, serious stuff.

Fast forward to the twenty-first century comedian Louis C. K. describing, on nationally syndicated radio, Sarah Palin holding her son at the Republican national convention. Louis C. K. took to the mic and described the scene in a torrent of baroque profanity: 'She was on stage at the f*cking convention that just came out of her disgusting f*cking c*nt … her f*ing retard-making c*nt.'[158] Another comedian, Marc Maron, stated on national television that he hoped Michele Bachmann's husband 'f*cks her angrily, because that's how I would. And I've thought about it.'[159] *Playboy* ran a feature called 'Ten Conservative Women I'd Like to Hate F*ck'.[160] On ESPN radio programme the *Larry Brown Sports Show*, Mike Tyson (a man who has commented, 'Do I think it's right to beat up a woman? No – hell no… Have I hit a woman before? Hell yeah. Was I wrong? Hell yeah.'[161]) said:

> You want [Palin] to be with somebody like [Dennis] Rodman getting up in there. Pushing her guts up in the back of her head … you want someone like Rodman – yeah baby! Imagine Palin with a big old black stallion ripping – yeehaw … some people need to get it so hard that their lower intestines get wrapped around their esophagus. She could always get boned out by a black person – a vote to bang her.

Larry Brown, the host of the show, calls these violent and sexual comments from a convicted rapist 'hilarious'.[162] It's quite disturbing the way these men have dehumanised another person to the extent they can talk about violence being done to her – violence which one has gone to prison for – and they don't even realise that it's a real woman they're talking about. Palin's just a sexual object to them.

Drummer Questlove, who's the leader of the house band on *Late Night with Jimmy Fallon*, broadcast on NBC, enjoys making fun of guests on the show by introducing them with songs he thinks are appropriate to their foibles. When Michele Bachmann went on the show, Questlove played Fishbone's 'Lyin' Ass B*tch', and tweeted that he was going to do it beforehand, and told *Rolling Stone* he'd planned it, even though he said afterwards that it was a 'spur of the moment decision'.[163] Questlove whined that people had been rude to him on Twitter about the incident, though why that would bother him when he felt free to call a woman a 'b*tch' on national television is somewhat puzzling. Questlove is yet another example of a progressive man who feels free to express latent sexism and prejudice towards strong women by using vulgarities and juvenile comments to insult them. Sexist prejudice is a very difficult thing to overcome, and what we've learned in the last four years is that men are unwilling to let go of a lot of their stereotypes of what a woman can be and do. And instead of trying to overcome their fear and prejudice, they retreat back into sexist vulgarities and violent fantasies. A *New York Magazine* editor, Joe Adalian, also expressed his admiration on Twitter for Questlove's song choice – again, a man who probably considers himself a feminist has no problem publicly calling a woman a 'b*tch' instead of making an actual objection to her opinions or policies. Conservative women provide a safe outlet for progressive men to release their prejudice about women.

If men, when confronted with a female candidate with whom they disagree, take the opportunity to indulge their desire to berate and insult, women indulge in virulent jealousy. As a feminist myself, having to confirm the stereotype of women being jealous of other women, especially pretty, successful, happy women, really makes me sad. But unfortunately, that does provide a compelling explanation of why there's such a bizarre fascination with and anger towards conservative women that seems out of proportion to the role they play in most women's lives.

Jessica G., at the women's blog 'Jezebel', encapsulated this jealousy perfectly when she wrote:

> For many of us looking back at high school, we can now feel a smug superiority towards the homecoming queen. Sure, she was pretty and popular in high school, catering to the whims of boys and cheering on their hockey games, but what happened to her after high school? Often, she popped out some kids and ended up toiling in some not particularly impressive job. We can look back and say, we might have been ambitious nerds in high school, but it ultimately paid off. What's infuriating, and perhaps rage-inducing, about Palin, is that she has always embodied that

perfectly pleasing female archetype, playing by the boys' game with her big guns and moose-murdering, and that she keeps being rewarded for it.[164]

Isn't it sad that we never really escape high school? Palin's one of those lucky people who achieved success in a man's world and for many supposedly feminist commentators, instead of being proud of her achievements despite political differences, they feel it has to come down to a comparison between them and her. They feel 'Palin's doing better than I am so I'm going to HATE HER!' Shouldn't adult women have outgrown the territorial struggles of female adolescence? *New York Times* columnist Maureen Dowd also gets stuck in the teenage years, observing of the women candidates in the 2010 elections: 'We are in the era of Republican *Mean Girls*, grown-up versions of those teenage tormentors who would steal your boyfriend, spray-paint your locker and, just for good measure, spread rumors that you were pregnant.'[165] It's not exactly clear from Dowd's column exactly how pushing a message of smaller government and more accountability and transparency equates to stealing boyfriends and spray-painting one's locker, but if you remember the movie *Mean Girls*, the queen bees were reviled but also envied. Perhaps Dowd is locked in that teenage catch-22 of hating and yet desperately wanting to be one of the Mean Girls herself.

James Taranto, a columnist at the *Wall Street Journal*, asked a young, progressive friend of his why her progressive friends hated Sarah Palin so utterly, and she came back with an extremely revealing answer. She said:

Because the devil in the red dress wasn't orating like a professor, it roused an unquenchable forest fire of rage and loathing in the breasts of many women, perhaps of the toiling gray mouse variety, who projected onto her their own career resentments and personal frustrations. I am amazed at how people still abhor her… I can tell you, being privy to the endless, incendiary rants this past week about her, coming from hordes of liberal women – age demo 25 to 45 – they rip her to pieces, they blame her for everything, and the jealousy/resentment factor is so clear and primal. I've never seen anything like it.[166]

Do you feel the sense of outrage she describes amongst her friends? How dare someone who doesn't speak like a professor be successful? How dare a woman from some horrible Alaskan backwater be richer, more influential, even happier than an upper-middle-class woman who's reached the pinnacle of upper-middle-class life – a decent full-time job in New York? Just like people who project their disappointment with the performance of the Obama administration onto the Tea Party and Republican candidates, women, struggling to succeed in their jobs, hate that Sarah Palin, some dumb chillbilly, was able to do it better than they were. It makes them so angry that they seethe.

If sexist insults and irrational envy won't neutralise a female candidate, you can just make stuff up about her – after all, it worked to stop Palin from gaining political power! The phrase 'fake but accurate' comes from a CBS producer, Mary Mapes, who was caught red-handed faking a story that alleged President George W. Bush got preferential treatment during the Vietnam War. Mapes said that even though the evidence was false, the story was true … but she couldn't prove it. All sorts of writers have had a terrific time writing all sorts of 'fake but accurate' stuff about Sarah Palin (and to a lesser extent Michele Bachmann) that wasn't exactly true, but played into the stereotypes of how Palin was supposed to be.

Michael Gross wrote a piece in *Vanity Fair* about Palin, in which he accused her of tipping badly, her 'temper veering wildly' after losing the 2008 election, walking out of stores after people insulted her in public, and missing her children when they weren't around.[167] Numerous feminists suddenly began to sit up and notice that these kinds of criticisms were pretty sexist. Melissa McEwan, a feminist blogger, said: 'Most of what's in it is the sort of sh*t that is considered (rightly or wrongly) the mundane business of doing politics, and yet is somehow ZOMG SHOCKING when done by Sarah Palin.'[168] *Mother Jones* editor Monika Brauerlein tweeted, 'I didn't think anything could make me rear up in Sarah Palin's defence, but this *VF* profile is close.'[169] Not only did people realise just how offensive the piece was, it turned out that several stories in the piece were just plain old lies. How fake stories made it into a major magazine of record is something that Gross and his editor must discuss, but political writer Ben Smith said 'My takeaway from the magazine piece is that you can really write *anything* about Palin.'[170] It's a bit worrying when fact-checking and accuracy go out the window in pursuit of a message, but when it comes to keeping women in line and voting for the Democratic party, I guess the message is so important that, sometimes, these editors possibly feel their integrity as writers and the trust readers have for the publication has to be sacrificed.

In the late summer of 2011 there was a small sensation in the celeb journalism world as tabloid writer Joe McGinniss, a man who earned the gratitude of multitudes of Manhattan and LA-based journos by taking one for the team and actually moving to Wasilla to write his book, released a tome about Palin called *The Rogue: Searching for the Real Sarah Palin.* It was a terrifically exciting read, filled with all sorts of sensational allegations like Palin having an affair with her husband's business partner, Todd having sex with a hooker, Palin's children being drunks and druggies, and Palin herself snorting cocaine with some friends on an overturned oil drum. Wow! Splashy stuff!

It's very difficult in the United States for a public figure to sue for libel. However, many attorneys think that Palin might have a test case. The book's author Joe McGinniss wrote an email checking back with one of his sources because Random House (his publisher) lawyers had said there was no 'factual evidence' for any of the salacious claims. McGinniss hoped to elicit some back-up, for without it the 'startling new revelations' would presumably have to be omitted from the book.[171] But despite the lack of evidence, Random House went ahead and published the rumours anyway, with no documentation other than a few citations from *National Enquirer* stories. Just so we're clear, a respected publishing house (as I write this) looks as if it published innuendo and smears about a public figure despite the fact the stories were not documented properly – but hey, because it's a woman nobody in New York likes, it's fine!

This case study, like Palin's 2008 interview with ABC News, should make you very, very afraid for political coverage of the 2012 election. Random House isn't some small imprint that publishes trashy quickie books – it's one of the largest and most famous publishing houses in the United States. Let's reiterate what happened – a major mainstream publishing house released a potentially libellous book about a private citizen. How do you feel now about trusting the stuff that comes from Random House? How do you know anything it publishes is true? Has Random House done a good thing for American politics by publishing this book? It's a disgrace that the book was released but, even more importantly, it has poisoned the relationship of trust that Random House had established with its readers. I wouldn't trust a Random House book about Mitt Romney; it's likely to be filled with gubbins. A major publisher with a track record of publishing totally unfounded rubbish for political gain is not healthy for a democracy, although it is excellent for political fundraising. By the way, Random House employees donated over $47,000 to the Obama campaign in the 2008 election and nothing to John McCain.[172]

Finally, if nothing else works to get conservative women to stay away from politics, their critics might as well threaten violence. If conservative women are too scared to run for office, there's no way other women can be convinced by their arguments. Perhaps that's why so many celebrities are threatening to do violence against prominent conservative women. In the 2008 election, comedienne Sandra Bernhard promised violence against Palin should the governor step onto the island of Manhattan – 'I'll tear her apart like a Wise natural kosher chicken'[173] – and also said that should a visit to Gotham occur, Palin would 'be gang-raped by my big black brothers'.[174] Radio talk show host Montel Williams urged Michele Bachmann to kill herself, saying, 'Michele, slit your wrist. Go ahead ... or, do us all a better thing [sic]. Move that knife up about two feet. Start right at the collarbone.'[175] If enough people say enough violent, disgusting and horrible things about a candidate they disagree with, it will discourage other women from running – who needs to deal with gang-rape threats and encouragements to behead oneself Khalid Sheik Mohammed style? Even Madonna got into the Palin violence, singing a little jingle at a concert about how she will 'kick her ass if she don't get offa my street'.[176] Again, there are lots of politicians who get lots of threats, but usually the threats come from crazies and people whose tinfoil hats are just a little too tight. These attacks are coming from multimillionaire pop stars and mainstream popular commentators, who are threatening violence because they feel like it's the right thing to do to get attention for their preferred candidate, and because their sense of humanity stops at an (R) after someone's name.

How can we get a woman elected to national office in the United States? If there's one thing that the 2008 election showed, it's that a woman can't count on the affinity of other women the way Obama could depend on support from the African-American community. The climate for women politicians is too divisive thanks to traditional female jealousy and male prejudice. But Americans aren't going to accept a president or vice president who represents the traditional female politicians in American politics – the smiling, progressive woman from an affluent, coastal area who fight for a woman's right to choose, accessibility of sex education and birth control, and extra breast cancer funding every October. A woman who will win a national audience will be the kind of person who is equally comfortable talking about economic policy as she is about defence policy. Cultural scholar Camille Paglia has said, 'As a dissident feminist, I have been arguing since my arrival on the scene nearly twenty years ago that young American women aspiring to political power should be studying military history rather than taking women's studies courses, with their rote agenda of never-ending grievances.'[177] There's no reason why women can't compete toe-to-toe with men to be commander-in-chief of the United States, but it's a difficult task to achieve. She's got to convince women that she's both competent and relatable, and men that she's non-threatening yet able to achieve great things in diplomatic and military situations.

6

SOCIAL ISSUES IN AMERICAN ELECTIONS

British and other international observers who have an interest in American politics are often mystified by the importance social issues have in US elections. It seems like we all are obsessed with abortion, school prayer, gay marriage, displaying the Ten Commandments, Christmas displays and other issues that affect a tiny minority of Americans but seem to command an awful lot of the airtime. Why is it that issues that touch on the lives of so few of us seem to hold such interest? And why do these issues seem to drive us crazy?

In late September 2008, CBS News aired a series of interviews between anchor Katie Couric and Sarah Palin. Those interviews are largely remembered for Palin either being unable or unwilling to tell Couric which newspapers she read, but the questions touched on a wide variety of topics, including the social issue flashpoints of abortion, sex ed. and gay marriage. Here's the transcript of the exchange about abortion:

COURIC: If a fifteen year old is raped by her father, do you believe it should be illegal for her to get an abortion, and why?

PALIN: I am pro-life. And I'm unapologetic in my position that I am pro-life. And I understand there are good people on both sides of the abortion debate. In fact, good people in my own family have differing views on abortion, and when it should be allowed. Do I respect people's opinions on this? Now, I would counsel to choose life. I would also like to see a culture of life in this country. But I would also like to take it one step further. Not just saying I am pro-life and I want fewer and fewer abortions in this country, but I want them, those women who find themselves in circumstances that are absolutely less than ideal, for them to be supported, and adoptions made easier.

COURIC: But ideally, you think it should be illegal for a girl who was raped or the victim of incest to get an abortion?

PALIN: I'm saying that, personally, I would counsel the person to choose life, despite horrific, horrific circumstances that this person would find themselves in. And, um, if you're asking, though, kind of foundationally here, should anyone end up in jail for having an ... abortion, absolutely not. That's nothing I would ever support.[178]

The day after this exchange aired, I happened to be screening calls for the radio programme I worked on. We played this clip to illustrate Palin's feelings about abortion, and Couric's obsession with it, and moved on. I noticed an incoming call, picked it up, and was greeted by a very angry gentleman shouting, 'You're a liar. Fox News are such liars. You're all liars.' When I gently inquired as to what Fox News was lying about, he said, 'You just said Sarah Palin wouldn't criminalise teenage girls who had abortions. She would. She's going to throw girls who have abortions in jail. And you're lying about it!' With some bewilderment, I pointed out we just played the clip in which *Palin herself* said she wouldn't put anybody who had an abortion in jail. But he kept calling me a liar and became increasingly agitated, so I had to bid him farewell.

People can go a little nuts about social issues during election cycles. Abortion has been the single most polarising issue in politics since the US Supreme Court decision *Roe vs. Wade* removed state and local restrictions on abortion in 1973. It and social issues such as gay marriage, prayer in schools and the display of religious paraphernalia strongly feature in American politics, and presidential politics, in a way that is unique to the United States. Why? Who cares that some place in East Bumblebee, Alabama, happens to have a big statue of the Ten Commandments on the public school lawn?

America's early history is peppered with religious dissidents coming to the North American continent to enjoy religious freedom. The Pilgrims went to Massachusetts to escape persecution from the Church of England; Roman Catholics founded the Maryland colony for the same reason. Quakers found a friendly home in Pennsylvania. Rhode Island was founded to be a haven for both political and religious dissidents. Both Pennsylvania and Virginia put religious freedom statutes into their own code of laws. Woven into the fabric of America's founding was the freedom to worship in whatever way a citizen's conscience led him. Even in the Constitution itself, religious freedom is enshrined, and not only in the Bill of Rights, but also in the 'religious test' clause in the Constitution, which asserts that nobody may be denied public office on the basis of his or her religion (as was the case in England at that time). With so much emphasis on religious tolerance, it's not surprising that the new nation was a haven for immigrants who wanted the freedom to worship in any way they chose. This is why America, alone among industrialised nations, still retains its theist heritage; because it's not part of American tradition to persecute religious believers, but rather to allow people to pursue any avenue of religious practice they wish, belief in God has become part of the fabric of everyday life.

From the 1790s to the 1840s, a cultural movement known as the Second Great Awakening emerged in the United States. This was a flowering of religious sentiment and Church membership that occurred throughout the country, but most notably in New York State, in which so many different denominations and churches rose it got the name 'The Burned-Over District'. But one feature that particularly characterised the Second Great Awakening was the rejection of intellectuals as religious leaders. Instead, common people began to take the reins of power in religious observances, and made religion part of popular culture. Theologian Nathan Hatch writes:

> The most dynamic and characteristic elements of Christianity during this time [were] the displacement from power of the religious people of ideas by those who leaned toward popular culture; the powerful centrifugal forces that drove churches apart and gave new significance to local and grass-roots endeavors; and the stark emotionalism, disorder, extremism, and crudeness that accompanied expressions of the faith fed by the passions of ordinary people.[179]

In some ways it was a good thing that clergymen like Cotton Mather were no longer scaring their congregations with hellish visions like 'Sinners In the Hands of an Angry God', but in other ways the new evangelicalism, divorced from the intelligentsia of the day and placed in the hands of local, grassroots religious groups, was yet another illustration of the American class struggle. People of comparatively low socio-economic status wanted to wrest the levers of power and status away from what they saw as the priestly class. In 1792, 83 per cent of southern churches were evangelical; there were a similar number of evangelical churches in the Midwest. To clarify, an evangelical church refers to its members' emphasis on personal conversion, an understanding of the importance of Jesus Christ's death and resurrection, and an interest in spreading the Gospel of Jesus Christ. We can see the historical legacy of the evangelical movement in the rise of mega-churches like Saddleback church in California, with its emphasis on popular music, casual clothing and short services with entertaining sermons.

As the class divisions in religious life deepened in the nineteenth and twentieth centuries, the lines became clear; the upper and upper-middle classes were going to mainline Protestant Churches (Episcopalian, Lutheran, Methodist) or the Catholic Church, while the middle and working classes were involved with denominations such as the Baptist Church. As upper and upper-middle-class faith in traditional institutions began to decline after the Second World War, membership in mainline Protestant Churches began to decline as their members pursued more individualistic choices. Rules of morality like keeping yourself a virgin before marriage or not dating lots of boys or not taking a birth control pill seemed terribly outmoded and people began to feel that Church had nothing to offer them. At the same time, people in the middle and working class weren't losing their faith in traditional institutions at all but still found their Churches to be an important part of their life – indeed, almost a bulwark against the societal changes that were happening in the 1960s and 1970s. We can now see the split that's going on, the exact mirror of the class struggle that happened at the time of the Second Great Awakening. Class elites felt they no longer needed Churches (and the Churches that remained strained to match their values to the new individualistic values of their members), whereas people lower down the socio-economic scale embraced religion, and the social issues religion touched upon, as the marker for their identity and their guide for making their way in the world.

Today, we experience the battles over social issues as yet another manifestation of the American class struggle. Elites mock and deride the religious beliefs of those they consider lower class to make sure they can't gain power, whereas the working class, who hold their religious beliefs very dearly, are attempting to achieve a political and cultural revolution. Because religious belief is very widespread in the United States, politicians can use their faith to appeal not only to the middle and working classes, but also to those urban, educated professionals who share those beliefs. Irreligious elites will find it harder to succeed in American politics, because their class status is too rare for the majority of Americans to relate to. Because everyone cares deeply about social issues due to their relation to our personal beliefs, the endless struggle over social issues is just class warfare conducted in another language; the bourgeoisie are trying to keep the proles away, while the proles are trying to start a Third Great Awakening.

But that has to be balanced against America's history of religious tolerance, which has transformed, over the years, into a very individualistic and libertarian attitude to how others live their lives. Most Americans couldn't care less if their gay neighbours are married or if their cousin wants to go to the Peace Corps or Occupy Wall Street, as long as it doesn't impinge on their lives. But that doesn't stop many progressive commentators from entertaining a notion that Christian conservatives are plotting a secret government takeover – and this is a fear that progressive advocacy organisations have found particularly fruitful for both fundraising and political support. Progressives are obsessed with the notion that fundamentalist Christians are taking over the Republican Party and getting ready to install a theocratic Christian government that will oppress all those who haven't accepted Christian Gospel. They're not wrong about the fact that there are Republican candidates (as well as Democratic ones) who have strong Christian beliefs, and that there have been presidential candidates from the Republican Party who have said things that are kind of crazy regarding religion. But there have not been any mainstream Republican candidates who've said they want to create a Christian-dominated theocracy in America. Nonetheless, there does seem to be a cultural push to create the fear of a Christian right-wing crusade, which serves the interests of the media and advocacy organisations just fine. The problem is that the people peddling the concept don't seem to be doing it particularly well.

Matt Taibbi, a political writer somewhat given to moments of hysteria (he's described Sarah Palin as 'the tawdriest, most half-assed fraud imaginable, twenty floors below the lowest common denominator, a character too dumb even for daytime TV'[180]), wrote an article about Michele Bachmann for *Rolling Stone* magazine called 'Michele Bachmann's Holy War'. Taibbi, who, remember, has to shift magazines off the news-stand shelf, gets himself into full-throated panic about the three-term Congresswoman from Minnesota:

> Bachmann is a religious zealot whose brain is a raging electrical storm of divine visions and paranoid delusions. She believes that the Chinese are plotting to replace the dollar bill, that light bulbs are killing our dogs and cats, and that God personally chose her to become both an IRS attorney who would spend years hounding taxpayers and a raging anti-tax Tea Party crusader against big government. In modern American politics, being the right kind of ignorant and entertainingly crazy is like having a big right hand in boxing; you've always got a puncher's chance. And Bachmann is exactly the right kind of completely batshit crazy. Not medically crazy, not talking-to-herself-on-the-subway crazy, but grandiose crazy, late-stage Kim Jong-Il crazy – crazy in the sense that she's living completely inside her own mind.

Taibbi imagines himself as the bulwark of civilisation against the barbarian. Conspiracy theories abound in this passage; he espouses the belief that the enemy somehow is able to bring the world as you know it to an end. Taibbi even decides to throw a bit of red meat to the bourgeoisie quaking in their boots about some redneck

Christian Congresswoman exciting the dull flyover proletariat, and gets down with the class war:

> Snickering readers in New York or Los Angeles might be tempted by all of this to conclude that Bachmann is uniquely crazy. But in fact, such tales by Bachmann work precisely because there are a great many people in America just like Bachmann, people who believe that God tells them what condiments to put on their hamburgers, who can't tell the difference between Soviet Communism and a Stafford loan, but can certainly tell the difference between being mocked and being taken seriously. When you laugh at Michele Bachmann for going on MSNBC and blurting out that the moon is made of red communist cheese, these people don't learn that she is wrong.[181]

Those hillbillies are so silly and moronic; they're ignorant of everything but their own self-respect! To Taibbi, people in New York and Los Angeles – coastal redoubts of right-thinking, decent people – know the truth about life, but you can fool the Midwestern rubes with a few fairy tales and wishful rumours!

As it turned out, the nice people in LA and New York were also fooled by fairy tales and wishful rumours. Taibbi actually copied most of the Bachmann quotes in the hit piece from articles and blog posts by 'Minneapolis City Pages' blogger G. W. Anderson, and when called on it, *Rolling Stone*'s executive editor admitted to deleting the attribution due to 'space concerns'. In addition, local reporters blasted Taibbi on how inaccurate his knowledge was of local issues described in the article and, to finish the pile-on, Anderson, who's a journalism professor, said of Taibbi's piece 'I do know that if a student handed in a story with that particular lack of sourcing, not only would I give it an "F", I would probably put that student on academic fraud.'[182] But in the end, it didn't matter – a lot more people read the *Rolling Stone* than read the corrections, so a lazy and paranoid piece has now shaped the views of nice progressive people up and down the coasts of America and internationally as well. It's the Palin Effect; Taibbi's got to shift magazines, and he knows perfectly well that concocting conspiracy theories about creeping Christianisms titillate his audience and pampers their vanity about being cultured and sophisticated. So he went with it and they believe it to this day.

New Yorker writer Ryan Lizza wrote a better sourced hit piece on Bachmann, but he still got lots of his facts wrong. Lizza's point was that the books Bachmann has read and the mentors she's had have made her a Dominionist – a Christian warrior who wants to establish a biblical theocracy in American government. Lizza provides this example:

> One of the leading proponents of Schaeffer's version of Dominionism is Nancy Pearcey, a former student of his and a prominent creationist. Her 2004 book, *Total Truth: Liberating Christianity from its Cultural Captivity*, teaches readers how to implement Schaeffer's idea that a Biblical world view should suffuse every aspect of one's life. She tells her readers to be extremely cautious with ideas from non-Christians ... the overall systems of thought constructed by nonbelievers will be false – for if the system is not built on Biblical truth, then it will be built on some other ultimate principle... Bachmann told me [*Total Truth*] was a 'wonderful book'.[183]

This all sounds very interesting, except that it turns out Lizza had no idea what he was talking about. Numerous journalists and commentators have questioned Lizza's assertions,[184] but perhaps the most telling criticism is that Nancy Pearcey herself says that Lizza was just making stuff up:

The takeaway from Ryan Lizza's hit piece on Michele Bachmann in the *New Yorker* is this: 'Dominionist' is the new 'Fundamentalist' – the preferred term of abuse, intended to arouse fear and contempt, and downgrade the status of targeted groups of people. Never mind that most of those people have never heard the term – including me. Lizza labeled [me a] Dominionist. Dozens of liberal websites have picked up the story and repeated the charge. I had to Google the term to discover whether there really is such a group.[185]

If the person who you claim is a Dominionist has to google Dominionism, then there's a flaw in your argument. But again, Ryan Lizza is a respected reporter for the *New Yorker*, a magazine beloved of bien pensants on the Upper West Side. Why shouldn't everyone believe exactly what he says? And while Lizza is a bit less wild-eyed than Taibbi, he's got to sell magazines too, and if that means pandering to the anxieties and prejudices of his audience, then by gum he will do it.

This suspicion about Dominionism is everywhere. Historian Sean Wilentz writes:

> Dominionists, who have established themselves inside the Republican Party, believe in a reassertion of Christine Doctrine over American politics and government. They range from believers who claim that the United States is a Christian nation and that Christians should exert more political leverage, to outright theocrats who want to supplant the US Constitution with scriptural law.[186]

This is a Princeton historian who's used to dealing with evidence and making a case for his assertions, but in his particular argument, there is no evidence; just suspicion and fear. The Palin Effect has caused people like Wilentz to reject dispassionately trying to find evidence on how religious beliefs affect politics, and instead fire off volleys at an invisible enemy while lost in a fog of suspicion and paranoia. Audiences are responsive to the argument that a Christian theocracy is among us, papers, magazines and broadcast advertising inventories are sold, people get hysterical and send off their money to advocacy groups and candidates. And thus, a billion dollar presidential race is paid for.

Exploiting social issues and the class divisions in American religious belief is super-handy for raising lots of cash; as Diddy used to say, it's all about the Benjamins. As we've seen, the 2008 election was the most expensive in history; it was 27 per cent more expensive than the 2004 election. The party nominees themselves, Barack Obama and John McCain, spent $1 billion together, and Obama far outpaced McCain, raising more than $770 million in donations.[187] For 2012, President Obama is expected to raise $1 billion, which is completely unprecedented in US politics.[188] They need all the money for events, field staff, strategy staff, planes, cars, computers, field offices, signage, website builds, phone banks, 'get out the vote' efforts, the all-important TV and radio advertising ... and I'm sure I'm only scratching the surface. Presidential campaigns create their own economy; over $2 billion was spent on ads in the 2008 campaign and in 2010 analysts predicted ad spending would top $3 billion.[189]

But it's not just the candidates themselves that spend money on campaigns – it's the political parties, it's state political committees, it's unions, and it's ideological groups like Planned Parenthood and the National Right to Life Committee. According to the Center for Responsive Politics, in 2008 Obama raised money from donors in four main sectors. The biggest was finance, followed by business, then lawyers and lobbyists, and finally 'ideological/single-issue' groups. They raised $54 million for the official 'Barack Obama for President' campaign in the 2008 cycle alone.

Ideological organisations spent over twice as much on Obama as they did on McCain.[190] These organisations aren't regulated by the FEC and they have no upper limit on spending as long as they do not advocate for a specific candidate. In order to raise money for their preferred candidates, they run ads about whatever social issue they're devoted to. The most famous of the 527s (so-called because that's the section of the US tax code that covers them) is the Swift Boat Veterans for Truth, which had such a strong effect on the 2004 election, but there are many of them now on both sides of the aisle. Two of the largest and most effective progressive 527s are EMILY's List, which is dedicated to electing pro-choice candidates for office, and the Gay and Lesbian Victory Fund, which aims to elect more open gay and lesbian candidates.[191]

The business model for these organisations is to frighten their potential donors into believing that only they can save the world against the savages out to destroy it. Inhuman monsters are trying to tear down everything you believe in – and only you, with your dollars and your time, can save what's dear to you. In 'The Paranoid Style in American Politics' renowned political scientist Richard Hofstader notes:

> The central image [in the paranoid style] is that of a vast and sinister conspiracy, a gigantic and yet subtle machinery of influence set in motion to undermine and destroy a way of life ... the paranoid spokesman sees the birth and death of whole worlds, whole political orders, whole systems of human values. He is always manning the barricades of civilisation... Time is forever just running out.[192]

Again, note the dehumanisation of the enemy, the sense that the writer is defending civilisation against hordes of barbarians, the apocalyptic air of doom that hangs over the words like a thundercloud. Our adversaries are pressing in from all sides, say these blog-gers, and only you can save all that you hold dear! And, of course, this beautifully enraging language inflames your passions such that you want to send $25 to the organisation of your choice that will fight these vandals and be partially responsible for saving the world as we know it. It's no coincidence that two of the most success-ful 527s are dedicated to the two most controversial social issues in the American political landscape. How do you get people excited enough about politics to reach into their pockets and donate money? You excite either their passions or their fears. There are 527s and ideological organisations devoted to things like dental care access and improving local government, but those don't excite the passions like abortion and gay marriage do. This is is entirely understandable; those issues touch the most deeply held beliefs that we all have about life, family, the choices we make and our own bodies.

Take a look at some of the language that's used on both sides and you'll see what I mean about social issues' emotional pull. Amanda Marcotte, a pro-choice blogger and political consultant, explained why she believes pro-lifers think the way they do:

> When anti-choicers speak reverently of 'life' … they imagine things that are technically alive, but have no relationship to this word … a mindless foetus, a fertilised egg, a stem cell. They relate to these beings, who are not really living, and scrounge up nothing but anger and hatred at those of us who are perceived as actually living in the impure, disgusting, life-having world with connections to family and friends, brainy intellectual engage-ment with reality and of course, dirty, filthy, despicable sex. The impure wetness of real life disturbs them. They dwell endlessly on the medically disgusting aspects of abortion – aspects that exist in all medical procedures – because their minds are enraptured by hatred of the perceived filthiness of human bodies and life.

The world with all its squirming, actually living life – it's bother-some. Better to dwell on the imagined peace of the foetus, the immoveable quiet of a person in a vegetative state. Someone who is recognisably human but not really living – the purest, simplest, least disgusting way of being. Purity is always under threat, from fluoride to uncontrolled sexuality.[193]

And then contrast that with the language used by Sister Toldjah, a pro-life blogger:

I've read many, many studies, articles, interviews, documentaries, etc on the grotesque practice of the termination of unborn life and oftentimes walk away from the illuminating pieces of infor-mation absolutely disgusted with our 'me first' 'if it feels good do it' casual culture – a culture made fashionable in the 60s by 'progressives' who took the women's lib movement way too far to the point that not only was the institution of marriage and a stable two-parent family unit viewed as a symbol of the 'repressed, subservient woman', but also that the precious, fragile lives of the unborn were portrayed as a 'burdensome inconvenience' for the 'modern woman'. And as a result, she needed 'legal options' to be able to take care of the so-called burden … the 'pro-choice' culture of death is exposed for what it is: bloodless, soulless – and most of all, heartless.[194]

No doubt, as you're reading these two excerpts, you're feeling a visceral anger and disgust at one or the other. You're supposed to. This is language that appeals to the deeply emotional side of your brain, the kind of language which, when you read it and agree with it, your brain gets a little dopamine hit by thinking 'Yes! I'm right and this person expresses it for me!' But let's break down the rhetorical techniques that are being used. There's a very us-versus-

SOCIAL ISSUES IN AMERICAN ELECTIONS

them mentality – each writer believes she's got sole purchase on being right, without any room for compromise. The other side is evil, 'enraptured' or enslaved by a 'fashionable' 'casual culture'. One side hates sex, the other side hates family. Interestingly, if you look at the thrust of each paragraph, they each come to say more or less the same thing; Marcotte says that pro-lifers hate humanity, whereas Sister Toldjah says that pro-choicers hate people. It's the demonisation of the enemy in this ideological war.

Politics is a business. Lots of people are employed by it and those people have got to be paid. For example, at the time of writing, the lobbying industry alone has made nearly $2.5 billion in revenue. There are 12,193 registered lobbyists, who receive money from corporations to persuade friendly government officials to sway public policy their way. We've been talking quite a bit about individual contributions to political campaigns and advocacy groups, but corporations donate too, and one of the extraordinary things about corporate donations to politics is just how profitable they are. Take AIG. The multinational insurance corporation, whose credit default swaps played such a crucial role in the collapse of Lehman Brothers, was one of the firms that received a bailout in 2008. In the Stimulus Bill passed in 2009, companies that got a bailout were prevented from paying executives' bonuses. But Senate banking chairman Chris Dodd (D-CT) put in an exception for bonuses agreed to before February 2009, which applied to AIG. So taxpayers paid for $165 million in bonus payments to AIG executives, thanks to the good senator (though he did whine on CNN that the Treasury Department made him put the clause in the Bill).[195] Dodd got $5,700 in political donations from three AIG execs between 2004 and 2006 and, over the past twenty years, he's received $280,238 in campaign cash from AIG executives and political action committees.[196] So for AIG, Senator Dodd has been an excellent investment.

Political corruption, even though it ends up costing us a shedload of money, isn't nearly as exciting as arousing people's passions about school prayer or abortion or gay marriage. *Roe vs. Wade* has been the single biggest fundraiser for conservative causes since Joe McCarthy succumbed to cirrhosis of the liver. I dread to think how many tears have been shed in progressive charities and advocacy groups since George W. Bush stepped down from office, though fortunately they have a new *bête noire* in the Tea Party. These are not issues that make that much of a material difference to the American populace, but they're issues that everyone has an opinion on, and therefore advocacy groups use them to keep the money rolling in. Candidates, because they know they have to keep the cash flowing, make statements that appease or offend one advocacy group or another, which are picked up on by the media because it knows very well a full-throated statement on the evils of abortion gets better ratings than a discussion of the future of the US vs the European equity market. The blogosphere also picks up on candidates' statements on social issues, because their passions have been inflamed by the rhetoric and because 'everybody's talking about it'. The advocacy groups use what the candidates say for more fundraising operations and the money keeps on coming.

What this produces is a system where no real change can happen. These ideological wars are designed to be self-perpetuating; we've created an economy of outrage that must be kept propped up. An illustrative example of how this works is when then-Senator Hillary Clinton, in 2005, gave a speech to pro-choice groups in New York trying to find common ground with pro-life believers. She said, 'There is an opportunity for people of good faith to find common ground in this debate – we should be able to agree that we want every child born in this country to be wanted, cherished and loved … we do have deeply held differences of opinion about the issue of abortion and I, for one, respect those who believe with all their hearts and conscience that there are no circumstances under which any abortion should ever be available.'[197] The reaction to Senator Clinton trying to find any common ground between both sides was predictably negative. On the right, Tony Perkins, head of the Family Research Council, said, 'I think she's trying to adopt a values-oriented language, but it lacks substance, at least if you compare it to her record,' and on the left, the news reported that there were 'gasps and head-shaking' when Clinton expressed her respect for pro-life views.[198] And why should they agree with one another? If they did, what would be the reason for their existence? They'd all be out of a job if they said to one another, 'You know, the senator's right. Let's try to work together to reduce unplanned pregnancies.' Why would they want to self-immolate themselves by trying to come to some kind of accord? Clinton's outreach to pro-life groups was quickly forgotten. President Lyndon Baines Johnson used to say, 'come let us reason together', but with the financial realities of running a presidential campaign, it's in literally nobody's interest to do so.

There's a serious debate about whether the Tea Party is just a new guise for the Christian right or whether it represents a new conservative force in American politics. And, as always with these things, it's complicated. Two social scientists, David Campbell and Robert Putnam, published the results from a study in the *New York Times* for which they interviewed 3,000 people in 2006, and then interviewed them again in 2010, and discovered that the people who were Christians and partisan Republicans in 2006 were still Christians and partisan Republicans four years later, but now they supported the Tea Party as well. From these results, they concluded that the Tea Party was obviously composed of partisan, Christian Republicans, which seems to me to be a bit of a stretch.[199]

The Pew Research Center, which did a much more comprehensive survey of American attitudes about the Tea Party, came up with a startling conclusion. They found an interesting crossover between the two groups; 69 per cent of Christian conservatives said that they had heard of or supported the Tea Party, but only 46 per cent of people who considered themselves Tea Party members had heard of or supported Christian conservatives. So it seems fair to say that while most social cons are Tea Partiers, fewer Tea Partiers are social cons.[200] Indiana Governor Mitch Daniels, who briefly flirted with a run for president this cycle, suggested in February 2011 that there should be a 'truce' on social issues while the country figured out its mounting economic problems. Nearly two-thirds of Republicans agreed with him,[201] but he received criticism from many vocal social-conservative organisations, and eventually decided not to run. And it's certainly true that moral crusader Rick Santorum has not found a great deal of sympathy for his campaign, which is almost entirely focused on social issues – in fact, to get himself out of the single-digit doldrums, he's been desperately trying to claim that the economy is in fact rooted in morality, and we shouldn't ignore human life while trying to bring down the deficit.

It does seem that despite the claims of the *New York Times*, Republican primary voters are much more interested in economic issues in this election cycle. In a poll of South Carolina voters, who vote in one of the earliest primaries, 62 per cent of Republicans in this heavily conservative state said that jobs and the economy trumped all other concerns. In a straw poll taken by the South Carolina Federation of Republican Women, most respondents said the economy was the most important issue to them in this election – social issues ranked a lowly fifth.[202] CNN did a national poll in December 2011 asking Americans what was the 'most important problem facing this country today', and the overwhelming answer for 57 per cent of the respondents was the economy. Only 1 per cent of respondents answered 'Policies towards gays and lesbians.'[203] Abortion didn't even feature. Rick Perry cut an ad affirming his Christian faith, asserting he's not afraid to stand up for Christians, and not only did it become an immediate punchline in progressive internet circles, conservatives didn't want to defend it. As conservative blogger Bill Quick put it, 'Any politician who thinks he or she is going to ride those issues to victory in today's climate is simply delusional about what today's climate really is. And their supporters are *projecting* their concerns onto the big screen of their desire, which doesn't reflect the reality of the day at all.'[204]

And that holds true for Democrats as well as Republicans. Democrats like to use social issues as a cornerstone of their campaigns because it has, in the past, worked so well to keep its coalition of identity groups in the fold (women, LGTB voters, African-Americans), and because if it's easy to portray the opposition as a wild-eyed fundamentalist maniac, it's an efficient money and vote getter. But 2012 is different. Voters don't really want to hear that so-and-so is anti-gay or has had three marriages or whatever. They want jobs. They want to stop losing money in their pensions hand over fist. And the Obama campaign had better come up with an answer for them, or they might be packing their bags on 19 January 2013.

7

WHY ARE WE ARGUING ABOUT EVOLUTION ANYWAY?

On a muggy, hazy day in August 2011, Texas Governor Rick Perry was greeting and schmoozing voters in New Hampshire. An exchange with a young boy and his mother about science education in the Lone Star State was captured on video:

> MOM: He has a question for you.
> SON: How old do you think the Earth is?
> PERRY: How old do I think the Earth is? You know what, I don't have any idea. I know it's pretty old so it goes back a long, long way. I'm not sure anybody actually knows completely and absolutely how long...
> MOM: Ask him about evolution.
> PERRY: ...how old the Earth is. I hear your mom was asking about evolution. It's a theory that's out there, and it's got some [either 'gas' or 'gaps' – it was inaudible] in it. In Texas we teach both creationism and evolution in our public schools...
> MOM: [louder] Ask him why he doesn't believe in science!
> PERRY: ...because I think you're smart enough to figure out which one is right.[205]

There were two notable things about this encounter. The first is that it's not quite clear from the video exactly what Perry is saying about evolution. *ABC News* quoted him as saying there were 'gaps' in the theory,[206] which suggests that Perry either didn't believe in it or was trying to find some other explanation for the origins of life on Earth, whereas the *Atlantic* quoted him as saying there was 'gas' in the theory,[207] which implies that Perry might find evolution credible. We'll never know because the video is inaudible. The more important thing to note is that Perry was accosted by a woman pressuring her son to ask questions of the Texas governor that would portray him in a bad light. In other words, she wanted the evolution issue to become Perry's 'macaca moment', an embarrassing moment captured on video that would make him lose the election. Evolution is a hot political issue. It isn't just used to shore up support; it's also designed to be used as a cudgel to attack one's political opponents.

Why on earth do Americans have to have a biennial national freak-out over a scientific theory first propounded in the nineteenth century? It must seem mystifying to people outside the hothouse of US politics that we have to badger every political incumbent and challenger about what their thoughts are on evolution and whether it should be taught in public schools. Like abortion and gay marriage, it's one of those issues on which everybody's supposed to have an opinion. It's also one of those issues where there's clearly a 'right' and a 'wrong' side. The preponderance of scientific research is on the side of evolution; the fossil record, the geological record, even the fact that you can recreate evolution in a petri dish points to the truth of evolution. What purpose does it serve for political candidates to aver that it doesn't exist? And why do the media and other political and cultural elites delight in haranguing office seekers and holders about it, even going so far as to assign office seekers beliefs they don't actually hold? Jay Richards and David Klinghoffer wrote in the *American Spectator*: 'Evolution is the speed trap of presidential campaigns. Though a President doesn't have much influence over state and local science education policy, reporters lie in wait for the unwary candidate, ready to pounce with a question he's poorly prepared to answer yet that is important to millions of voters.'[208] It's not like the president has much to do with setting local education policy. Why bother pinning candidates down on a question that has no actual bearing on how a candidate will perform as commander-in-chief?

The evolution issue is the perfect microcosm of the American political class war. 'Everybody knows' that Democrats are over-educated, over-intellectual, over-sophisticated, snobby, latte-sipping wimps who tremble in fear at the sight of a muddy pick-up truck, just as 'everybody knows' that Republicans are Joe and Jane Sixpack, salt of the Earth, anti-intellectual, stupid, rural, dentally challenged idiots who'd rather die than crack the spine of a book. These stereotypes are exploited conveniently around election time for the delectation of the political audience and the delight of advocacy organisations. It's also a great story for the media. What could be a more compelling story, to excite audiences and stoke ratings, than that of an over-religious throwback who believes in a two-millennia-old Biblical account despite scientific evidence to the contrary? It touches all the passion points that an urban, middle-class professional wants to feel: that he or she is smarter than the average bear, that he or she understands more than the yahoos living in the middle of the country and, most importantly, he or she is making the right decision sending their children to expensive schools (or living in areas with expensive property taxes) because at least the kids are learning something about science, unlike the crazies running for president. This particular issue works to the advantage of Democrats rather than Republicans; nobody ever hears GOP primary voters say during the primaries that they're voting for one candidate or another based on their beliefs on evolution, but Democrats love citing evolution as a key reason why they won't be voting for a particular Republican candidate, like when actor Matt Damon said of Governor Palin in 2008, 'I need to know if she really thinks that dinosaurs were here 4,000 years ago. I want to know that, I really do. Because she's gonna have the nuclear codes.'[209] (As vice president, she wouldn't have the nuclear codes, but since Matt was really cute in *Good Will Hunting*, nobody seemed to mind his factual error.) The evolution issue plays to all the most deeply held stereotypes that progressives have about the barbarians in the American hinterlands: they're overly religious, they don't believe in science, they don't believe in critical thinking, they're stupid, backward and unable to think their way through a problem. If a Republican politician can be portrayed as anti-science because of the evolution issue, then it's game over. That's why candidates are constantly asked about it; if answered the wrong way, it becomes an instant campaign destroyer.

But like all things that people feel passionately about, if a political candidate tries to please everyone they end up upsetting at least some. So the fine line that all candidates have to walk is one that pleases the most Americans but upsets a lot of other people both in the USA and internationally. When most Brits look quizzically at their cousins across the pond, not only do they look across a great watery divide, but a big cultural one as well. Let's just come out and say it: Americans are religious. Ninety-two per cent of Americans believe in God, according to a May 2011 Gallup poll. This is the highest concentration of theists in the industrialised world. It also happens that 57 per cent of Americans believe in evolution. So for 157 million Americans, there's going to have to be a crossover between a belief in God and a belief that evolution occurred that is a satisfactory explanation for life existing on Earth as we know it. That's why most politicians espouse a position of 'I don't know' or 'God had a hand in it' or 'I see God in creation'. Al Gore, when he was running for president in 2000, said that while he favoured teaching evolution in public schools, he felt local school boards should be able to teach creationism as well.[210] John Edwards stated, when he was running in 2007, that he believed in evolution and that:

> it's perfectly possible to make our faith, my faith belief system, consistent with a recognition that there is real science out there, and scientific evidence of evolution... The hand of God was in every step of what's happened with man. The hand of God today is in every step of what happens with me and every human being that exists on this planet.[211]

Hillary Clinton said of her beliefs on evolution, 'I believe in evolution... I believe that our founders had faith in reason and they also had faith in God, and one of our gifts from God is the ability to reason.'[212] But it isn't just Democrats who espouse this position. Mitt Romney's beliefs go along with the standard politician's line. He said: 'I believe that God designed the universe and created the universe... And I believe evolution is most likely the process he used to create the human body. I've never found a conflict between the science of evolution and the belief that God created the universe.'[213]

Again, if you're a politician who doesn't want to seem like a complete ignoramus yet don't want to needlessly piss off the 157 million Americans who are able to both believe in God and evolution, you've got to be able to figure out some way to get God and Darwin to get along. As then-Senator Joe Biden said on *Real Time with Bill Maher* in 2008:

> I think the problem with a lot of élites in the Democratic Party, quite frankly, is that they communicate that they don't respect people's faith. People out there don't want them to believe like

they believe, but they want to know that they respect them. We have too many élites in our party who look down their nose on people of faith. The people of faith don't want us to share their view, they just want to know we respect them. That's the big problem with my party.[214]

People expect politicians to respect them and their faith; when politicians don't, it's no surprise that voters turn away. The religion issue has been difficult for Democrats to deal with; their constituents comprise both people who believe in God as well as those who don't, therefore they have found it difficult to be able to speak compellingly to both groups and avoid offending one or the other. That's why Nancy Pelosi made her caucus take religion classes after the Democratic election debacle of 2004 – it was felt Democrats weren't doing enough to reach out to people of faith.

You can't make everyone happy; pleasing the majority is bound to upset members of the minority. Atheists, of which there is a large contingent in the scientific community, really can't stand that politicians have to acknowledge both science and God. Take P. Z. Myers, a biologist at the University of Minnesota, who's a strict neo-Darwinist and atheist. Myers blogged:

> I'm sorry, but Romney's statement [regarding the lack of conflict between belief in evolution and the belief that God created the universe] is pure calculated bullsh*t with more acknowledgment of religion than science... What is particularly troubling is how far we've sunk that so many on the side of science are willing to ignore the unscientific promotion of an unevidenced supernatural entity and pretend that this is good for us.[215]

In one sense, Myers is absolutely right; God doesn't really belong in the laboratory. Faith and the *work* of science are two separate things. But Myers completely misunderstands what it is to have faith and be equally enthusiastic about the understanding we're able to glean from the human brain. We can marvel at the extraordinary fossil record and understand the evolution of, say, the trilobite, and still be able to keep God in that universe. William F. Buckley, a firm believer in the divine origins of man, once said:

> Skepticism about life and nature is most often expressed by those who take it for granted that belief is an indulgence of the superstitious – indeed their opiate, to quote a historical cosmologist most profoundly dead. Granted, that to look up at the stars comes close to compelling disbelief – how can such a chance arrangement be other than an elaboration – near infinite – of natural impulses? Yet, on the other hand, who is to say that the arrangement of the stars is more easily traceable to nature, than to nature's molder? … The skeptics get away with fixing the odds against the believer, mostly by pointing to phenomena which are only explainable – you see? – by the belief that there was a cause for them, always deducible.[216]

For many Americans, the gaps where the unknowable resides, the inscrutable mysteries, that's where God is. Many theist Americans believe that the unknowable – what created the human soul, the spark that separates the human spirit from mere flesh – comes from God. And while that's deeply unfashionable to atheists in the scientific community, or post-religious Europeans, in a country with religious freedom written into its founding documents, it's a belief held dear by millions of Americans. That's why an explanation of humanity maybe evolving from a reptile that might have had a mutation a billion years ago and, whoops-a-daisy, here we are, isn't going to be satisfactory to a lot of people.

Myers' criticisms do a lot to explain how for some, particularly for secular Europeans, it seems baffling that a mainstream, intelligent person like Mitt Romney (or John Edwards for that matter) can hold both a belief in God and a belief in evolutionary biology at the same time. To such people, believing that God designed creation through an evolutionary process is no different from believing in creationism; it's putting God at the beginning of things where He doesn't necessarily belong.

Many Americans reject this Myersesque notion of theistic evolution as 'calculated bullshit', but they wouldn't call themselves creationists. They believe in both a divine being and the process of evolution which science has revealed through experiments and evidence, and they're comfortable with both those ideas. Blogger Jazz Shaw, who believes in both God and evolution, wrote: 'If the development of the universe and our planet played out over billions of years and life "evolved" here as current theory suggests, I'm not so vain about my own intellect to claim that God couldn't have designed the entire shooting match to do just that.'[217] In the USA, 4.8 million people identify themselves as atheist or agnostic; 157 million Americans believe in both God and evolution. If you're a politician, which group of people are you going to appeal to? And since over half of Americans are both God-fearing and believers in science, isn't it likely that political candidates could be in that crossover group themselves? The lesson here is that no politician will make any friends among the swing voters of Ohio and Missouri by telling people that their ideas about science and the origins of man are 'calculated bullshit'. It's not fashionable among the academy, or in post-religious Europe, but a simultaneous belief in both the divine and the scientific is where the beliefs of a majority of the American population lie, and that's where at least the mainstream political dialogue will stay. There's just no upside in pointlessly angering millions of Americans who are both strongly theist and believe in scientific evidence. Don't expect that standard political attitudes about evolution will change until American demographics do.

But what about the candidates who aren't in the political mainstream? In this election cycle, there are indeed a couple of candidates who either say they don't accept evolution or say they accept 'intelligent design' (ID). And before we talk about ID, it's good to point out that there are lots of flavours of cosmological theories of the universe and life on Earth as we know it, most interesting among them being 'Young Earth' creationists. These people are folks who believe that the Earth is 6,000 years old, that God created the Earth and its inhabitants in six days, and that dinosaurs existed at the same time as humans.

There are also 'Old Earth' creationists, who believe that the world was created in six days like the Bible says, just that the six days actually represent periods of time that could have been longer – millennia, perhaps. There are no publicly declared Young or Old Earth creationists currently competing for the Republican presidential nomination in 2012 or who have prominent positions in the Republican Party. Huntsman has stated he believes in theistic evolution, like Romney and Newt Gingrich, who have said they believe God was behind evolution and that mankind has a divine origin. Ron Paul has said he does not accept evolution as a theory and that 'The creator that I know created us, each and every one of us and created the universe, and the precise time and manner... I just don't think we're at the point where anybody has absolute proof on either side.' Bachmann and Perry believe in 'intelligent design', which they both think should be taught alongside evolution in public schools, and Santorum, who also believes in intelligent design, thinks it shouldn't be taught in schools, but rather students should learn 'the problems and holes and I think there are legitimate problems and holes in the theory of evolution'.[218]

It's Bachmann's and Perry's position on intelligent design that seems most objectionable to non-theist, non-conservative people. ID is a concept that many object to because, it is often asserted, ID is no different from creationism – it's just given another name and dressed up as scientific theory. At its simplest level, ID is not particularly different from theistic evolution; *Slate* writer Daniel Engbert explained, 'Intelligent design adherents believe only that the complexity of the natural world could not have occurred by chance. Some intelligent entity must have created the complexity, they reason, but that "designer" could in theory be anything or anyone.'[219] But many commentators insist that ID is, in the words of John Cook from *Gawker*, 'a pseudo-scientific-sounding "theory"… a sort of stalking horse to sneak their creation myth into the public education curriculum'.[220]

Most people who believe in intelligent design, or at least teaching it in schools, don't publicly state they believe in creationism, or that they want to use ID to introduce creationism to students. Here's what Bachmann says about it: 'I support intelligent design… What I support is putting all science on the table and then letting students decide. I don't think it's a good idea for government to come down on one side of a scientific issue or another, when there is reasonable doubt on both sides.' And here's what Perry says about ID: 'I am a firm believer in intelligent design as a matter of faith and intellect, and I believe it should be presented in schools alongside the theories of evolution. The State Board of Education has been charged with the task of adopting curriculum requirements for Texas public schools and recently adopted guidelines that call for the examination of all sides of a scientific theory, which will encourage critical thinking in our students, an essential learning skill.'[221] Of the two Republican candidates for president that have the views that are most scientifically objectionable about evolution, it's interesting neither are calling for dogmatic instruction of creationism or intelligent design to children in public schools; they both want to 'teach the controversy', which, while having its own problems, is not the same as 'no evolution taught ever'.

The teaching of the 'controversy', such as it is, revolves around there not being enough evidence to support the idea of a completely atheistic evolutionary mechanic. ID theorists 'prove' their ideas by showing there are holes in the evidence which justify there being some sort of intelligent hand in the creation of the universe. Here's an example, given by a senior fellow at the pro-ID Discovery Institute in Seattle, Stephen Meyer:

> In 1953, when Watson and Crick elucidated the structure of the DNA molecule, they made a startling discovery. Strings of precisely sequenced chemicals called nucleotides in DNA store and transmit the assembly instructions – the information – in a four-character digital code for building the protein molecules the cell needs to survive. Crick then developed his 'sequence hypothesis', in which the chemical bases in DNA function like letters in a written language or symbols in a computer code. As [Richard] Dawkins has noted, 'the machine code of the genes is uncannily computer-like'. The informational features of the cell at least appear designed. Yet, to date, no theory of undirected chemical evolution has explained the origin of the digital information needed to build the first living cell. Why? There is simply too much information in the cell to be explained by chance alone.[222]

Meyer's point is that even though DNA molecules look like a language or a computer code, and function like a language or a computer code, there's never been any theory or experimentation on how this language or code came to be. Meyer hypothesises that the coded information in DNA is too complex to have occurred by chance over a random series of mutations.

What some theists object to about this particular flavour of intelligent design, and why it could be seen as a kind of creationism, is that it puts God into inappropriate places. Physicist and theologian Karl Giberson says:

> The fact that [blood clotting or the propeller on a bacterium] seem complicated and hard to explain through evolution doesn't suggest for one second that we ought to invoke the supernatural finger of God. I do think there are lots of things we don't understand about the world and maybe the intelligent design movement is doing us a service by shining a bright light on those. But when all is said and done, I don't think Christian theology wants to have a God who is one of several different factors in shaping natural history ... it turns God into a kind of conjurer, one who comes in every now and then to do a trick in nature. How is this a helpful model for God?
>
> In a sense it cheapens God to have Him everywhere – it becomes a kind of spiritual literalism where for everything we can't figure out we say 'God did it, God did it'. In this way, intelligent design suggests a kind of intellectual infancy and dependency, a surrender of the power of our own intellect. It takes away a bit of the awe of God and turns him into a harried parent performing magic tricks for slightly bored children. But again, while ID can put God into inappropriate places, it doesn't make a case that it supplants evolutionary theory with creationism.

Some scientists make the point that offering to 'teach the controversy' is itself the way to introduce creationism in schools. The weight of scientific evidence falls rather clearly on the side that evolution exists – there really isn't much evidence for intelligent design other than, 'this is too complicated to appear through random mutation'. So just the notion that there is any kind of controversy, many scientists feel, gives too much credence to any kind of belief other than evolution. As evolutionary biologist Richard Dawkins explains:

> What is wrong with the apparently sweet reasonableness of 'it is only fair to teach both sides'? The answer is simple. This is not a scientific controversy at all... If ID really were a scientific theory, positive evidence for it, gathered through research, would fill peer-reviewed scientific journals. This doesn't happen. It isn't that editors refuse to publish ID research. There simply isn't any ID research to publish... Never do they offer positive evidence in favour of intelligent design. All we ever get is a list of alleged deficiencies in evolution ... organs are stated, by fiat and without supporting evidence, to be 'irreducibly complex': too complex to have evolved by natural selection.

It's difficult to 'teach the controversy' when one side's argument consists largely of pointing out the flaws in the other's. Dawkins is right that there's no scientific evidence to prove that intelligent design exists; it largely serves as a kind of stop-gap explanation for things that either can't be or haven't yet been explained by science. By its nature it resists scientific verification. Even to acknowledge the 'evidence' behind intelligent design is to acknowledge creationist thinking.

The notion of 'presenting both sides' is appealing to many Americans. Why do politicians like Bachmann and Perry think this message would be more palatable to voters than saying, 'All public schools should teach intelligent design'? Why are so many Americans comfortable with saying, 'I believe in evolution, but I believe that humans are created by God?' It's because the explanations the scientific community have asked laymen to believe are not entirely satisfying. Part of the problem is that those in charge of conveying complex scientific findings to a lay audience often don't really have sufficient scientific understanding themselves. For example, the evolution of the X chromosome was explained by a reporter at the *Washington Post* as 'A conventional chromosome in a forebear of humans – probably a reptile of some sort – apparently underwent a mutation that allowed it to direct the development of sperm-producing testes.' Remember, this is stuff that is important – but that we all want taught well in public school classrooms. It just seems to be hard for the average person to believe that something that might have happened 300 million years ago to a reptile eventually led to the creation of modern humans. The kind of simplistic explanation just quoted, and many like it, leave too much to chance. Unfortunately, if public school students have queries about the explanations they're given, science educators are often not good enough to answer them. And so they go to their parents to find out the answers, but their parents, often themselves with an inadequate science education, use a mixture of what they've learned in school and in their faith communities. The result is that many laypeople end up relying for their scientific knowledge on a combination of what they learned in science class and the religious beliefs they learned within their families.

In a much-discussed media kerfuffle, the Miss USA 2011 beauty pageant contestants were asked whether or not evolution should be taught in schools. For a bit of background, beauty pageant contestants are now asked controversial political questions, because of a 2009 stunt in which producers decided to bring 'relevancy' to the pageant contest by having the judges ask the contestants whether they believed in gay marriage. Miss California, Carrie Prejean, said that she did not, causing a confrontation with pageant judge Perez Hilton. Prejean also received death threats, including one, bizarrely, from Conservative MP Alan Duncan, who said on the BBC's *Have I Got News for You*, 'If you read that Miss California has been murdered, you will know it was me, won't you?'[223] Despite the threats of violence, the controversy halted years of ratings decline for the pageant so, of course, from now on Miss USA contestants will face tough political questions.

The 2011 contestants, facing the evolution question, hedged their bets. 'Think Progress', a progressive political blog, lamented that only two candidates 'stood up for Darwin', but that's not so. Three said unequivocally that evolution shouldn't be taught in public schools, eighteen said it should and thirty-one said that 'both sides of the story should be taught'. It should be noted that many of those who endorsed both sides said that they personally believed in evolution but did not want to offend people of religious faith – as Miss Utah noted, 'it's tough because either way, someone will be offended'. After the Prejean incident, it's perfectly understandable they didn't want to upset anyone; what nice young woman wants to face death threats? The answer of 'teach both sides' is a dodge that attempts to please all and offend none; it's a way to reach all of us who have questions about combining evolutionary biology and theology that were imperfectly explained by both the education system and religious institutions.

Again it's very important to anyone who is interested in gaining the confidence of a popular majority of people, whether it's in an election or a beauty pageant contest, to make sure you don't unnecessarily alienate anyone. Gilberson says, 'I think there's a reckless extrapolation from what we know about evolution to an all-encompassing materialism... It overlooks the reality of human experience, overlooks that religious experiences are very common and meaningful for a lot of people.' The Myers and Dawkins emphasis on materialist causes for the development of modern humans is not only unsatisfying to many, it can make people of faith feel disrespected, which, as we know from Senator Biden, really turns people off. Yet there aren't very many theists who can publicly work through how it's possible to believe in God and science. We therefore end up with a situation where students and parents end up distrusting the school system and science education, which politicians capitalise on by expressing populist sentiment about it and advocacy groups use for scaring the pants off of voters and raising lots of cash. Think back to the class struggles over religion. Evangelical voters who take religion seriously are considered lower class, whereas upper and upper-middle-class folks don't feel the pull of religion in the same way. The evolution issue is another great manifestation of this. The upper and upper-middle classes see political candidates talking about intelligent design and 'teaching the controversy' and they instinctively recoil because that candidate's just announced *I'm not like you*. That was why so many progressive commentators were anxious to portray Sarah Palin as a creationist – even if she wasn't – because it stoked class anxiety in people who might be inclined to give her a look. The same thing will happen with the 2012 candidates; progressive pundits will be trying to place the class marker of happy-clappy religion on all of the Republicans in order to keep suburban professionals voting for Democrats. That's why that mother in New Hampshire wanted to catch Perry out saying that he didn't believe in evolution; if he'd cooperated, it would have been great video proving Perry was not the right candidate for professional, suburban America.

Determining whether a presidential candidate believes in evolution does have a practical use in a political campaign; if a candidate can't weigh evidence of a particular point of view, or if he or she ignores evidence in favour of another theory, then that doesn't speak much of his or her judgement and critical thinking ability. *Science* editor-in-chief Donald Kennedy wrote: 'I don't need [candidates] to describe their faith; that's their business and not mine. But I do care about their scientific knowledge and how it will inform their leadership.'[224] If someone wants to be the leader of one of the great scientific and technological powerhouses of the world, he or she must be able to think critically and rationally. But it must be noted that belief in evolution doesn't have a great track record of proving that a politician has superior judgement; Bill Clinton, for example, believes in evolution and his judgement has faltered on more than one occasion. But it seems odd that it's now evolution and climate change that's the litmus test for 'believing in science'? Why couldn't it be quantum field theory or plate tectonics?

As we know, the most resonant political issues are the ones that touch us personally. It's difficult to have an emotional political discussion about the Higgs boson particle, but it's easy to get people excited about an issue which touches on the most basic human questions: Who am I? Where do I come from? Where am I going? You had better believe that people are going to feel very strongly about that. Since the dawn of time humans have been searching for answers to those questions. One of the extraordinary things about human progress is that we as a species have managed to go from writing creation myths to using scientific methods to try to answer these questions rationally, though there is still much we don't understand. The facts that we do know provide a comforting framework for our inquisitive minds. And if someone questions a belief that we hold dear, even if we feel that it's supported by facts, we really don't like it. That's why the 'anti-science' charge has such emotional resonance, and why so many are desperate to use it against politicians they don't like. Here's what I mean. In September 2008, *Los Angeles Times* reporter Stephen Braun quoted Alaskan music teacher and progressive blogger Philip Munger who in 1997, had asserted that Sarah Palin told him 'dinosaurs and humans walked the earth at the same time' and explained away the fossil record by saying she had 'seen photographs of human footprints inside dinosaur tracks'. When asked about the statement, Palin's spokesman said, 'I've never had a conversation like that with her or been apprised of anything like that,' and said Palin never discussed her views on evolution openly.[225] Munger isn't the most credible source in the world – he is a political opponent, nobody was around to corroborate his story and Palin's spokesperson denied it – so it becomes he-said, she-said. But the progressive blogosphere was so anxious to push the story that Palin believed that dinosaurs and humans co-existed that they reported on it like it was gospel. In September 2011 googling 'Sarah Palin dinosaurs' resulted in 2,970,000 hits. This was a story that people wanted – needed – to believe. It didn't matter that it was unsupported by any corroborating evidence; it didn't matter that it only came from one source; it didn't matter that Palin's spokesman denied it. Jonathan Haidt, a social psychologist at the University of Virginia, gave a speech at the Society for Personality and Social Psychology conference in 2011. He shocked the audience by saying that the fact there were so few people who had conservative political beliefs was due to fear and prejudice, not statistical anomaly. He pointed out:

> [Social psychologists] had created a 'tribal-moral community' united by 'sacred values' that hinder research and damage their credibility – and blind them to the hostile climate they've created for non-liberals... Anywhere in the world that social psychologists see women or minorities underrepresented by a factor of two or three, our minds jump to discrimination as the explanation. But when we find out that conservatives are underrepresented among us by a factor of more than 100, suddenly everyone finds it quite easy to generate alternate explanations.

He also noted, 'If a group circles around sacred values, they will evolve into a tribal-moral community... They'll embrace science whenever it supports their sacred values, but they'll ditch it or distort it as soon as it threatens a sacred value.' The example Haidt then gave was Professor Daniel Patrick Moynihan's research into the rise of unwed mothers and welfare dependency among African-Americans. 'Moynihan was shunned by many of his colleagues at Harvard as racist,' Dr Haidt said. 'Open-minded inquiry into the problems of the black family was shut down for decades, precisely the decades in which it was most urgently needed. Only in the last few years have liberal sociologists begun to acknowledge that Moynihan was right all along.'[226] Haidt's research into the progressive political make-up of the 'tribal-moral' community of social psychologists is yet another example of the Palin Effect; his research suggests social psychologists developed 'alternate explanations' (or told comforting stories) about themselves to cover up the uncomfortable truth that they were discriminating against conservatives who wanted to join their field. This is a fascinating, and very common, human phenomenon. Similarly, the Palin Effect meant that many Americans were willing to believe unsupported allegations against Palin, even though the evidence was thin – they needed to believe she was somehow different, somehow lower class, somehow unsuited to be vice president.

It's hard to acknowledge if we ourselves have created a 'tribal-moral' community around our own sacred values – it's not really a conscious action. But it's a question that we need to ask ourselves if we're finding that we want to believe things that aren't true. Humans like to believe facts that confirm our already held beliefs and discard facts that contradict what we believe. The question must be asked: have people who consider themselves part of the 'reality-based' community, people who believe in rational thought and the power of evidence, created such a closed community around the 'sacred values' of science, rationality, evolution etc. that they can believe that Palin thinks dinosaurs co-exist with humans when there's very little evidence to prove that? Or read 'I see the hand of God in creation' as 'I believe the Earth was created in six days'? It's human nature to believe the evidence of things we support and reject evidence of things that go against our beliefs, but when it comes to decisions about politics it's important to make sure that our beliefs are backed up by actual facts, or else our thoughts and beliefs are simply tools for others to manipulate. The vested interests in making sure that we're terrified of creationists are excellent at raising plenty of cash for their cause. In 2010 the education industry spent over $120 million lobbying federal and state officials; it was the eighth largest industry spender on lobbying. Organisations like the National Math and Science Initiative, the National Association of Science Teachers and the Science Coalition give thousands of dollars every year to political candidates. How do they get this kind of money? By scaring the bejesus out of you about creationist political candidates.

Instead of spending so much money and time on frightening the populace about anti-science politicians, it'd be great if the science education lobby could improve the dismal state of American science education. If you think it's depressing to know that only 57 per cent of Americans believe in evolution, let me give you some more cheerful stats. According to the Trends in International Mathematics and Science Study, 27 per cent of adults are considered 'scientifically literate'. Forty-nine per cent of American adults believe that genetically modified tomatoes have genes, but regular ones don't. Forty-five per cent of adults believe antibiotics will kill viruses as well as bacteria and 41 per cent of Americans think that astrology has some basis in science.

The study also looked at the scientific knowledge of students from ages five to eighteen and their scores also weren't so hot. The United States ranked eleventh in scientific knowledge. Students from affluent backgrounds tended to score higher on the tests; urban, largely African-American districts did not score as highly. Teachers blamed the poor scores on economic differences as well as an education system that required the memorisation of scientific concepts rather than reasoning out and understanding scientific theories. One professor said:

> [I visited] an elementary school one time where the principal proudly told me that every student in the school was required to memorise the order of the planets. I said to him, 'I'm not going to argue with that, but when you have them learn that, don't do it during science time because it has nothing to do with science.' The science question is how do we know Venus is closer to the Sun than the Earth, or how do we know the Earth goes around the Sun?

Alex Berezow, a microbiologist and the editor of *Real Clear Science*, points out that neither party has the monopoly on being anti-science. As one example, he cites vaccine scepticism, stating that there is a higher rate of non-compliance in counties where there is a Whole Foods. Eighty-nine per cent of counties containing a Whole Foods supported Barack Obama in the 2008 election, meaning that nice, progressive, affluent, middle-class people believe erroneously and against scientific advice that there is something wrong with getting their kids vaccinated against potentially deadly diseases, thereby exposing large communities to illnesses like measles and whooping cough. Scientists also support measures like animal testing, constructing nuclear power plants and producing genetically modified food, yet progressives are constantly agitating against them. In 2009, the London School for Hygiene and Tropical Medicine concluded the world's largest study of the nutritional value of organic vs non-organic food, and discovered that there were in fact no health benefits to organic food, yet people still believe quite firmly that organic food is healthier. Again, these tribal-moral communities that we build around ourselves, where we justify our own self-beliefs, are actually shielding us from the evidence in front of our eyes. Are we really any better than a creationist clinging to a Biblical belief about the nature of the universe if we cling to a belief that organic food is somehow healthier despite scientific evidence to the contrary?

North Carolina is one of the few states that's actually managed to successfully transition its economy from agriculture and low-value manufacturing (tobacco and textiles). This is due in part to a successful knowledge economy and a high-value manufacturing base, but also because of good investment in science and technological education. But Doug Edgeton and Ed Kitchen, North Carolina tech entrepreneurs, are worried that a lack of college graduates in science and technological fields will destroy the economic growth North Carolina's seen. They say:

> The National Science Foundation estimates that 80 per cent of the jobs created in the next decade will require some form of STEM skills [and] a survey of local technology CEOs reports that 87 per cent believe that having a supply of STEM-trained workers is critically important. Our lack of STEM-skilled workers is a leading factor in the loss of high-paying jobs to other regions. One local company, TIMCO, the world's largest privately owned aircraft maintenance, repair and overhaul provider, has had to move program work to other states because it could not find the trained workers it needed here.[227]

Shouldn't these science education lobbies be working on how to get more kids interested in science as a career, rather than worrying about what Michele Bachmann thinks of evolution? Should they be sacrificing the American economy for the sake of a few donation dollars on the back of Rick Perry's endorsement of intelligent design? The President of the United States has called for

10,000 new qualified science teachers and 10,000 new engineers – which we desperately need, particularly for the new infrastructure projects he wants – and we're not going to get them. What do we get instead? Fearmongering about intelligent design. Hooray.

Instead of obsessing about evolution for the purpose of massaging class anxiety and destroying political candidates that we don't like, what if we as a society took the opportunity to take on the poor science education we're saddling our children with? Isn't a much more relevant question for politicians, 'How would you get American children back to the top of the science education rankings?' Wouldn't that tell us much more about a potential candidate's leadership abilities and judgement than 'Do you believe in evolution?' We really need to convey more understanding of scientists and how they perform their research to the general public. I've been using the word 'layman' quite specifically, because at the moment it does seem that scientists are some kind of high priests transmitting their wisdom to those of us outside the holy community. This isn't a good situation – more people should understand science so we're not blindly following the beliefs that we might have heard somewhere or somebody's aunt's neighbour's cousin's folk wisdom. All of us should be clamouring for more – and better – science education, so that our children and grandchildren actually understand the scientific issues that are facing the world today.

But if we do that, there would be fewer chances to ridicule and belittle people we don't like, and fewer ways to make sure that class anxiety keeps voters from exploring different political parties, and fewer exciting debates and interviews on television. As a result, the question 'How should we improve science education?' will never become the litmus test of scientific knowledge the way 'Do you believe in evolution?' has.

8

THE TEA PARTY'S INFLUENCE
ON AMERICAN POLITICS

Barack Obama won the 2008 election on the promise that his administration would deliver 'hope and change' to an American electorate who badly needed it after war and economic crisis. But, for a number of reasons, both external and due to the Obama administration itself, the promised hope and change never arrived. The economy has stayed in the doldrums, unemployment has remained relatively high and the country seems trapped in malaise. According to a Real Clear Politics poll average in late November 2011, the percentage of Americans who believe that the country is heading in the wrong direction is over 73 per cent.[228]

What's been particularly interesting to see since 2008 is the rise of grassroots, populist movements that express frustration with the political system as it is and offer solutions for change. On both the left and the right, we've seen ordinary people express their displeasure with politics as they find it. The Tea Party is one of the largest of these movements, and it has already had a profound impact on the American political landscape. Springing up in early 2009, expressing long-held anger with the size and expenditures of the federal government, the Tea Party became a rallying point for all those who were concerned about deficit spending, the role of the government in people's lives, the importance of being able to rely on ones' self and one's local community in a crisis, and the imbalance of power between federal, state and local government. Tea Partiers have vociferously expressed an interest in returning to a Constitutional notion of what the federal government should do and a deep concern about how far the government, particularly federal government, should reach into citizens' lives.

The Tea Party is repeating a pattern in American history that we've seen numerous times. There has always been a streak of resistance to big government in politics, ever since the Whiskey Rebellion in the 1790s. To pay off its national debts, the new US Congress used its new Constitutional authority to levy an excise tax on distilled spirits. While this didn't cause much controversy in the east, in the west of the country it was a major problem indeed. Michael Hoover from the Alcohol, Tobacco and Tax Trade Bureau explains:

> While eastern farmers could readily transport their grain to market, westerners faced the hard task of moving their crops great distances to the east over the mountains along poor dirt roads. Given this difficulty, many frontier farmers distilled their surplus grain into more easily transportable whiskey. In doing so, their grain became taxable distilled spirits under the 1791 excise law, and western farmers opposed what was, in effect, a tax on their main crop. Usually cash-poor, frontier residents also used whiskey to pay for the goods and services they needed. Naturally, many westerners quickly came to resent the new excise tax on their 'currency'. Other aspects of the excise law also caused concern. The law required all stills to be registered, and those cited for failure to pay the tax had to appear in distant Federal, rather than local, courts. In Pennsylvania, for example, the only Federal courthouse was in Philadelphia, some 300 miles away from the small frontier settlement of Pittsburgh.

A tax on the primary form of currency and the only way to escape it is to travel for 300 miles on foot or horseback? It's no wonder this caused major resentment in American frontier towns. Also, the tax brought out major class resentment from western farmers, who didn't much like city dwellers in the east threatening their lives and livelihoods. In 1794, anti-whiskey tax protesters precipitated violent protests throughout western Pennsylvania. In fact, when several thousand of them gathered at Braddock's Field outside Pittsburgh in July of that year, President Washington invoked the Militia Act of 1792, sent a proclamation asking the protesters to disperse and sent nearly 13,000 militiamen to quell the rebellion. The militia arrested 150 of the rebels, but most of them had to be released due to a lack of evidence. The issue became a major sticking point in the 1800 presidential election and because Thomas Jefferson sided with the farmers, he was able to defeat John Adams. Congress repealed all internal taxes, including the whiskey tax, in 1802.[229] Another popular rebellion occurred in the 1790s, instigated by a poor farmer named Daniel Shays, a Revolutionary War veteran. The Massachusetts state legislature had enacted a law to pay off the state's revolutionary war debt; taxes rose more than 60 per cent and numerous farmers in the western part of the state felt that the burden was falling disproportionately on them. When Shays's farm was threatened with foreclosure, to pay for a war he'd fought in, he'd had enough. He and his fellow farmers threatened an arsenal and temporarily closed the courts. While the rebellion was quashed by the militia, the point was not lost on the general population, and at the next election, debt relief, not continuing the foreclosure, won a popular majority.[230]

The pattern presented itself again amongst the pioneers of the nineteenth century, charged with settling the American West. In the beloved, semi-autobiographical books by Laura Ingalls Wilder (ghostwritten by her daughter Rose, one of the founders of the American Libertarian movement), the author describes her neighbour's reaction to politicians entering the settlement town of DeSmet, South Dakota:

'I'm aiming to go far West this spring,' he said. 'This here country, it's too settled-up for me. The politicians are swarming in already, and ma'am if there's any worse pest than grasshoppers it surely is politicians. Why, they'll tax the lining out'n a man's pockets to keep up these here county-seat towns! I don't see nary use for a county, nohow. We all got along happy and content without 'em… I don't aim to pay taxes.'[231]

This neighbour of the Ingalls family doesn't see the point of remaining in a county town when the only thing that you pay taxes for is to support politicians. Politicians don't provide more food or help with the livestock or build haystacks or do anything useful; and it's the towns people's taxes that support these 'pests'.

Even though the rural-urban struggle is a common pattern in American history, it isn't just farmers and settlers that rebel against the federal or even state governments – it isn't always about hicks vs sophisticates. States and locales often rebel against the federal government in the name of issues that are very dear to progressives' hearts. For example, in 1998 Oregon voters passed Ballot Measure 67, which removed state criminal penalties for possession of medical marijuana and created a medical marijuana registry, despite opposition from the federal government. Another example is San Francisco declaring itself a 'sanctuary city' from federal immigration statutes: in 2007 Mayor Gavin Newsom said he would discourage federal authorities from conducting immigration sweeps, proclaiming 'I will not allow any of my department heads or anyone associated with this city to cooperate in any way shape or form with these raids',[232] rebelling against what they considered the federal government's abuse of power. In Michael Pollan's *The Ominvore's Dilemma*, a book beloved by progressives about the American food industry, a conscientious farmer, who wants to sell well-treated, clean meat to his customers, describes the thicket of federal regulations he must go through in order to process his own meat without adding to the cost. Pollan says:

> The problem with food safety regulations, in Joel's view, is that they are one-size-fits-all rules designed to regulate giant slaughter-houses that are mindlessly applied to small farmers in such a way that 'before I can sell my neighbor a T-bone steak I've got to wrap it up in a million dollars' worth of quintuple permitted processing plant'. For example, federal rules stipulate that every processing facility have a bathroom for the exclusive use of the USDA inspector. Such regulations favor the biggest industrial meatpackers, who can spread the costs of compliance over the millions of animals they process every year, at the expense of artisanal enterprises like Polyface.[233]

It can't be a good thing to force small, artisanal food producers, who take time and effort to make sure that the food they produce is of the absolute best quality, to adhere to federal standards that they can't afford to meet and that are not really applicable anyway. If federal regulations drive artisanal food producers out of business, making it harder for local people to buy produce from local farms, who is that a victory for? If you care about things like compassion towards immigrants, or gay marriage, or supporting local food producers, then you understand the point that sometimes the federal government can be ineffective when it comes to enacting regulations; local and state government can sometimes do it better, depending on what the regulations are.

The catalyst that set off the Tea Party movement happened on 19 February 2009. CNBC reporter Rick Santelli was on the floor of the Chicago Board of Trade doing an interview on the morning programme *Squawk Box* with anchor Joe Kerner and fellow reporter Carl Quintanilla. The day before, the Obama administration had announced a $75 billion mortgage rescue programme by which homeowners having trouble repaying their mortgages could either refinance through government-backed mortgage entities Freddie Mac and Fannie Mae, or could modify the terms of their sub-prime mortgage agreement. Kerner asked Santelli for analysis of the Obama administration's new programme.

In a now-famous moment, Santelli, live on television, said:

The government is promoting bad behavior. Because we certainly don't want to put stimulus forth and give people a whopping $8 or $10 in their check, and think that they ought to save it, and in terms of modifications... I'll tell you what, I have an idea.

You know, the new administration's big on computers and technology. How about this, President and new administration? Why don't you put up a website to have people vote on the Internet as a referendum to see if we really want to subsidise the losers' mortgages; or would we like to at least buy cars and buy houses in foreclosure and give them to people that might have a chance to actually prosper down the road, and reward people that could carry the water instead of drink the water?...

This is America! How many of you people want to pay for your neighbor's mortgage that has an extra bathroom and can't pay their bills? Raise their hand.

(Booing)

President Obama, are you listening?

TRADER: How 'bout we all stop paying our mortgage? It's a moral hazard.

KERNEN: Hey Rick, how about the notion that, Wilbur pointed out, you can go down to 2 per cent on the mortgage...

SANTELLI: You could go down to −2 per cent. They can't afford the house.

KERNEN: ...and still have 40 per cent, and still have 40 per cent not be able to do it. So why are they in the house? Why are we trying to keep them in the house?

SANTELLI: I know Mr. Summers is a great economist, but boy, I'd love the answer to that one.

REBECCA QUICK: Wow. Wilbur, you get people fired up.

SANTELLI: We're thinking of having a Chicago Tea Party in July. All you capitalists that want to show up to Lake Michigan, I'm gonna start organising.[234]

Santelli's point, loudly supported by the traders with him, is that if you've been working hard to pay your mortgage, you won't necessarily want to support people who've made bad decisions, particularly if they've made such a bad decision they can't afford the payments on their house even if the interest rates went down to 2 per cent. That's what's meant by a 'moral hazard'; if you reward, or don't penalise, bad behaviour, there aren't any consequences to teach the badly behaved person not to do it again. So, if people who made bad mortgage decisions to begin with were rewarded by the government, who is to say there wouldn't be another housing bubble ten or twenty years down the line? There will be a sub-prime mortgage crisis every generation if we don't instil the message that you can only buy what you can afford, and going into mountains of debt to have a big house is a really bad idea.

It was Santelli's words 'Tea Party' that really captured the imagination of people who hadn't heard a mainstream cable TV journalist actually say these sorts of things before. The day prior, blogger and activist Keli Carender organised an anti-stimulus protest in Seattle, WA. Keli, who's thirty-one and a former maths teacher living in Seattle, Washington, is considered the founder of the modern Tea Party movement, although she says modestly, 'I think that gives me too much credit.' Anti-stimulus protests were soon organised in Denver and Mesa, AZ, and word quickly spread via social media – soon it was a nationwide movement. As blogger and University of Tennessee law professor Glenn Reynolds says, 'Rick Santelli said July, but nobody wanted to wait till then, so there were numerous protests the next weekend, and then even bigger ones around Tax Day on April 15.'[235] Reynolds wrote in an op-ed for the *Wall Street Journal* that more than 300 Tea Parties took place all around the country that day.[236]

A wide variety of people showed up at Tea Party rallies all over the country. From my interviews with Tea Party members and leadership, I can tell you that they are teachers, students, members of the military, writers, entrepreneurs, salesmen – a real cross-section of American society. You can find Tea Party members in every state, even in heavily Democratic areas of the country. They come in all religions, creeds, ethnicities and beliefs. And all of them talk about not being heard in the cash donation-based political system.

Jonathon Baloga is the chair of the Knoxville Tea Party. In early 2010, he was at university and was thinking about joining the local Tea Party in time for the elections. However, when he looked up the Tea Party leaders, he discovered the group had disbanded, so he decided to start it up again.

'We just put ads in the local papers, that's all we did,' Jonathon told me. 'I think I put ads in two papers, and about ninety people showed up to our first meeting.' He said that he had been think-ing a lot about how he personally could contribute to society, and came to the realisation that it was as 'an individual' that he could be of greatest help, which is why he wanted to join the Knoxville Tea Party in the first place. But interestingly, he discovered that assuming that everyone knew what the Tea Party was and what it stood for was the 'wrong approach'. He said, 'I focused on organi-sation, not the idea of the Tea Party.' So in talking about the Party's philosophy, he discovered that the united message was the glue that held the local group together. That message was, as Jonathon told me, 'We want a smaller government that lives within its means and abides by the Constitution.'

Lisa Miller, the founder of the Washington, DC, Tea Party, is an independent businesswoman working in the financial services industry, and she says the animus for her to get involved in the Tea Party was the objective to return to individual rights and responsibility. She says that because she is an independent practitioner, she feels tax increases very keenly, because not only is she taxed on her own income, as an employer (of herself) she must pay employer taxes on social security, healthcare etc. 'I pay property, state and local taxes as well,' she pointed out. 'Taxes went up by 45 per cent in Arlington last year,' she said of the DC suburb she lives in. 'There was a 10 per cent increase this year. Every year I have less and less income, and the same is true of my clients themselves – the unemployed to CEOs of corporations. We all have less.'

Keli Carender told me that it was the lack of government accountability that inspired her to join the Tea Party. She'd grown up in Washington State, 99 per cent of the people she knew were liberal, and she said that she didn't pay attention to politics until the 2008 election. The candidates bothered her, because she felt that none of them were conservative. Federal spending worried her: 'The bailout under Bush bent the straw and the stimulus broke the straw. It was a long slow burn about how much money they were spending and how much debt they were getting us into.' So after the Stimulus Bill, 'which rolled into the healthcare debate', she decided to get involved and call her Congresswoman. She laughed ruefully, 'I had the naïve idea that you could elect someone in your party and they would do right by you.' So she called, and called, and called, and realised that no one cared. 'Nobody had a clue what was in the Health-care Bill. There was a 400-page amendment!

It's their job to read the bills! They just seemed so arrogant – there was a pretend rush to get it done. They could have put it out there, gotten some public input, but they weren't interested.'

Ali Akbar is a 26-year-old small business owner, and says he got interested in the Tea Party because of his 'single mother upbringing'. He clarifies:

> I did a lot to take care of my two younger brothers while my mother went to school full-time and worked full-time. We were latch-key kids, but understood that our mother loved us very dearly and was doing everything she could to provide a better opportunity for us. This story is shared by African-American kids like myself everywhere… I can't help but think that my humble upbringing helps play a role in all of this.[237]

Despite the fact that these people got into the Tea Party for various reasons, in the end, as Jonathan says, it's the idea of the Tea Party that unites them. It's the coalescing of the philosophy that is the movement's strength. Not every Tea Partier has the exact same opinion about the exact same thing, but their beliefs tend to congregate along two lines. The first is a notion that the US federal government has abrogated too much power to itself, and a lot of that power should belong to the states. As Keli Carender says:

> The federal government needs to be cut back to size and we need to restore states' roles. The decision-making authority should be with the states. If there's fifty different models, then we have choices about where we live. The big goal is to get the states back to what they should be doing.

Why should it matter whether federal or state government handles any particular issue? Here's where we must detour into a bit of

American constitutional history. Colonial America consisted of thirteen colonies, which had their own laws, their own cultures, their own rules regarding religion and their own forms of taxation. They were, by and large, small separate nation-states of their own. After the Revolutionary War, they banded together as states in a loose collective under the Articles of Confederation, which ostensibly provided some sort of national government under a unicameral legislature, but it was considered by many contemporary politicians as too weak to govern a full nation because it had no provision for gathering federal taxes or negotiating trade with all the states. The Constitutional Convention came about to provide a stronger federal government to deal more effectively with these issues. That said, though, people in New York and Connecticut weren't exactly excited to throw in their lot with people in Virginia and Georgia. Their populations were different, their economies were different – even the landscape was different. It was difficult for them to relate to one another and, quite frankly, the states wanted to be in charge of their own affairs as they always had been.

In 1787, as the new US Constitution was sent to the states for ratification, pro- and anti-Constitutional campaigns rose up in the press. The most famous of these were the 'Federalist Papers', published in the *New York Packet* between 1787 and 1788. John Jay, Alexander Hamilton and James Madison argued for the Constitution under the pseudonym 'Publius', and attempted to quell concerns that the federal government would be taking too much authority away from the states. Madison argues, for example, that under a constitutional government states would be able to resist the federal government if they felt it was encroaching too much on their powers. He wrote:

> But ambitious encroachments of the federal government, on
> the authority of the State governments, would not excite the

opposition of a single State, or of a few States only. They would be signals of general alarm. Every government would espouse the common cause. A correspondence would be opened. Plans of resistance would be concerted. One spirit would animate and conduct the whole. The same combinations, in short, would result from an apprehension of the federal, as was produced by the dread of a foreign yoke; and unless the projected innovations should be voluntarily renounced, the same appeal to a trial of force would be made in the one case as was made in the other. But what degree of madness could ever drive the federal government to such an extremity?[238]

In the extremity of the federal government encroaching on the rights of state government to govern the people, Madison imagines that the states would resist, that the government closer to the people would act as a bulwark against the overreaching hands of the national central government. And that is the way that the Tea Party sees itself – as the Madisonian bulwark against an ever-increasing federal government.

Discussion of federalism can descend into the notion of 'states' rights'. This phrase has had an unsavoury whiff ever since the Civil War. It's easy to see how the phrase 'states' rights' has acquired a connotation of slavery and segregation. Alabama governor and intractable segregationist George Wallace said that instead of saying 'Segregation Now! Segregation Tomorrow! Segregation Forever!' he should have said 'States' Rights Now! States' Rights Tomorrow! States' Rights Forever!' and the Dixiecrat Party headed by Strom Thurmond was officially called the 'States' Rights Party'. But these facts shouldn't make us afraid to have the discussion. As law professor Ann Althouse puts it, 'Americans cannot contemplate state and local government autonomy without having flashbacks to the nation's history of slavery, segregation and racism …

this flood of bad memories is disabling Americans from thinking accurately about – dare we say it? – states' rights.'[239] But because these admittedly horrible events occurred, does that mean that we should grant the federal government rights to deny people medical marijuana, stop gay marriage, prevent people from buying good, clean, decent food for their kids from local farmers? Because the Civil War happened 150 years ago, do we have to hand over all governance to the federal government? Do we have to allow obscenity laws to be defined equally for Pierre, South Dakota and New York City? Most reasonable people would say no, that local communities should be allowed to create laws that reflect their communities' values. As William R. Mackay, legal counsel for the Canadian province of Nunavut put it:

> The point is to allow normative disagreement amongst the subordinate units so that different units can subscribe to different value systems. In a similar manner to citizens, sub-units in a federal state may act as they choose within the scope of the right, regardless of the practical result. When the larger nation state acts within the scope of the sub-unit's rights to obtain the results it desires, that right is abrogated.[240]

The United States is not North Korea or Stalinist Russia; citizens don't have to submit to a diktat from some faraway capital. Our federalist system allows us the flexibility to create a nation out of wildly diverging values. If you appreciate Gavin Newsom standing up to Arnold Schwarzenegger and marrying gay couples on the steps of San Francisco's City Hall, or state officials suing the Environmental Protection Agency (EPA) to regulate air pollution, you must at least acknowledge that the Tea Party, whatever you think of its aims, is doing the same thing. They are exercising the right of citizens and members of state and local government to disagree on an issue with the national government, and to act as a safeguard to the appropriation of too much power in too few hands.

The other philosophical strand the Tea Party gathers around is the issue of the deficit. There's no question that the US budget deficit is at an absolutely frightening level – as of January 2011 it stands at $14 trillion and for fiscal year 2011 it was $1.3 trillion, the second highest level ever (highest was the budget deficit for fiscal year 2009, $1.42 trillion). There was a lot of wailing and gnashing of teeth when Standard & Poor's downgraded the United States' credit rating after the protracted debt-ceiling negotiations – with Democrats calling Republicans 'terrorists' and 'hostage takers' and so forth – but other agencies, such as Egan-Jones, downgraded the USA not because of the debt-ceiling arguments, but rather because of the US debt load standing at more than 100 per cent of the country's gross domestic product.[241] The United States is still, for the moment, the most powerful economy in the world, even it doesn't make enough money to pay back its bills for a year. That's frightening to many people and it raises a philosophical point – if the United States can no longer support itself, does that mean that we should or could continue with the kind of spending that has got us so far into this hole? If we're spending so much that the United States is no longer a going concern, does that mean we should rein it in for the health of the economy? Or does it even matter? If we can run the country with a huge deficit, should we?

The United States has the exact same problem as every other developed country in the world. We've got to pay for social security, medicare and medicaid (this is what's referred to as 'entitlement spending'), and since people are living longer and longer, more of our budget has to pay for these items. In addition, falling fertility rates means that there are fewer workers to pay for the increasing numbers of people who are dependent on social security and medicaid. Americans can find an excellent tax calculator

at http://wheredidmymoneygo.com (Brits can find their version at
http://wheredoesmymoneygo.org) which explains exactly where
your taxes go each year. I won't tell you how much I made in 2009,
the latest year that's available, but even though I lived in the UK I
was liable to file US taxes. My tax dollars would have gone to the
following: 16 per cent on social security, 17 per cent on national
defence, 16 per cent on medicare (health insurance for the elderly)
16 per cent on income security (federal unemployment, pensions
for federal civil service workers, military retirement, and very small
amounts for child nutrition and assistance for needy families), 10
per cent on interest payments on the budget deficit, and 8 per cent
on medicaid (health insurance for poor families). These six things
take up 83 per cent of my tax receipts for the year, leaving just
17 per cent for foreign aid, protecting the environment, improv-
ing the transportation infrastructure, education, federal scientific
initiatives etc.[242] People are always shocked by this – they figure the
vast majority of American spending goes to the military or foreign
aid. But no, it's entitlement spending – the money we promised
to the elderly and the ill – that's taking up the lion's share of the
federal budget.

Reasonable people can argue about whether or not that's a
good thing, whether we as a country should be solely occupied
with using our tax dollars to take care of the poor and the sick. Tea
Party Senator Marco Rubio said in a speech at the Reagan Library:

> It was institutions and society that assumed the role of taking
> care of one another. If someone was sick in your family, you took
> care of them. If a neighbor met misfortune, you took care of
> them. You saved for your retirement and your future because you
> had to. We took these things upon ourselves and our communi-
> ties and our families and our homes and our churches and our
> synagogues. But all that changed when the government began to

assume those responsibilities. All of a sudden, for an increasing number of people in our nation, it was no longer necessary to worry about saving for security because that was the government's job. For those who met misfortune, that wasn't our obligation to take care of them, that was the government's job. And as government crowded out the institutions in our society that did these things traditionally, it weakened our people in a way that undermined our ability to maintain our prosperity.

Rubio's point, echoed by many libertarian conservatives, is that community institutions and families used to do a lot of the jobs that the government does now – taking care of the old, the poor and the sick used to be a job that we all shouldered together, and now we pass it along to a bureaucrat. And Rubio wants to honestly ask the question, has it made life better for the old, the poor and the sick? It's easy to demonise him and say, 'Oh, he's a heartless jerk, he wants to cut the funding to Grandma,' but the point he's really making is that by passing the buck of our family and community responsibilities to someone else far away, it perhaps is us who are a bit heartless. Tea Partiers believe that it is not the job of the federal government to do this, and anyway we can't afford it. As Jonathon, leader of the Knoxville Tea Party, told me, 'It's hard for people to wrap their minds around $14 trillion, so I explain that for every $50,000 we take in, we spend $86,000.' Lisa, who heads the DC Tea Party, says that 'fiscal responsibility' is one of the planks of the Tea Party platform – she says that people in DC are 'disconnected from reality' because if they take away the capital small businesspeople earn, 'then we can't use it to hire anyone else or invest in other companies'. Wilson Getchell, a 'fiscally responsible punk rock' musician, captured the heart of the Tea Party and the libertarian blogosphere with the ditty 'You're Gonna Pay', questioning whether or not it was necessary to use federal funds for 'cowboy poetry festivals' or keeping troops in Europe. Comedian Felonious Monk says, 'This message is for the government ... all we want you to do is pay your *$^#@ bills.' A 2010 Gallup poll showed that 61 per cent of Tea Partiers said the federal debt was their number one concern.[243] Laurie Newsome, the leader of the Gainsville, Florida, Tea Party, put it in stark terms; if America's debt was your family budget, you'd be pulling in just over $21,000 in salary, and seeing just over $38,000 go out in annual expenses, and your total credit card debt would be $142,000. She says 'We had discussed about how any citizen needs to understand what the proposed cuts mean... One of our members had figured it out and put it in terms of a household budget. If you ran a household with these numbers, you would see that it's simply not enough.'

After ten years of jumping up and down and yelling about the deficit, and nothing being done about it, Tea Party members decided it was time to take a very serious stance. A lot of the desperation and passion that I heard both from Congressional Tea Party members and the grassroots Tea Partiers comes from the fact that they feel as if no one is listening to them and that no one has been listening for a long time. They want action on the federal debt and want it now, because they see it as a seriously hazardous situation. That's why Eric Cantor, the House Majority Leader, promised Congressional Tea Party freshers that there would be 'more than one bite of the apple' at cutting federal spending and getting the debt under control, and that the debt ceiling fight would be the first one. But it was a hard fight among the Republican caucus, as Rep. Cantor told the *Wall Street Journal*: 'Most people who were elected this time [in 2010] feel they were elected to change the system.'[244] Tea Partiers did object to federal spending under the Bush administration. Lisa Miller told me, 'I objected to Bush's spending,' she said, 'He was not a conservative. The private sector declined under his administration. Oh, the letters I wrote to the White House! They must have gotten sick of me!' Indeed, 68 per cent of Tea Partiers objected to the debt settlement;[245] they wanted to go further. *Investor's Business Daily* reported that despite claims from Paul Krugman of the *New York Times* and others that the 'age of austerity' the USA was entering was killing the economy, federal spending is in fact going up by $120 billion in fiscal year 2011 (one wonders why the economy isn't doing better, then, Professor Krugman?).[246] So there's no question that Tea Partiers are disappointed, and may well punish their representatives at the ballot box in November 2012. But as Jonathon said to me, 'This is a long-term thing – keeping vigilant with efforts to teach the people about this philosophy. You might get this Bill or that Bill passed but if nobody understands why, then you won't achieve a long-term effect of a generation of Americans who get it.'

It's not a bad idea to have a serious discussion about the Tea Partiers' philosophy and approach to governance. It's worth thinking about whether the Tea Party actually represents a Madisonian rebellion against encroachment of federal power on state power. Does it hurt us actually to think about whether government programmes like Obamacare or the stimulus package represent the kind of 'ambitious encroachments' that Madison described? Does the Constitution even apply to the modern problems and philosophical question of society? Knowing the wide variety of opinions the American people have about issues ranging from farming to gay marriage, shouldn't we adopt a more federalist approach to governing? Wouldn't that solve the perennial plaint that America simply is 'too big to govern'? It's not like Tea Partiers are perfect about always maintaining high-minded political discourse either. It's a form of name-calling and less than intellectually honest to dismiss Obama as a 'socialist' in regards to Obamacare – how to solve the problem of lack of access to healthcare is a serious problem that demands a solution. Equally, thinking about how the pension crisis in America when states and localities are being crippled by legal contracts to provide endless pensions to public servants isn't helped by calling public sector workers selfish and greedy. Is it right to balance localities' budgets on the backs of teachers, policemen and firefighters? Is there another solution?

These are interesting and hard philosophical questions, and demand more than just quick soundbites to grapple with them. Thanks to the Palin Effect, though, not many of these questions have been asked. Instead of carrying out a serious analysis of Tea Party policy ideas, a number of political commentators use class anxiety and political division to try to dismiss the movement. For example, the BBC did an excellent job in illustrating just how icky urban British professionals found these heartland Americans. During the 2011 debt ceiling debacle, Mark Mardell, the BBC's North America editor, sighed in an article about the situation that 'it's that Tea Party again', and quoted UK Business Secretary Vince Cable as saying that 'a bunch of right-wing nutters' were putting the world economy in peril. It was interesting that no one from the Tea Party was given the chance to respond to Mr Cable's remarks.[247]

If the Tea Party got cultural prejudice from the BBC, they got an all-out snarling hissy fit from CNN. Reporter Susan Roesgen found a member of the Tea Party in Chicago during the 2009 Tax Day protests and peppered him with questions while not allowing him to speak – 'Why be so hard on the President of the United States? Did you know you get a $400 tax credit? What does all this have to do with your taxes? Did you know the State of Lincoln gets $50 billion out of this stimulus?' She then concluded with, 'It's anti-government, anti-CNN, since this is highly promoted by the right-wing conservative network, Fox.' Being around the Tea Party and hearing criticism of the President discomfited her so much she wasn't able to act professionally. Roesgen got fired for her performance.

It's telling that so many of the attacks on the Tea Party are class-based rather than on actual policy disagreements. California Congresswoman Loretta Sanchez made fun of Tea Party-backed members of Congress on a syndicated radio show by mocking a slow Southern drawl. *The Guardian's* Jonathan Raban noted:

> The Tea Partiers I met were Republicans and independents, but (with a couple of exceptions) they weren't racist bigots, nor were they foaming-at-the-mouth right-wing hyenas. What led them to join the movement was less their anger than their perplexity… Palin and her kind have put heart into people who previously imagined themselves merely confused or ill-informed, and now see themselves as proud sceptics, resisting the tide of received professional opinion.[248]

It doesn't say much about this reporter's esteem of Tea Partiers if he characterises them as confused ignoramuses willing to follow the lead of a right-wing maniac leader. After the previously quoted study that social scientists David Campbell and Robert Putnam published in the *New York Times* that Tea Partiers are in fact religious, there was a small cottage industry of commentators who tried to prove that the Tea Party was, in the words of *Daily Beast* writer David Sessions, 'the Christian Right in disguise'. Sessions remarked of the new Tea Party members of Congress, '[it is] suddenly populated with home-schooling activists, youth ministers, abstinence proponents, former members of radical anti-abortion groups and even a Mennonite'.[249] But in a country where 78 per cent of the inhabitants are Christian, and 50 per cent go to church regularly, wouldn't one expect there to be some crossover between the conservative/Republican demographic, and the Christian, religiously conservative one? Wouldn't there be some crossover amongst the candidates themselves? In which case, why is it surprising there'd be some Christians in Congress? With a basic understanding of statistics, it shouldn't come as a shock that there's a crossover between people who believe in Christianity and people who believe in limited government. The real question is whether social conservative activism or fiscal responsibility is the main animus behind the Tea Party. Lisa Miller told me, 'I'm a libertarian – do whatever you want as long as I don't have to pay for it.' Ali Akbar said, 'Tea Party groups leave out social issues. This is a fiscal reform movement dedicated to fundamental reform in the way business is done in the federal government.'[250]

Not only did a number of political commentators try to use class-based attacks to make the Tea Party go away, they also tried a racism smear to make sure nobody took the Tea Party seriously. The most often cited charge against the Tea Party is that they're unreconstructed racists who only object to President Obama because he's the first black president. Celebrities in particular are very fond of calling Tea Partiers racists. Sean Penn, Morgan Freeman and Samuel L. Jackson all announced that they thought the Tea Party was racist. MSNBC has made accusing the Tea Party of racism a regular feature of its programming. Keith Olbermann announced that everything the Tea Party was concerned about was really code for the fact they didn't like Obama's skin colour; as he put it, 'facts don't matter when you're looking for an excuse to say you hate this President – [STARTS WHISPERING] but not because he's black'. *Washington Post* columnist Eugene Robinson dismissed Tea Party concerns about lobbyists in government and Bush-era levels of spending (if he'd interviewed Tea Partiers, he might have discovered they agreed with him on those issues) and asserted, 'Obama [is] black. For whatever reason, I think this makes some people unsettled, anxious, even suspicious.'[251] African-American Congressman Andre Carson insisted that Tea Party members wanted to see African-Americans 'hanging from a tree'. There are people who still insist that a racial slur was yelled at four African-American Congressmen at a rally in 2010, although a cash reward exists for hard evidence of such an occurrence that hasn't been collected yet. Even the President of the United States believes that part of the animus driving the Tea Party is racial prejudice. Kenneth Walsh, in his book *Family of Freedom: Presidents and African Americans in the White House*, says:

> But Obama, in his most candid moments, acknowledged that race was still a problem. In May 2010, he told guests at a private White House dinner that race was probably a key component in the rising opposition to his presidency from conservatives, especially right-wing activists in the anti-incumbent 'Tea Party' movement that was then surging across the country. ... A guest suggested that when Tea Party activists said they wanted to 'take back' their country, their real motivation was to stir up anger and anxiety at having a black president, and Obama didn't dispute the idea. He agreed that there was a 'subterranean agenda' in the anti-Obama movement – a racially biased one – that was unfortunate.[252]

It's quite revealing that none of those who talk about the Tea Party being racists have actually spoken with any of them, or explored exactly what their concerns and solutions are. The racism charge just seems to be a way to dismiss this political movement without seriously engaging with its ideas.

Or perhaps the racism charge covers up other anxieties. Former National Public Radio (NPR) executive Robert Schiller summed up the belief that the Tea Party is racist when he told an undercover filmmaker that 'this group has hijacked the Republican Party' and that they are 'just Islamophobic, but really xenophobic, I mean basically they are, they believe in sort of white, middle-America gun-toting. I mean, it's scary. They're seriously racist, racist people.'[253]

Schiller's prejudice here, expressed in oddly broken sentences, represents a deep insecurity he has about himself. People who live in cities feel superior to people who live in 'middle America' or 'flyover country', and when such people have a voice on the public stage, the class anxiety urban professionals feel about this makes them very anxious and defensive. Schiller is the type of person who prides himself on recognising and celebrating diversity, a distinction he draws against the 'whiteness' of Tea Partiers. No wonder, then, Schiller might project his anxiety about NPR coming under fire from the National Association of Black Journalists for not having enough people of colour in its management onto what he perceives as a racist movement.[254] He blames the Tea Party for deficiencies he himself wants to cover up.

The one thing that's clear, however, is that accusing the Tea Party of racism derails any discussion of their policies. This means that a person who uses the racism charge is unable or unwilling to engage in serious policy debate. Keli Carender made this point clear by saying:

> It's the most insulting thing you can say, to call somebody a racist. It hurts my feelings. I don't even know a racist. My parents were involved in the civil rights movement. People who call me racist don't know anything about my family or what's in my heart. What an easy way to get out of arguing politics in one fell swoop. And calling someone a socialist isn't the same. You can still be a good person and be a socialist. You can't be a good person and be a racist. How many times have I been to a protest with educated, intelligent people and the media finds the one goofball

and interviews him. It's cowardly and it's rude. How do you fight that? There's no burden of proof on people who want to call me a racist. Not one of them knows me. It's so unfair for people who don't have a legitimate criticism of my beliefs to criticise me on this. And why don't they address the racism in their own ranks? Michael Steele's social security numbers were stolen. Colin Powell got called an Uncle Tom. Even Harry Reid said Obama was only electable because he's light-skinned. How come they don't police their own side?

I asked her if she had ever seen anything prejudiced at a Tea Party rally. She told me she had to kick out a man who was carrying an anti-Semitic sign: 'It had to be taken care of.'

It would be wrong to say that there weren't racists in the Tea Party – there are people who hold up racist signs and say racist things. But to say that individuals who do bad things represent the whole is sloppy thinking. Just as we rightfully object to those who say 'All Muslims are terrorists' when some Muslims commit terrorist acts, we equally must object to saying 'all Tea Partiers are racists' when clearly not all of them are. And it's important to remember just how hurtful these smears are. These days we tend to meet people who disagree with us as flickering words on a Twitter feed or as fleeting images on the television screen. We forget that our political opponents are human beings with thoughts and feelings just like the rest of us. Every time some progressive calls a Tea Party a racist, they hurt another person. We should all ask celebrities like Sean Penn to show a little human compassion. Going around insulting people you disagree with doesn't make you a good person or a courageous fighter for your cause. It makes you a jerk.

In a political system that depends on frightening people to raise money, it's important for political parties, political action committees (PACs) and advocacy groups to make sure that people are well and truly afraid of a genuine populist movement. Populist movements are part of a grand American tradition. The Tea Party members have views that are convincing and in line with mainstream American belief; they're not threatening, they're law-abiding, they look like your grandparents and they pick up after themselves. This can't be countenanced by the opposing political party and progressive advocacy organisations; it might convince people to rethink the positions they've been fed or perhaps even join it. So, demonise them by calling them racists and they'll make most nice people shrink away from even thinking about the Tea Party in any other way. And that's all the racism charge is – baseless, pointless demonisation designed so nice people pay up. Because it can't be proven or disproven, it's the refuge of the irra-tional. Anyone who uses the racism charge sounds like a broken, demented alarm clock, shouting 'RACIST! RACIST!' at random opportunities. Eventually, the broken clock becomes part of the background noise.

What does the future hold for the Tea Party? It's going to play a big part in the 2012 election process, as its goals include taking both the Senate and the White House. Indeed, a lot of the twists and turns in the soap opera that is the Republican nomination process is the testing of various candidates in the Tea Party crucible and seeing whether they've been found wanting or not (most of them have). A number of national Tea Party-linked organisations like Americans for Prosperity and FreedomWorks, which provide financial and organisational support for local Tea Party groups, are on track to donate almost $100 million to the 2012 election.[255] It will be interesting whether local Tea Partiers see the entrance into the big-money world of presidential poli-tics as a betrayal of their values. But they've got other goals as well; Jonathon Baloga has his eyes set on local government.

He says, 'In 2010 we got four politicians elected – it was a land-slide. Being a ragtag group, that's a pretty big achievement, we've never been involved in politics, but we have the right ideas. For rank amateurs to do that is pretty outstanding and we want to continue.'

The Tea Party consists of human beings who arrived at their conclusions not because they're stupid or childlike or because Sarah Palin told them to or because they hate the colour of Barack Obama's skin, but because their rational judgement of their experiences led them to think so. Actual conversations with Tea Party members reveal that they're not malevolent maniacs; they're not strange and horrible and alien. Because until we get over the hump of hating the people we disagree with, we won't be able to cure the sickness in American politics. And they really are quite ordinary people, just like the rest of us. As Keli told me, 'People assume that we're 100 per cent anti-tax, anti-government, anti-regulation. We're not. We're boringly normal.'

9

INCOME INEQUALITY IN 2012

The global economy, particularly in the Anglosphere and Western Europe, is suffering serious structural problems. After the collapse of the sub-prime mortgage bubble in 2007 and with the continuing lack of economic growth since, Brits and Americans have been facing a lack of jobs, the loss of a generation of young workers, and populations drowning in debt. In addition, a real crisis in public spending is beginning to emerge; localities have to make incredibly hard choices between paying for the public services we all want and paying the public workers who deliver those services. Debt in most Western countries is out of control and the payments to service the debt are growing ever more expensive.

These are not easy issues to deal with; they resist the usual dialogues of partisan politics. We're not going to be able to solve the public pension crisis with the usual political bickering; we can't think about how we're going effectively to deliver schools, policing, firefighting etc. in a time of decreased public revenue if we're insulting each other Palin Effect-style and spreading rumours and innuendo. For both parties, American political culture means cooperation and bipartisan understanding is nearly impossible.

But for a few moments in late 2011, it seemed like a change was going to happen. There are few movements that both represent the potential to create a culture-changing moment in American politics and the failure to be able to do so better than the Occupy movement. The Occupy movement is a popular, grassroots movement that addresses so many people's frustrations with the structural problems in the American economy and the unfairness of the political establishment's reliance on financial donations. The Occupy movement approached from the left the same frustrations that the Tea Party approached from the right: a government beholden to donations from corporations might not govern in the best interests of the people; the lobbying industry is hurting good, transparent government; and the lack of jobs is seriously hurting opportunities for all Americans. Even the public spending crisis that Tea Partiers worry about and the student loan crisis that concerns Occupiers are inextricably linked.

But instead of taking the opportunity to cooperate with Tea Partiers and create a broad-based, populist movement to create political change and perhaps find a way to unshackle politics from its total dependence on financial donations, both sides chose instead to view each other with Palin Effect-tinted lenses of enmity and suspicion. It was perhaps most disheartening that Occupiers became violent – knocking down elderly ladies and threatening to assassinate political leaders. If they'd been able to put their partisan divisions aside and reach out to people from opposite sides of the political spectrum, it could have been a real watershed moment in American politics. But the years of Palin Effect messaging were too great – many Occupiers and Tea Partiers simply could not overcome the feeling that the Other was the enemy.

On 17 September 2011, a group of protesters calling themselves 'Occupy Wall Street' marched in New York's financial district and occupied Zucotti Park, an open park in the area. By the end of the month, the Occupy movement had spread to Boston, and by the middle of October the protests had spread to 951 cities in eighty-two countries. The protests had been planned for a while, with Canadian magazine *Adbusters* providing some initial inspiration with its call for a 'Tahrir movement … against the greatest corrupter of our democracy', echoing the populist protests that had been occurring in the Middle

East. Social media spread the word about the rallies and the Occupy movement grew in size and scope. In London protesters campaigning outside St Paul's linked their portion of the movement to the public service cuts proposed by the coalition government: as Scrapper Duncan, a blogger and participant in Occupy London put it:

> The last government broke the convenant with the army. The age old understanding was that our soldiers, sailors and air force would do whatever we asked of them and in exchange we would see to it that they were properly equipped to do it. This government is now attempting to break the covenant with the public service workers. Without this arrangement, we will not attract staff of the right quality into our public services. Excepting the 1 per cent and the bankers who caused the current crisis, we will all suffer the consequences.[256]

Tent City University, which is part of the Occupy London movement, organised a 'teach-out' during the student fees protests in November 2011. 'People are excited but also determined,' said Neil Howard, one of the organisers. 'Everyone gathered here realises that this is not a simple fight for education but for the welfare state more broadly.'[257]

It seems clear that the philosophical underpinnings of the Occupy movement are as multitudinous as those of the Tea Party, but they do coalesce around several things – the overwhelming influence of corporations, particularly from the financial sector, in government; the feeling that young people, who did everything they were supposed to do by staying in education and getting a degree, are being cheated out of the opportunity to start their own lives and are saddled with massive college loan debt to boot; and a concern that the 1 per cent of the richest Americans hold the majority of the nation's wealth, to the detriment of the other 99 per cent.

Occupy movement leaders that I talked to were quite frank that they had a philosophical bond with the Tea Party. I spoke with Matt Renner, a New York City resident and community organiser working with Occupy Wall Street, and director of development and communications at Truthout, an independent media platform. Matt told me, with a smile in his voice, 'I was there the first day, bringing supplies, tarps and ponchos, but I had to leave after that as my wedding was supposed to happen a week later, and I wasn't allowed to get arrested before I got married.' The conversation turned, though, to his particular passion point about the kind of revolution that he envisioned from these protests – a removal of the influence of money from politics:

> I once was a Democrat. When I was nineteen my best friend started a campaign in Berkeley to finance elections, to reform how they were funded. It was called Measure H and the idea was to make sure that candidates had a demonstrable element of popular support so that candidates who had ideas that people liked could run, excluding people who enter a race simply because they had money to fund it. Measure H lost because of bad ballot language, but now I see the problem is getting even worse. For a rather small donation – thousands of dollars – corporations are profiting from millions of dollars in tax breaks and benefits. The whole industry is incredibly profitable to them. We've got to tear down the cosy relationship between corporations and politicians. I fear that democracy is going to collapse unless there's a people's revolution like this one.

When I pointed out to him that his point about the corporate influence in politics was similar to things I'd heard Tea Party members saying, he agreed. 'There's a lot of common cause between us and the Tea Party. The media has driven these stories to divide the people on the left and the right – it's to hide the institutional corruption that they themselves are part of. There's no question that the government is part of the problem here.' He did point out that they approached the problem from two different angles – 'the left attacks the bribers and the right attacks the bribees' – and also said that he admired the change in the Republican Party that the Tea Party had brought about and wondered if they could do the same for the Democratic Party. 'The Tea Party has split the Republican Party into the old corporate way of doing things and a new radical direction. You need a left version of that to really make a change. Isn't there room for a third party? You have at least one unaffiliated senator – why couldn't there be more?'

Matt then shared his true passion and his vision – a radical rethinking of the way America selects its leaders. 'Essentially what we have to do is create a new constitutional structure to get money out of politics. We need elections to be publicly funded; we need to force the media to give airtime for free to politicians like in European countries and we need to limit the amount of commercials that can go on the air.' Matt told me that the presidential campaign of former Louisiana Governor Buddy Roemer, who refuses to accept any donation larger than $100, is a model for a candidate truly supported by the people. 'If you could provide money for a candidate on the national stage who had qualified at the local level by showing bona fide state support, that would get rid of some of the financial barriers to running for office.' He acknowledged that enacting any kind of constitutional change would be difficult – 'three quarters of the states must agree, which is an incredibly high bar to reach at the moment. But look at Congress – it's got a 12 per cent approval rating! There is an appetite for change now – why not take advantage of it?'

I also spoke with J. A. Myerson, who's in the media and Labour Outreach Working Group for Occupy Wall Street. He said that the movement had surpassed their wildest dreams: 'Six weeks ago it was fifty guys emailing too much and now there are 100,000 people involved in it all over the world.' He said that the main challenge they're facing is how to accommodate the size of the movement without compromising its principles:

> We have to figure out how to accommodate this many people – the folks who started it are committed to democracy. We're trying to work with a spokescouncil, a model that had been in radical politics. The scope of focus and speed of the movement's rise is unprecedented – it's difficult for people outside the movement to comprehend it, so they think about it in terms of leadership. But this is not a movement centred around leadership or politics. This is a structural change, a radical restructuring of democracy.

He addressed Adbusters' idea that Occupy Wall Street was connected to the revolution that took place in Tahrir Square:

> It's tempting to think that, but that was a revolt against an autocracy, a revolt against the deprivation of freedoms, and while there are serious problems, we're not in that position in the United States. The connection is really a rejection of entire assumptions about what power has made internationally. Occupy Wall Street is a rejection of plutocracy and we are trying to expose our democracy as a façade. People whose only aim is to gain wealth run the country.

I asked if this was only a problem for the Republican Party or if both sides were equally accountable, and he said, very firmly:

Both sides are extremely guilty. Liberals are in a difficult position, though, because they have to pretend to care about the poor. The GOP are in a slightly easier position, because they don't have to pretend that they're not in the sway of plutocrats. Dems have to pretend not to do this, but it's expensive to run a campaign. The system puts pressure on people to solicit money, and they have to sell out to run. That's why you have scandals like Billy Tauzin, a pharmaceutical lobbyist, basically writing the Health-care Bill. We won't see change unless we stand up and demand it.

I asked J. A. about the commonalities in what he was saying with what I'd been hearing from the Tea Party. He said, quite frankly:

There's a tremendous opportunity for cooperation with the Tea Party. We share the same concerns with populist libertarians. To be sure, there's not much common cause between the solutions we'd propose, but imagine what a powerful movement it could be if anti-corporatists from the right and the left joined together. We have libertarians in our movement now and it makes us stronger. We get along great. It's a philosophically cogent set of beliefs we share and we can get behind each other.

To underscore the point, J. A. said something that I'd heard many times from Tea Partiers – 'There's no way of solving our problems until politicians are more scared of the people than they are of losing political donations.'

I found it extraordinary that both Matt and J. A. were so frank in acknowledging the commonalities between Occupy Wall Street – as he sees it – and the Tea Party. Yes, the fixes that they'd have for the problems they see would be radically different from one another, but both have fixated, laser-like, on the same problem that's preventing American government from actually being a service that can help most Americans.

As Chris Miles, the editor of political blog 'PolicyMic' pointed out:

> Both of these movements claim they represent the voice of average Americans, and they are right. Many Americans who are disillusioned with government's ability to handle the on-going economic crisis sympathise with these demands. But if these movements represent the 'normal' American voter's views, what does that say about where most citizens stand on the political spectrum? The emergence of the hard-right leaning Tea Party and left-leaning Occupy Wall Street movements is an indication that rhetoric aside, Americans are not polarised, but rather share similar goals and objectives. Different groups may spring up seeking to tackle the same political problems, but they aren't limited to solving the puzzle based on one-sided political ideology.[258]

As we've said many times, the political industry of media commentators, advocacy organisations and professional pundits needs a Manichean battle between good and evil to create drama and excitement, which sells papers and gets eyeballs watching TVs. But that doesn't actually represent the reality experienced by many Americans. Frustrations about the inefficient economic system, the inability to escape the clutches of a corporate-led economic policy and the necessity to make sure politics isn't the playground of the rich are common to everyone, not just one political side or another. But because political candidates, opinion columnists and advocacy groups are trying to capitalise on Occupy Wall Street, and turn it into a movement for their own advantage for the upcoming elections, divisions between the two movements, which could together be a powerful advocate for change, are deepened.

The sad thing is that no matter what Matt and J. A. say about common cause with the Tea Party, ordinary Tea Partiers and Occupy Wall Streeters still think the ideological differences are too great to overcome, based on years of divisive stereotyping by the media, the blogosphere and their peers. The *Daily Caller* has video of Occupy DC protesters knocking down elderly women attending a conference sponsored by progressive *bêtes noires* the Koch brothers, and screaming at the poor reporter 'Fuck the *Daily Caller*! How are you going to twist this?'[259] Numerous Tea Party-affiliated bloggers malign Occupy Wall Street as 'smelly hippies'.[260] The arguments on Twitter are as intense as ever, with Tea Partiers calling Occupiers selfish, petty and juvenile, and Occupiers saying Tea Partiers are soulless, racist and endorse thievery. We have a moment that could seriously turn into a popular groundswell to create actual change from the circus act we currently have, and instead all we've got are people sniping at each other. The Palin Effect has done its work. The Occupy movement, which could have had a shot at really engaging the public if they'd been able to work with the Tea Party, instead chose to commit violence against old ladies and children, killing any chance for public sympathy. And if the Tea Party had taken on the Occupy movement's concerns about student loans and corporate influence in politics, rather than deriding it (as Newt Gingrich did –'take a bath and then get a job'), they might have been able to win some left-leaning independent support. But sadly, because of the pointless political divisions that we've built up over the years, this opportunity was squandered. The other dilemma is that many of Obama's supporters refuse to see that both sides are part of the problem. J. A. and Matt were both quite forthcoming about the fact that Democrats are equally as guilty of accepting corporate money, and using that money to do the will of the corporations at the expense of others, but a lot of Occupiers and their sympathisers don't see things that way. Jonathan Demme, for example, said that the American public didn't support Obama enough after his election and that's why the economy's gone wrong.[261]

Part of the challenge of presidential campaigning is hitting on just the right message. Candidates have to pick the slogan and the words that will not only appeal to primary voters when they start out, but when they finish nearly two years later. Obama hit on a perfect message in 2008 when he chose 'Hope and Change' and 'Yes We Can'. One provides vague, unspecified optimism; the other suggests collective optimism about the future. For a country tired of the constant arguing about the war on terrorism, weary of the endless battles about Iraq and Katrina, concerned about the handling of the economy, the notion of change and positivity was a most welcome one, despite the lack of specifics.

We're now heading into the fourth year of the Obama administration and an electoral showdown; to say that he hasn't delivered on the promise of hope and change is something of an understatement. Not only has the economy stayed in the doldrums, as we've seen, but some of the endemic problems with the political system itself, that both Obama and the Democratic party said they wanted to fix, have stayed almost exactly the same, or have even gotten worse. Promises made to end what Nancy Pelosi memorably called 'the culture of corruption' and the revolving door from government to K Street have been flagrantly broken. Obama promised not to take money from lobbyists, but he counts numerous lobbyists among his donor pool, and they even say so on their FEC filings – they just don't happen to be registered federal lobbyists. In addition, at least fifty former lobbyists now have positions in the Obama administration, and after they're done working for him, they'll go back through the revolving door between lobbying and government, just like Obama's former budget chief, Peter Orzsag, who's now at Citigroup, and Greg Craig, who's lobbying for Goldman Sachs.[262] Progressives are deeply underwhelmed by Obama's ability to deliver government initiatives important to them, like action on climate change, while independents are frustrated and alarmed by the effects of Obama's legislative adventurism, such as the drawbacks of well-meaning efforts like the Dodd-Frank financial reform Bill. In fact, the only real successes that Obama can point to are the scalps of enemies like Osama bin Laden and Muammar Gaddafi; and trying to build a campaign around that will be awkward indeed for the 2009 Nobel Peace Prize winner.

But a campaign must be delivered for the 2012 election, and since Obama can't run on his record, he has two options. The first is to blame somebody else for his troubles, which he's lavishly done: George W. Bush, the Republican House of Representatives, political gridlock, Libya, Europe, the media, the American people themselves ('they've gone a little soft'), the internet and, amusingly, ATMs, have all found themselves the scapegoat for the lack of progress on really any issue (except killing terrorist leaders) since 20 January 2009. His other option is to provide a red herring, a distraction for people to become obsessed about in lieu of thinking about and assessing his performance as president. His campaign's oppo researchers are thinking even now about 'character issues' that will occupy and distract people about his eventual opponent but, almost by accident, a new issue has emerged that not only allows people to stop thinking about him, but might just help him pin the blame for the bad economy on Republicans: income inequality.

A lot of media outlets had been banging on about income inequality for some time; back in 2007 the *New York Times* called the millennial boom years 'The New Gilded Age' and worried about the concentration of wealth at the very top of the income distribution pile, which had only happened to the same degree at one other

point in American history, right before the First World War.[263]
But in late 2011 there was a critical mass of worries about whether
it was income inequality that was holding the economy back or
whether 'the rich', squirrelling away their money in untouchable
bank accounts and avoiding the tax man, were making America's
deficit problems and economic problems worse. Senator Bernie
Sanders, an Independent from Vermont, started a campaign called
'Shared Sacrifice', where he identified corporations that he felt
weren't paying enough in corporate taxes. Warren Buffett, one of
the USA's richest men, wrote an op-ed in April, saying that his tax
burden of 17.4 per cent was less than his employees' average tax rate
of 34 per cent, and that he personally would be willing to pay more
tax, and that other members of what he called 'the super-rich club'
should be willing to pay more as well. He said, 'I know well many
of the mega-rich and, by and large, they are very decent people.
They love America and appreciate the opportunity this country has
given them... Most wouldn't mind being told to pay more in taxes
as well, particularly when so many of their fellow citizens are truly
suffering.'[264] If he wants to pay more taxes, one must wonder why
his company, Berkshire Hathaway, the eighth-largest company in
the world, owes back taxes from 2002 to 2009. This has deprived
the government of nearly a billion dollars.[265] But that peccadillo
aside, Buffett touched a nerve in a lot of people. In September,
in response to Buffett's op-ed, President Obama proposed a new
tax rate for millionaires, which he called the 'Buffett Rule'. 'This
is not class warfare, it's math,' thundered the President, 'the plan
... observes the Buffett Rule – that people making more than
$1m a year should not pay a smaller share of their income in taxes
than middle-class families pay.'[266] This touched off a debate in
Washington about whether targeting the rich in this way actually
was class warfare, and whether such a tax would actually work.
However you feel about the proposed 'Buffett Rule', it achieved

the desired effect of getting attention off the Obama administration's failed efforts to help the economy.

The Democratic Party is already using Occupy Wall Street's (OWS) message to sell its presidential candidate. Obama's political advisor, David Plouffe, turned OWS' opposition to corporatism in politics into an attack on Republicans by saying, 'If you're concerned about Wall Street and our financial system, the President is standing on the side of consumers and the middle class and a lot of these Republicans are basically saying, you know what, let's go back to the same policies that led us to the great recession in the first place.'[267] Moveon.org, an advocacy group that raises money for Democratic candidates, used Occupy Wall Street for its own fundraising effort, emailing supporters a missive which pleaded, 'In addition to providing all the support we can to Occupy Wall Street, we're scrambling to launch a huge campaign to make Wall Street pay… Can you chip in $5?'[268]

Democratic senatorial campaign committee director Guy Cecil admitted that Democratic candidates for the Senate in the 2012 cycle will be running on Occupy Wall Street's message, saying:

I think the message of income disparity, of how do we make sure that working-class families and middle-class families have a chance, how do we make sure their kids get to college, is going to resonate in almost every state … our candidates will talk about income disparity, talk about the level playing field. They will talk about the issues around corporate tax deductions and whether or not we should eliminate those as a way to pay down the debt and make sure we can afford unemployment benefits.[269]

Former New York City mayor Rudy Giuliani tried to tie Occupy Wall Street to Democrats in an effort to frighten Republicans, by saying, 'Barack Obama owns the Occupy Wall Street movement, it would not have happened but for his class warfare.'[270] All this, of course, plays beautifully to the campaign that Obama will run in 2012; it'll stop us from thinking about whether we're better off now than we were four years ago, because we're going to be so busy arguing with each other about which class of people we can demonise more.

Income inequality in the United States is not the economy-killer that a lot of progressive thinkers like to say it is – there are other economic problems facing Americans that are a lot worse. The Congressional Budget Office released a report in October 2011 that found that between 1979 and 2007, income grew by 275 per cent for the top 1 per cent of households, but only 18 per cent for the bottom 20 per cent.[271] Those are some pretty stark figures, but there's more to this story than just this particular study. Research from the University of Chicago's Bruce Meyer and Notre Dame's James Sullivan discovered that 'median income and consumption both rose by more than 50 per cent in real terms between 1980 and 2009… Our results provide strong evidence that the well-being of the middle class and the poor has improved considerably over the past thirty years.'[272] What this suggests is that while the top households have certainly seen the most growth in their income over the past thirty years, the improvements that the rest of the population has seen have been enough profoundly to improve their lives. The Congressional Budget Office data shows that the top 50 per cent of earners saw their income grow by an average of 35 per cent and despite a seeming disparity between wages and productivity, economist Robert Gordon points out that globalisation and big-box stores like Wal-Mart actually have shrunk that gap by reducing the prices people must pay for necessities. So actually, the gap between rich and poor only grew by 0.16 per cent per year.[273] In addition, the fate of the top 1 per cent of American earners hasn't been quite as fortuitous as people who want to take political advantage of the income inequality issue would have you believe. The University of Chicago's Steven Kaplan shows that despite government bailouts, the 2008 and 2009 adjusted gross income of the top 1 per cent fell to 1997 levels, a 20 per cent income hit as opposed to the 7 per cent hit the bottom 9 per cent took. And that money will never come back.[274] Another interesting point that *National Review* writer Reihan Salam posits is that in the 1980s executives had longer job tenure and higher marginal tax rates, so their salaries included more perks like lavish expense accounts and executive washrooms. As tax rates came down, and CEOs changed jobs more frequently, those perks were converted into salary. This makes income inequality look like it's gotten much worse in the past twenty years, but if you convert benefits into salary, it hasn't changed that much.[275] And, finally, it is true that tax rates used to be much higher in American history, but there were so many deductions and loopholes that not very much revenue was collected at all. There were numerous cases of millionaires who simply were not paying any federal income tax whatsoever. To respond to this, President Richard Nixon sent a tax reform package to Congress in 1969 which would close some of the tax loopholes; this is called the Alternative Minimum Tax, and still exists today.[276] Tax rates are lower than they used to be, but more Americans pay taxes now.

The worries about income inequality assume that economics is a zero-sum game, where there are absolute winners and losers. But it's not, as writer David Harsanyi points out: 'If the wealthy get wealthier, no one has to become one penny poorer. This childish idea … appeal[s] to the populist sentiments of the so-called 99 per cent or to the envious nature of some others or to the emotions of many struggling through this terrible economy.' And even if we did want to repair income inequality, what would we be willing to do about it? Who would get to decide what was fair pay for everyone to take home? Harsanyi says, 'Are Americans prepared to take on a massive social engineering project that entails politicians, commissars and czars making biased and arbitrary assessments about who deserves what and who doesn't?'[277] Who on earth would we trust to create and adjudicate such an income-levelling endeavour?

The real problem isn't the top 1 per cent of households confiscating the wealth that the bottom 99 per cent want, but rather the whole notion of the median – the middle class – coming apart. Law professor Kenneth Anderson suggests that there are actually two middle classes, one of which is much better equipped to survive in the new global economy than the other. The upper tier, he says, has been able to leverage expertise and access to technological markets on a global scale, commanding huge premiums in the process, but now that this expertise is globally commodified it is coming back to the USA to take on privileged positions in both the public and private sector. But as for the other sector, he writes:

> It is characterised by a status-income disequilibrium … it cultivates the sensibilities of the upper tier New Class, but does not have the ability to globalise its rent extraction [and therefore command salary premiums]. The helping professions, the professions of therapeutic authoritarianism (the social workers as well as the public safety workers), the virtuecrats, the regulatory class, etc., have a problem – they mostly service and manage individuals, the client-consumers of the welfare state … the machine by which universities trained young people to become minor regulators and then delivered them into white collar positions on the basis of credentials in history, political science, literature, ethnic and women's studies – with or without the benefit of law school – has broken down. The supply is uninterrupted, but the demand

has dried up. The agony of the students getting dumped at the far end of the supply chain is in large part the [agony of] OWS.[278]

Anybody who can leverage their education and experience to a business with global implications – finance being the main example, technology being another and senior positions in government being a third – will still do pretty well in today's compressed economy. The trouble is that for those who are unwilling to enter those fields, a university degree in some kind of humanities no longer guarantees a job in journalism or arts administration or publishing or a charity organisation or a cabinet department, as public spending is drying up and the traditional content production companies that are the traditional homes for humanities majors are disappearing because of the growth of the internet. Just having a history degree doesn't guarantee you a job any more if you're unable to deploy experience that will be useful in a professional situation.

I've often wondered if Michelle Obama, when she says that traditional 'high-powered jobs' are less fulfilling than service jobs, isn't doing young people a disservice. She is fond of saying things like 'I had to ask myself whether, if I died tomorrow, would I want this to be my legacy, working in a corporate firm, working for big companies ... the resounding answer was, absolutely not... There is nothing more fulfilling [than public service]. It's an opportunity to put your faith into action in a way that regular jobs don't allow.'[279] But considering the openings for these kinds of jobs at non-profits or regulatory industries are growing ever scarcer, she should be encouraging people to leverage their education and intelligence into industries where there's a demand for employees.

The *New York Times* published a rather depressing piece on the lack of science majors called, 'Why Science Majors Change Their Minds (It's Just So Darn Hard)'. President Obama and industry groups have asked colleges to graduate 10,000 more engineers a year and 10,000 more science, engineering and maths teachers, but it simply isn't going to happen because the process of getting a science major is reputed to be not very interesting and can lead to failure. A researcher at Cornell discovered that STEM students are both 'pulled away' by high grades in their courses in other fields and 'pushed out' by lower grades in their majors.[280] These low grades are discouraging to many students at elite colleges who are used to succeeding. And the problem is there's a huge demand for engineers, applied maths graduates and skilled machinists – so much so that employers can't fill their positions – with jobs that can reach salaries of $60–80,000 a year. North Dakota and Minnesota, bucking the national trends, have unemployment rates of 3.3 per cent, and they've got more jobs than skilled workers to fill them – they need architects, teachers, skilled mechanics and even drivers[281] – but what self-respecting middle-class progressive kid from an urban area wants to live in an unglamourous place like North Dakota, even if you can easily get a job there? Middle-class kids, their heads filled with dreams of joining a non-profit, becoming a filmmaker, publishing small chapbooks filled with lovely poetry, of living in Manhattan and San Francisco, find themselves totally unable to get a job and completely unprepared to pay off thousands of dollars in student loan debts. It's worth reiterating that the value of all outstanding student loans exceeds $1 trillion.

The pain that onerous student loans is causing a generation is truly a major economic worry. An example is Occupier Nate Grant. Nate is twenty-two years old, and was an honour student in high school, so he could have gone to his local public university for free. Nate decided he didn't want to do that and instead chose to rack up $90,000 in debt at Ithaca College, a much more prestigious university in upstate New York. Initially, he was majoring in filmmaking, but he became disenchanted with that so became an English major instead. Since graduation, he has been living with his parents and doing odd jobs, and wondering if his brother, who didn't go to college and is a UPS driver, didn't do the smarter thing. 'I'd do anything to get this monkey off my back… [My brother] is married and debt-free except for his mortgage, and here I am with $90,000 and a piece of paper… Well, in a weird way I regret the whole college thing.'[282] There's no question that what's happened to a generation of Americans is deeply depressing. Losing thousands of people who ought to be entering the workforce to unemployment and disillusionment is a terrible loss of human capital. But at the same time, there's a certain amount of responsibility that we all need to take for ourselves and to realise that there's not a huge market out there for filmmakers and English majors without any kind of work experience. And if you are going to be like Nate and wilfully choose to rack up a ridiculous student loan bill – when a cheaper option is available – you don't look exciting and revolutionary when you blame it on somebody else. You look like an idiot. Alex Pareene wrote in *Salon Magazine*, 'What unites the outraged 99 per cent is that we have all "played by the rules", only to learn belatedly that the game was rigged. Having been promised modest rewards for working within the system, by taking on debt or voting the party line, we find ourselves, bluntly, shit out of luck.'[283] But what Nate Grant and Alex Pareene fail to see is nobody owes anybody anything – if you want to be able to succeed, it isn't a question of 'if I do x, then y will occur', it's a question of what opportunity in the market is there and how do I fill it? That's how you make enough money to have an apartment and a successful career in New York City and then maybe make enough to donate to your favourite Democratic politician. If you go to university and major in political science, nobody is going to throw you a party and hand you a job. You can rail against the rich as much as you like, but in the end, the only person to blame for Nate's problems is, well, Nate.

But on the other hand, students, who make up the backbone of the Occupy movement, are at the forefront of dealing with the rapidly changing American economy. Since states and localities now have to make do with reduced revenue from property taxes, thanks to the implosion of the housing market, they've got less money to fulfil the pension and compensation contracts of their public sector workers. California is ground zero of the public spending crisis; in 2011 the officially recognised gap between the money it had on hand and what it was legally obligated to pay workers was about $105 billion; thanks to clever accounting tricks, the actual amount is probably twice that. David Crane, Governor Arnold Schwarzenegger's former economic advisor, said that the state would pay $32 billion in 2011 for employee pay and benefits, to the detriment of state higher education and public health, both of which are down 5 per cent. A University of California student paid $776 for tuition thirty years ago; he or she now pays over thirteen grand per year. With public workers' pensions growing ever more expensive as they live longer and longer, states and localities now have to make hard choices about how to spend limited public dollars and, unfortunately, some of the losers are public college students. A local journalist in Cosa Mesa, California, one of the worst hit states for unfunded public pension liabilities, points out that the University of California system has a $21 billion unfunded pension liability, which means it owes $21 billion in pensions that it simply doesn't have the money to pay. So what do the universities do to raise the money? They hike tuition fees by 32 per cent. It would be fine if the students could find jobs to pay off their student loans to pay tuition, but they can't.[284] This is the current economic situation in America – the hijacking of the economic fortunes of the young to pay for the retirement of the old, and a concentration of wealth and property among the elderly and retired, not young working professionals.

And what do we do? Everyone recognizes that that the current college education bubble is unsustainable, and that we as a society have to have a major rethink about how we prepare young workers to enter the economy and whether the American economy is handling them as well as it used to. This could have been a moment for Occupy Wall Street and Occupy London to start an important policy discussion about the nature of education and the future of the economy and the future of the middle class. It would have been difficult, and fractious, and wouldn't have lent itself well to chanted slogans and mottoes on placards. But it would have done its members a great service and would have been useful to American society. That's not the choice they made.

Young voters are part of the coalition the Democratic Party needs to win elections, so there's an impetus for the Dems, and Obama in particular, to make sure that 18–25-year-olds are happy, because they turned out for him in record numbers in 2008. He needs them to do it again in 2012. So Obama has rolled out a 'student loan forgiveness package', the suggestion of which made budget hawks tremble in fear, because where are we going to find a trillion dollars to pay off student loans? But the plan is going to expedite the timeline for an already approved loan repayment plan with lower monthly payments for those whose burden of debt is disproportionate to their earning potential.[285] There are arguments about how helpful the plan actually is, and whether it will save people much money, but in the end it's a great campaign ploy to make sure that people will pull the lever for Obama in November.

What Occupy (Your City) represents is an opportunity lost. We need to talk about the future of young people in America. We're risking losing an entire generation to unemployment, not unlike what happened in the Great Depression. We need to talk about what's happened to the middle class and if there's any way we can regain the kind of economy we had from 1945 to 1975 when trade is global and moves at lightning speed. And if there isn't, we need to find something to replace it. There's no reason why America still can't be an economic superpower in the twenty-first century. The Occupy movement chose not to instigate that conversation. People who self-identified as progressive and elite chose not to listen to the Tea Party trying to instigate that conversation. And, yet again, Americans as a people are having to pay the price for these pointless and baseless political divisions.

10

THE STORY OF 2012

I often get asked, 'Who do you think will win the election?' Here's what I can tell you – it'll probably be a man. But seriously, Obama is already planning his national strategy and I predict with confidence that Mitt Romney is too. If we imagine an election as like a television show, which it is, the difficult bit is imagining what the episodes will be like. You can't really predict the weird twists and turns the story will take, and each election has its own flavour. But what we can predict quite easily is the election's story arc – we have a sense of the timing, the setting and the characters in the story. We know which states will be battlegrounds, we know the demographic groups that will be targeted, and we have a good idea of each candidate's lines, for the most part.

Larry Sabato, the political genius at the University of Virginia, has broken down what he thinks the electoral vote trajectory of 2012 will be. Just as a quick primer, each state is assigned a number of electoral votes based on its population (Congressional seats plus senators' seats), and when you vote for president, you vote for the state's electors, who in turn vote for the president directly later. This is designed to prevent mob rule. There are 538 total electoral votes and a presidential candidate needs 270 to win.

Because voting is quite predictable, thanks to the segregation of the American populace, we know pretty much, barring some sort of total collapse on either Obama's or the Republican nominee's part, what the electoral map looks like now. Obama is assured of 175 electoral votes from deep blue states. He's likely to get twenty-one more from Maine, Minnesota and Oregon, and the odds are good for Michigan, New Mexico, Pennsylvania and Wisconsin. The Republican nominee will get his deep red states plus likely wins in Arizona, Georgia and Texas. Indiana, North Carolina and Missouri are all leaning Republican. That gives Republicans 206 likely electoral votes and Democrats 247.[286]

This means that the presidential election of 2012 will be largely fought in a grand total of seven swing states: Colorado (9), Florida (29), Iowa (6), Nevada (6), New Hampshire (4), Ohio (18) and Virginia (13). That's not too unusual – these days elections are often fought in just a handful of states – but it's interesting that these states are all relatively small, with just a handful of electoral votes.

This is going to be a big election fought on a small stage. With all this money, and so few battleground states, these seven states are going to be utterly carpeted with political ads. Every yard will have a sign, every car will have a bumper sticker, every sizeable town will have a field office for each candidate. The local television and radio stations will have a bonanza of revenue – it'll be like Christmas.

The secret to Obama's success in 2008 was that he was able to encourage turnout from people who didn't usually vote, particularly from young people and African-Americans. Sixty-four per cent of the American public voted in that election. In 2010, young voter turnout dropped dramatically, from 51 per cent to 20 per cent. There are generally fewer votes in a mid-term election than there are in a presidential election but, even so, a 30-point drop is precipitous. Youth turnout was 10 per cent worse in 2010 than in 2006, when Obama wasn't even on the ballot in any way. The problem is that young voters are experiencing what's called an 'enthusiasm gap'. In 2008 they couldn't wait to vote for Barack Obama, but in 2010 they didn't listen to his exhortations to vote for Democrats in Congress. Thanks to the bad economy and poor opportunities for people just starting out in their careers, as well as the student loan crisis, he probably won't be able to recapture their votes at nearly the same margins. And it's a tough loss for him, because in 2008 they helped clinch victories in four major swing states – Ohio, Pennsylvania, Virginia and Florida – three of which he needs to win this year.[287] Thanks to the bad economy and his failure to achieve policy victories on issues these constituencies care about, like climate change, he won't be able to count on them, though he's tried with his student loan forgiveness plan.

Obama won't lose support from African-Americans – he won 96 per cent of their support in 2008 and that percentage has held steady at 95 per cent – but African-Americans represent only 13 per cent of the population. They are clustered in states like North Carolina, Virginia and Florida, and the President's campaign is already setting up field offices to target African-Americans in those states. The unemployment rate among African-Americans is much higher than it is for the general population, and one might think that economic woes might be enough to get at least some African-Americans to switch to the GOP. The Republican Party has tried to reach out to African-Americans before; in 2006, then-Republican National Committee chairman Ken Mehlman recruited Michael Steele to run for Senator of Maryland, Ken Blackwell to run for Governor of Ohio and former NFL star Lynn Swann to run for Governor of Pennsylvania. All of them lost, and huge percent-ages of African-American voters pulled the lever for their white, Democratic opponents. The reputation of Republicans for being racist was just too great for African-American voters to ignore.

The poor performance of African-American Republicans is fascinating; what it suggests is that African-Americans do not vote on identity but rather on policies. When an African-American national candidate emerged espousing Democratic policies, they supported him enthusiastically, but when African-Americans run for statewide senatorial and gubernatorial (governors') offices as

Republicans, the demographic runs in the opposite direction. Poverty rates among African-Americans suggest that their universal support for Democrats has not been helpful to them but, so far, Republicans have been unable to convince African-Americans it's in their economic interest to vote for the GOP. Could the insistence by progressive commentators that Republicans are racist actually be harming the economic progress of African-Americans? The greatest period of civil rights progress, between 1964 and 1974, occurred in a period when both parties were fighting for the African-American vote; if one party is locked out of that contest, what incentive is there for Democrats to woo African-Americans?

Hispanic-Americans, the fastest growing demographic group, broke for Obama over McCain at a margin of two to one in 2008, and carried the Latino vote in states with large Latino populations by huge margins. This helped put him over the top in Florida, Nevada, New Mexico and Colorado.[288] But things have gotten worse for him in the intervening three years. In Florida he's lost 9 per cent of Hispanic support, and in New Mexico he's lost 11 per cent. Nobody expects the Republican nominee to win the Hispanic vote entirely – the immigration issue makes that difficult – but in an election that's bound to be as close as this one, it's all about the margins. In states like New Mexico or North Carolina, Obama can't afford to lose too much of his 2008 support from minority voters, or he'll lose those states altogether. This is why Republicans have been working hard to cultivate a bench of young, charismatic, conservative Republican Hispanic senators, and they might have their secret weapon in Florida Senator Marco Rubio, the son of Cuban immigrants. Also, Mitt Romney has said that a possible vice presidential pick could be Susana Martinez, the Governor of New Mexico. If a vice presidential nominee such as Rubio or Martinez can help deliver Florida, Colorado, North Carolina and New Mexico, it's speech circuit time for Obama.

Unlike the African-American community, Hispanics have shown some willingness to vote for both parties, which is why around election time you'll often hear about issues dear to Hispanic voters, like immigration (though because of the Palin Effect, we never get to a solution for it).

On the other side of the aisle, the support of Tea Party affiliated conservatives will be crucial if the nominee wants to make any headway against Obama. Forty-one per cent of voters in the 2010 mid-terms said that they supported the Tea Party, and considering that election was a success for Republicans, it's hard to imagine that a Republican would be able to make any kind of headway, particularly in states like Wisconsin, Georgia and Missouri, without Tea Party support. Wisconsin is an interesting state because its Tea Party-backed governor, Scott Walker, has cut back on union benefits and collective bargaining rights to try to solve the state's budget deficit; it's become one of the most bitterly politicised states in the union, with constant protests, recall elections and ugly political scenes. So far Scott Walker seems to have succeeded in his aims, but there's no way that Wisconsin Republicans will turn out in force to deliver their electoral votes to the Republican nominee unless he supports their message of fiscal sanity.

Nate Silver, the political statistician at the *New York Times*, has gamed out several scenarios, based on various data inputs, of what might happen in the upcoming election. He modelled the chances of several Republican nominees, Jon Huntsman (the former Governor of Utah), Romney, Perry and Bachmann, based on various forms of economic growth. Based on his data, there's no way that Bachmann could win the nomination, unless we see the economy shrink by 1.6 per cent or more. If the economy stalls, Huntsman, Romney and Perry can expect to gain a majority of the popular vote. If the economy grows sluggishly, both Huntsman and Romney can win over the President, and even if the economy grows as much as 4 per cent, Huntsman could still win. But in the most likely scenario, with Romney as the nominee and sluggish economic growth, Silver forecasts a 60 per cent likelihood that Obama will win, which are not terrific odds for the President. If the economy grows by less than 2.3 per cent over the next year, it's Romney in a walk. Silver thinks that independents will break for the Republican if the nominee 'represents a credible alternative [to Obama] and fits within the broad political mainstream'. These studies were conducted before Gingrich surged ahead in the polls, so Silver didn't do an analysis of his chances.

Every presidential election has a theme. In 2000 it was 'Who seems like a nice guy like Bill Clinton?' In 2004 it was, 'Don't get rid of the 9/11 President.' In 2008 it was, 'Finally, we get to get rid of George W. Bush and experience racial reconciliation. Yay!' And we're beginning to see a theme emerge for 2012. People have laughed at the high number of debates in this year's Republican primary, but it's actually served a very important purpose. President Obama is going to raise a billion dollars for his campaign war chest and while the Republican nominee can't possibly hope to compete with that, he's going to need every cent in order to keep up with the Democrats' coming onslaught. So, quite intelligently, the Republican Party has scheduled these debates to keep the primary relatively inexpensive and to save all the money for the general election. The media anoints one front-runner or another in order to have a storyline, and polls reflect the changing fortunes of one candidate or another.

But the theme that's emerging in this election is that conservatives, Tea Partiers, and Republicans are all deeply hungry for philosophical debate in this election. The theme is 'Which way do we go?' Conservatives feel that the country is at a crossroads, fiscally and legally. They think the country could head down the road that Obama is taking them, with further central government control, more and more federal spending, more and more authority handed over to the federal government, and more legislative adventurism. Or, the country could head down another path of less government control, more authority handed to localities, and less money for public employees. And they believe quite strongly that in order to make their case in a presidential election, they need a leader who can articulate these things in a way that will make the media and progressive commentators not turn away from Obama (because that certainly isn't going to happen), but rather make them see that the progressive way isn't the only way. *Daily Caller* reporter Matt Lewis says:

> The latest narrative – and I think there's truth in it – is that voters are hungry for someone who will 'take it to Obama'. Clearly, Gingrich's debating ability is key. Republicans are champing at the bit to see him debate Obama. But I think this urge is deeper than a desire to simply watch him beat up or attack the president rhetorically – they also want him to *intellectually* flatten him – to out-debate him.

After what happened in 2008, no matter how ill-deserved it was, conservatives feel they can no longer afford to have their ideas and philosophies dismissed as stupid and idiotic. So it's not surprising that Newt Gingrich and Mitt Romney, two candidates who anyone would be hard-pressed to describe as stupid, have risen to the top of the pack. In Gingrich's case, it's not only that he will be an equal sparring partner to Obama in the debates, it's that he refuses to accept progressive orthodoxies that their ideas – about anything – are better. James Taranto writes:

> [Gingrich] was aggressive in refusing to accept the smug presumption of moral and intellectual superiority – a left-liberal

presumption that rankles conservatives, that is very common among the leaders of cultural institutions, and that Obama very much personifies... Gingrich is popular among conservatives because he refuses to be browbeaten by liberal bullies. One can easily imagine him bringing out the least attractive qualities of Obama, who does not like to be challenged.

Progressive orthodoxies which television journalists champion – that the Iraq War, for example, was disastrous and illegal, that all conservatives think bombing things is the answer, that all conservatives want to take food out of children's hands and throw Grandma out on the street – aren't shared by wide swathes of the country, but most political candidates meet journalists on their own terms. Gingrich refuses to do that. Sarah Palin sat back and took Charlie Gibson's browbeating, but Gingrich would have called him on his factual errors. Conservatives deeply want to see that happen in the upcoming election.

But it's not just intellectual browbeating and a refusal to be bullied that's appealing to conservative voters right now. Democrats are fond of saying that the Republicans are the 'party of no', that they like to criticise Democratic economic plans without offering any of their own. That's not quite true; Wisconsin Congressman Paul Ryan, who is part of the brain trust of the Republican Party, has offered very detailed plans about entitlement reform. While there are lots of flaws with his plan, hey, at least he's offered one and, more importantly, he's been willing to engage with the extremely difficult legal and economic problems posed by taking a serious stab at fixing the enormous unfunded budget liabilities that social security, medicare, and medicaid represent. Because of this, Ryan earned untold respect from all wings of the Republican Party for grappling with this issue (except for Gingrich, who criticised the plan, which nearly doomed his candidacy).

Eric Waxman, who is a self-described conservative, says that what people who have political beliefs like him want is someone who can not only demonstrate rhetorical leadership, but real thought leadership. There's a hunger, Waxman says, for someone who not only says the right things, as Romney does, but someone who seems to understand the philosophical underpinnings of modern American conservative thought. Waxman says:

> The claims that this is a special time and a critical juncture are legion and usually the product of hubris and misperception. Not so for 2012. Many sense a tipping point. If entitlements are not restructured, if ObamaCare reaches 2013 unrepealed, if the debate is not engaged now, then we will lack the will and the votes to address the issues later. 'It's getting late' is a tired refrain, but may apply here and now.

Neither the Tea Party nor Occupy Wall Street have been able to get the debate going, to get America really thinking about its economic future for the next century. The country has not been able to have a national conversation about that yet. Will the 2012 election be a chance to do so? If so, conservatives want a candidate who can hold his own in that conversation. This is why they changed loyalties from one candidate to another – they listened to each of the debate performances and judged the candidates based on what they heard. This sounds like a reasonable way to pick a candidate for a general election.

Despite not being the ideological warrior that most conservatives crave, what if it turns out that Romney is the nominee that independents, not conservatives, most like? This is the problem that Tea Party activists have to face. If there is no economic growth in the next ten months and, let's be frank, there isn't likely to be, we are very likely looking at a President Romney, should he be the nominee. Tea Partiers want nothing more than to get Obama out of office, as they feel he's been a bad president. But Romney, many Tea Partiers feel, is a pragmatic squish and a flip-flopper – he doesn't have strong conservative ideological underpinnings. Plus, since Mitt Romney spearheaded a form of universal health-care while he was Governor of Massachusetts, it will be difficult for him to run against Obamacare, which conservatives want to repeal as soon as they get the key to the Oval Office. As one Tea Party activist put it, 'If he's the last man standing, would you see people charge up the hill – maybe myself included – to try to beat Barack Obama? Probably… I admitted to my wife, there are far worse things than Mitt Romney being our nominee.'[289] During the 2010 election, Republicans like Karl Rove criticised more ideological fiscal conservatives like Sarah Palin and Jim DeMint for supporting fringe candidates like Christine O'Donnell (whose nomination was probably a mistake) over more moder-ate Republican candidates like Chris Coons. Their answer was simple. What's more important: having people in Congress who understand where we're coming from philosophically or having people in Congress who have an (R) after their names, who caucus with Republicans, but don't really understand the philosophy of small government? Is it more important to have a majority in the Senate and the House, or is it important to make sure the Congressional delegation fights for the philosophical beliefs his or her constituents adhere to? Tea Party conservatives have to ask themselves: what's more important – getting Obama out of office or having an ideologically correct president of the United States? Again, we return to the theme of this election: 'Which way do we go?' If you believe the country's on the wrong track, is electing Romney enough to divert the train? Or do you need more of a pure ideology? And, either way, is anyone thinking about what happens after 6 November? It's all very well to think about who can beat Obama, but how are they actually going to deliver the change conservatives want?

As for Obama, the theme for him in this campaign is 'Mitigate the losses'. *New York Times* political writer Tom Edsall wrote a much commented on piece in the 'Gray Lady', which explicitly stated that Obama would be giving up on white working-class voters, the ones who handed the election to Bill Clinton in 1992 and 1996. Edsall writes:

> All pretense of trying to win a majority of the white working class has been effectively jettisoned in favor of cementing a center-left coalition made up, on the one hand, of voters who have gotten ahead on the basis of educational attainment – professors, artists, designers, editors, human resources managers, lawyers, librarians, social workers, teachers and therapists – and a second, substantial constituency of lower-income voters who are disproportionately African-American and Hispanic.[290]

This says two things. The first is that the Obama campaign will do whatever it can to make sure the eventual Republican nominee is portrayed as a hick rube from the sticks who is unpalatable to and unacceptable for modern progressive Americans to serve as president of the United States. That will be tricky for Romney but they will try, probably by appealing to religious bigotry against Mormons. There will also be a lot of accusations of racism. And they will be very weird. If driving a pick-up truck and saying the words 'break him' are now markers of racism, I can only imagine what new unsayable phrases will emerge from the campaign. 'Radish'? 'Toothbrush'? The mind boggles.

The other thing that will emerge is that because of the economic pattern of settlement in the United States, where affluent, college-educated professionals and ethnic minorities cluster in very small districts, this is an election that won't just be fought in a few states, it will be fought in a very few neighbourhoods in selected cities. Think about it: if Obama needs to appeal to the affluent, minorities and the young, he needs to find places where they are not already overrepresented, like California and New York. The secret to Obama's success in 2008 was to get people who ordinarily didn't vote to vote for him. He can't count on that now, so he needs to win places where his constituency can tip the balance for him. Affluents and minorities tend to live in deep blue states, which are rich in electoral votes but not enough to get him to the magic 270. He's got to make inroads into purple states that might ordinarily be inclined to vote against him. That's why he needs to focus his campaign on places where his coalition can rack up electoral votes for him – places like Fairfax, Virginia, Chapel Hill, North Carolina and Denver, Colorado. He's got to find the members of his coalition in swing states and do intense, targeted campaigning to get them to tip their states into the blue column. In swing states, people in the Obama coalition tend to live in very proscribed areas such as the cities listed above – those living in these places are going to be targeted, massaged and analysed in order to get them to vote Democrat.

This kind of targeting means that 2012 is the perfect election to run via social media. Digital fundraising was pioneered by Joe Trippi of the Howard Dean campaign in 2004, and perfected by the Obama campaign in 2008. Since then, social media platforms have become more pervasive and sophisticated. We will literally be unable to escape political messages as all of our friends will be sharing articles, opinions and urban legends, as more of us get interested in the presidential contest and Palin Effect messaging begins to gain purchase on our brains. But social media will play a bigger role than just a platform for every amateur pundit to play armchair political analysis. Micro-targeting of ads will be a major factor; because we can now segment audiences by not only demographics but interests and keywords, you will get bespoke political ads delivered to you on Facebook that will be expertly calibrated to you and your interests. You won't have to see an ad on Facebook for a candidate who's in an opposing political party. In addition, the ranking of status updates on Facebook means that you're more likely to see status updates that you'll agree with (unless you have a habit of disagreeing politically with your friends) and see articles shared that complement your worldview. Twitter is also getting into the political ad market; after some negotiation, Twitter will create promoted accounts for at least five campaigns. Sources say that two of the campaigns are Mitt Romney's and the Democratic senatorial campaign committee. Political advertising on Twitter will be targeted like Facebook advertising; you may not see ads for political candidates with which you disagree. Mark Zuckerberg, the founder of Facebook, called this 'serendipity design', which means that social media platforms will mediate what you see on them – they will be in charge of delivering messages they think you'll like, rather than allowing you to discover things by happy accident. Political messages will be tailored to your demographic and location, which is exactly what candidates want. Both sides have a pretty sophisticated understanding of social media now, so it will be quite intriguing to see how they use the message and advertising tools that social media platforms offer.

Will 2012 be the firestorm that 2008 was? No. 2008 was one of the most dramatic elections in living memory and it will be tough to repeat. What 2012 will be, though, is an election where the Palin Effect is put to the test. Democrats don't want to fight this campaign on the issues, because they have a real chance of losing. Republicans don't want to fight this on anything but issues. Can the Democrats make this election about personality and social issues? Can Republicans keep their focus on fiscal matters? Will the conservative standard bearer live up to conservatives' expectations? Will Obama defy conventional wisdom and get his 2008 supporters to turn out for him one last time?

I can't wait for it all. Can you?

11

HOW TO DEFEAT THE PALIN EFFECT

On 16 November, 2011, 26-year-old Nathan Shafer heard about the arrests of nineteen Occupy Columbia protesters who were camped outside the South Carolina State House. Shafer, angry at this and Governor Nikki Haley's Facebook post about how she 'appreciate(s) freedom of speech', commented on her post, 'I hope someone murders you before I do. How's that for freedom of speech?'

The mere fact that someone would joke about murdering another human being, even if they're from the opposing political party, means something has gone deeply wrong. Shafer arguably has the right to say what he says. We can disagree about whether it was appropriate for the police to investigate the threat and lawyers to prosecute him for it, and we can disagree whether, as a public figure, threats against governors should not be legally actionable unless there is 'actual malice' involved in making the threat, which is very hard to prove.

It's not the action of Shafer threatening to kill another human being that's the trouble, it's what it signifies. It's the leap that humans are taking in finding another political opinion so odious, so horrible, so malevolent, that one feels compelled to stamp the owner, another human being, out. We all joke about killing each other all the time: 'Please don't shoot me' or 'I'm going to kill you', but we don't often talk about murder in cold blood. Mr Shafer's politics led him to dehumanise another person to the extent that he could say, in public, 'I hope someone murders you before I do.'

Politics is the most human sport; its practitioners prey upon our human weaknesses and frailties to manipulate us into doing what they want. And it's tough, believe me, to resist this kind of manipulation. When every impulse is telling us to agree with what we're hearing, to go ahead and be nasty about people we don't know, to go along with what everyone else is saying to fit into the tribe, it's very hard to say no. We're so used to thinking of political debate as an endless dichotomy that it's difficult to think about it any other way.

The Congressional approval rating is 9 per cent, at the time of writing. Just 9 per cent of Americans think Congress is doing a good job. When asked about how to solve our problems in Washington, most people give the answer, 'throw all the bums out'. But we try that every election and it doesn't really work very well. We simply trade one set of bums for another.

We need to come up with a new way of thinking about politics. We need to stop conceiving of ourselves as Democrats and Republicans, liberals or conservatives; we need to get over the idea that conservatives are country yokels and progressives are latte-drinking snobs. We have to realise that we are all in this together. As a certain senator from Illinois once said, 'There is not a liberal America and a conservative America, there is the United States of America.' He might have forgotten it, but we don't have to. We don't have to be stuck in this endless rut forever.

But this kind of change demands a leap of faith. It demands that we let go of tribalism and stereotypes and all the messages we've been hearing for so many years, and reach out to people we disagree with. It demands that we let go of making fun of political candidates because David Letterman tells us they're stupid or sharing pictures of Occupy Wall Streeters defecating on a cop car. It demands us to stop calling conservatives selfish and progressives crazy. It demands that we have to go outside our comfort zone and talk to people who hold opinions that we find anathema.

You don't have to be like Joe Klein and go all the way to Arkansas to find people you disagree with, but it helps. You might not live that far away from people who hold very, very different opinions from you. I grew up in Northern Virginia, in some of the bluest counties in the country, where everybody had a college education and worked for the government or tech companies. When I was a teenager we moved two hours down the road to central Virginia, where people hunted for fun and farmed for a living. I was so glad to have the experience of meeting a more diverse group of people, who had different life experiences and philosophies and ways of making the world make sense. It enriched me immensely and I don't doubt it would do the same for others. Two hours down the road from almost anywhere in the United States, you will meet people who think differently than you do (you might have to drive a few more hours in places like Texas or Wyoming). You'll experience the good effects of diversity; you'll be able to get along with a wider variety of people, you'll find your mind enriched, and you'll find yourself better able to express your ideas. But most importantly, you'll find out why people think they way they do – it's not because they're evil or alien, but because they had different experiences and their intellect has led them to process their opinions about these in a certain way. And if people in red state America took a trip to their local metropolis and talked with the locals, they might find this has a similar effect.

NBC News famously sent a man dressed in traditional Muslim garb to a NASCAR rally in Virginia, hoping they'd get some compelling video of rednecks being racist. Disappointingly for NBC, everyone was just as polite as they could be. Exposure to intellectual diversity won't cure the seriously endemic problems in American politics like corruption and undue corporate influence, but it will stop us threatening to murder each other. Let's learn our lessons from the Palin Effect. In 2012 I challenge you to have a conversation with a person you disagree with. Find out about his or her beliefs. Find out how their life experiences led them there. Figure out the evidence he or she is martialling to make their case. It will help you understand your opinions better, will make American politics less of a soap opera and, most importantly, it will revive our civic duty to be engaged in the democratic process of selecting the leader of the most powerful nation on Earth.

NOTES

1   'Top 10 MTV moments', http://www.time.com/time/specials/packages/
     article/0,28804,1963569_1963568_1963528,00.html

2   CNN broadcast, 29 August 2008.

3   *The McLaughlin Group* broadcast, 31 August 2008

4   Dowd, Maureen, 'Vice in Go-Go Boots', *New York Times*, 31 August
     2008, http://www.nytimes.com/2008/08/31/opinion/31dowd.
     html?_r=1&em&oref=slogin

5   Mallick, Heather, 'A Mighty Wind Blows Through the Republican
     Convention', CBC 5 September 2008, http://www.heathermallick.ca/cbc.
     ca-columns/a-mighty-wind-blows-through-republican-convention.html

6   Cho, Margaret, 'I want to steam up those glasses', 19 September 2008,
     http://www.myspace.com/margaretcho/blog/434054382

7   Kamiya, Gary, 'The Dominatrix', Salon, 9 September 2008, http://www.
     salon.com/news/opinion/kamiya/2008/09/09/mistress_palin

8   Kurtz, Howard, 'Katie Couric, on the Move', The Daily Beast, 25 October
     2010, http://www.thedailybeast.com/articles/2010/10/25/katie-couric-on-
     her-contract-cbs-and-love-of-the-campaign-trail.html

9   *Real Time with Bill Maher*, HBO, 26 June 2011, http://www.realclearpoli-
     tics.com/video/2011/06/24/nyts_david_carr_middle_places_home_of_
     low_sloping_foreheads.html

10   (Quoted in) Strong, Jonathan, 'Obama wins and Journolisters rejoice',
     The Daily Caller, 21 July 2010, http://dailycaller.com/2010/07/21/
     obama-wins-and-journolisters-rejoice/2/

11   Reid, Tim, 'Barack Obama's "guns and religion" blunder gives Hillary
     Clinton a chance', *The Times*, 14 April 2008.

12   (Quoted in) *The Brussels Journal*, 24 June 2006, http://www.brusselsjour-
     nal.com/node/1126

13   Leith, Sam, 'Cultural Notebook: the Days of the Undead', *The Prospect*, 18
     November 2009.

14   Marx, Karl and Engels, Friedrich, *The Communist Manifesto*, 1848

15   Meacham, Jon, 'The Palin Problem', *Newsweek*, 3 October 2008.

16   Martin, Iain, 'Sarah Palin and the Wasilla Hillbillies', *Daily Telegraph*, 7
     November 2008.

17   'Rick Perry's Redneck Guide to Fixin' the Gov'mint', 9 September
     2011, http://open.salon.com/blog/frank_michels/2011/09/09/
     rick_perrys_redneck_guide_to_fixin_the_govmint

18   Parker, Kathleen, 'Why the GOP fell for Newt Gingrich', *Chicago Tribune*,
     6 December 2011, http://articles.chicagotribune.com/2011-12-06/news/
     ct-oped-1206-parker-20111206_1_newt-gingrich-mitt-romney-herman-cain

19   Dillow, Chris, 'The Purpose of Columnists', *Stumbling and Mumbling*,
     26 August 2011, http://stumblingandmumbling.typepad.com/stum-
     bling_and_mumbling/2011/08/the-purpose-of-columnists.html

20   Garofalo, Janeane, interview with *Ecorazzi* magazine, 12 February 2009.
     http://www.ecorazzi.com/2009/02/12/woodstock-fas-exclusive-janeane-
     garofalo-preaches-obama-palin-and-bacon/#more-13424

21   'Dumbass Liberals At It Again', The Daily Retard, 11 December 2009,
     http://dailyretard.com/dumbass-liberals-at-it-again/

22   Damron, David, 'Grayson unloads on "chillbilly" Palin after she calls him
     out in Orlando', *Orlando Sentinel*, 15 March 2010, http://blogs.orland-
     osentinel.com/news_politics/2010/03/grayson-unloads-on-chillbilly-palin-
     after-she-calls-him-out-in-orlando.html

23   Jones, Owen, *Chavs: The Demonization of the Working Class*, (Verso:
     London, 2011), p.1

24   Marx, Karl and Engels, Friedrich, *The Communist Manifesto*, 1848

25   Of course, in a true Marxist analysis, the means of production would still
     remain in the hands of the bourgeoisie, so it wouldn't be a proper proletar-
     ian revolution. Still, a Palin political victory would make the American
     elite mighty uncomfortable.

26   Rius, *Introducing Marx*, 6th edition, (Icon Books: London, 1999)

27   De Tocqueville, Alexis, *Democracy in America*, translated by Henry Reeve,
     (Lawbook Exchange Ltd: 2003), Vol. 2

28   Fussell, Paul, *Class: A Guide Through the American Status system*,
     (Touchstone: Florida, 1992), p. 17

29   Ibid, p. 37

30   Orwell, George, *The Road To Wigan Pier*, New Ed edition, (Penguin
     Classics: London, 2011)

31   Wardin, Andrew, 'Finance Sector Swells Obama Poll Funds', *The Financial
     Times*, 17 July 2007, http://www.ft.com/cms/s/0/0dd41b74-33ff-11dc-
     9887-0000779fd2ac.html#axzz1Xeqd2P8r

32   'Shifts in Political Giving Toward Democrats among Top Voter Segments',
     Marketing Charts, http://www.marketingcharts.com/direct/shifts-in-

political-giving-toward-democrats-among-top-voter-segments-2884/
nielsen-presidential-primary-donations-top-ten-segments-trendsjpg/

33 'Average Income per person, by state', *USA Today*, 24 March 2011, http://
www.usatoday.com/NEWS/usaedition/2011-03-25-personalincome25_
TB_U.htm

34 J. T. Young, 'Who're You Calling the "Party of the Rich"?' *The American
Spectator*, 5 April 2011, http://spectator.org/archives/2011/04/05/
whore-you-calling-the-party-of#

35 Stanley, Tiffany, 'Things Fall Apart: How Democrats Gave Up on
Religious Voters', *The New Republic*, 18 December 2010, http://www.tnr.
com/article/politics/80162/democrats-faith-based-outreach

36 Steyn, Mark, 'If a Presidential Candidate Falls in the Woods…' *Daily
Telegraph*, 27 July 2004.

37 Sen. John Kerry, remarks in Independence, IA, 3 July 2004.

38 Kristof, Nicholas, 'Lock and Load', *The New York Times*, 13 November
2004.

39 Fowler, Mayhill, 'Obama: No Surprise that Hard-Pressed Pennsylvanians
Turn Bitter', *Huffington Post*, 11 April 2008, http://www.huffingtonpost.
com/mayhill-fowler/obama-no-surprise-that-ha_b_96188.html

40 Podhoretz, John, 'Obama Drips, Drips, Drips', Commentary, 11
April 2008, http://www.commentarymagazine.com/2008/04/11/
obama-drips-drips-drips/

41 Lander, Christian, 'Knowing What's Best for Poor People', Stuff
White People Like, 10 February 2008, http://stuffwhitepeoplelike.
com/2008/02/10/62-knowing-whats-best-for-poor-people/?cp=70

42 Joyner, James, 'Obama on Guns, God, and Hate in Rural America',
Outside the Beltway, 12 April 2008, http://www.outsidethebeltway.com/
obama_on_guns_god_and_hate_in_rural_america/

43 Quoted on *Countdown* with Keith Olbermann, 19
January 2010, http://hotair.com/archives/2010/01/20/
olby-massachusetts-suddenly-turned-racist/

44 Initial coverage from Larry O'Connor of Breitbart TV, 16 August 2011,
http://www.breitbart.tv/outrage-nbc-news-ed-schultz-uses-deceptive-edit-
to-paint-rick-perry-as-racist/

45 Magleby, David, *The Change Election: Money, Mobilzation and Persuasion
in the 2008 Federal Elections*, (Temple University Press: Pennsylvania,
2011), p.43

46 'Soft money political spending by nonprofits tripled in 2008 election',
CFI Press Releases, pp. 1–7, http://www.lb5.uscourts.gov/ArchivedURLs/
Files/10-30080(1).pdf

47 Luce, Edward, 'The crisis of Middle Class America', *The Financial Times*,
    30 July 2010, http://www.ft.com/cms/s/2/1a8a5cb2-9ab2-11df-87e6-
    00144feab49a.html#axzz1Xeqd2P8r

48 'Economic Mobility in America', Pew Trusts and the Brooking Institution,
    20 February 2008, http://www.pewtrusts.org/our_work_report_detail.
    aspx?id=35528

49 Ibid.

50 'Inside the Middle Class: Bad Times Hit the Good Life', Pew Research
    Center Publications, 9 April 2008, http://pewresearch.org/pubs/793/
    inside-the-middle-class

51 Luce, Edward, 'The crisis of Middle Class America', *The Financial Times*,
    30 July 2010, http://www.ft.com/cms/s/2/1a8a5cb2-9ab2-11df-87e6-
    00144feab49a.html#axzz1Xeqd2P8r

52 Ibid.

53 Usborne, David, 'President Mom: On the Stump with the Tea Party's
    Michele Bachmann', *The Independent*, 23 April 2011.

54 Weisberg, Jacob, 'Palinisms: Did Sarah Palin really say that?', Slate, 5 April
    2011, http://www.slate.com/articles/news_and_politics/palinisms/2011/04/
    palinisms_6.html

55 Ibid.

56 'Part 1: Obama Talks War on Terror, Iran and Pakistan in First-
    Ever Interview with O'Reilly', *The O'Reilly Factor*, 5 September
    2008, http://www.foxnews.com/on-air/oreilly/2008/09/05/
    part-1-obama-talks-war-terror-iran-and-pakistan-first-ever-interview-oreilly

57 Lutz, Hendricks and Scholleman, Todd, 'Student Abilities During the
    Expansion of U.S. Education, 1950–2000', 16 February 2011, http://www.
    lhendricks.org/Research/paper_abil.pdf

58 Morella, Michael, 'Harvard, Stanford, Yale Graduate Most
    Members of Congress', US News and World Report, 28 October
    2010, http://www.usnews.com/news/articles/2010/10/28/
    harvard-stanford-yale-graduate-most-members-of-congress

59 Malcolm Harris, 'Bad Education', N+1 magazine, 25 April 2011.

60 Bila, Jedediah, *Outnumbered: Chronicles of a Manhattan Conservative*,
    (USA, 2011), p.22.

61 Ridenour, Amy, 'Michael Steele Oreo Eyewitness Report', National
    Center Blog, 23 November 2005, http://www.nationalcenter.org/2005/11/
    michael-steele-oreo-incident.html

62 Wagner, John, 'Democrat Pleads Guilty in Steele Case', *The Washington
    Post*, 25 March 2006, http://www.washingtonpost.com/wp-dyn/content/
    article/2006/03/24/AR2006032401726.html

NOTES

63 Gardner, Amy, 'Moran Upsets Jewish Groups Again', *The Washington Post*, 15 September 2007, http://www.washingtonpost.com/wp-dyn/content/article/2007/09/14/AR2007091402171.html

64 York, Byron, 'Barack Felix Obama', *The National Review*, 2 December 2006, http://www.nationalreview.com/corner/133912/barack-felix-obama/byron-york

65 Allen, Jonathan, 'Sources: Joe Biden Likened Republicans to Terrorists', Politico, 1 August 2011, http://www.politico.com/news/stories/0811/60421.html

66 Karl, Jonathan, 'Say What? Democrat Compares Republicans to Nazis', The Note, ABC News, 19 January 2011, http://abcnews.go.com/blogs/politics/2011/01/abc-news-jonathan-karl-reports-the-newfound-civility-didnt-last-long-political-rhetoric-in-congress-doesnt-get-much/

67 'Joy Behar: Republicans Illogical, Evil, Immoral, Unethical, Stupid', Maggie's Notebook, (broadcast of the Joy Behar Show, HLN), 22 February 2011, http://www.maggiesnotebook.com/2011/02/joy-behar-republicans-illogical-evil-immoral-unethical-stupid/

68 Brodesser-Anker, Taffy, 'I Can't Believe My Best Friend Is A Republican', *Salon*, 5 April 2011, http://www.salon.com/life/feature/2011/04/05/my_best_friend_is_a_republican

69 Steyn, Mark, *After America*, (Regnery: 2011), p.239.

70 Weinstein, Jamie, '10 Questions With the Author of I Can't Believe I'm Sitting Next to a Republican', The Daily Caller, 16 January 2011, http://dailycaller.com/2011/01/16/10-questions-with-i-cant-believe-im-sitting-next-to-a-republican-author-harry-stein/2/

71 Tierney, John, 'Social Scientist Sees Bias Within', *New York Times*, 7 February 2011

72 Bishop, Bill, *The Big Sort: Why the Clustering of Like-Minded America is Tearing Us Apart*, (Mariner Books: 2008), p.22.

73 Ibid, p.4.

74 Miller, Laura, 'America Closes the Book on Education', *Salon*, 15 February 2008, http://www.salon.com/2008/02/15/susan_jacoby/

75 Bishop, Bill *The Big Sort: Why the Clustering of Like-Minded America is Tearing Us Apart*, p. 41.

76 Bishop, Bill, *The Big Sort: Why the Clustering of Like-Minded America is Tearing Us Apart*, p. 143.

77 Bafumi, Joseph and Herron, Michael C., 'Leapfrog Representation and Extremism: A Study of American Voters and their Members in Congress', http://www.dartmouth.edu/~herron/LeapFrog.pdf

78 De Tocqueville, Alexis, *Democracy in America*, p. 121, then p. 138.

79 Bishop, Bill, *The Big Sort: Why the Clustering of Like-Minded America is Tearing Us Apart*, p. 77

80 Carter, Jeff, 'Out of the Closet Conservative in a Democratic City', Points and Figures, 24 September 2011, http://pointsandfigures.com/2011/09/24/living-in-a-democratic-city/

81 Radosh, Ron, 'Joe Klein Takes a Road Trip and Partially Gets It!' *Ron Radosh*, 24 September 2011, http://pajamasmedia.com/ronradosh/2011/09/24/joe-klein-takes-a-road-trip-and-partially-gets-it/

82 Text of Arizona SB 1070, http://www.azleg.gov/legtext/49leg/2r/bills/sb1070h.pdf

83 Michaels, Sean, 'Shakira Attacks Arizona Immigration Law', *The Guardian*, 30 April 2010, http://www.guardian.co.uk/music/2010/apr/30/shakira-attacks-arizona-immigration-law

84 Gorman, Anna, 'Jewish Group Denounces Comparisons of Arizona to Nazi Germany', *LA Times*, 14 May 2010, http://articles.latimes.com/2010/may/14/local/la-me-0514-arizona-wiesenthal-20100514

85 'Mexico's Drug War Heats Up Near Arizona Border', Associated Press, http://www.msnbc.msn.com/id/38093155/ns/world_news-americas/t/mexicos-drug-war-heats-near-arizona-border/#.TpsYNGC2Tps

86 Trinko, Katrina, 'Obama: Not Always a Fan of Raising the Debt Ceiling', National Review, 3 January 2011, http://www.nationalreview.com/corner/256199/obama-not-always-fan-upping-debt-ceiling-katrina-trinko

87 Rago, Joseph, 'Obama and the Narcisissm of Big Differences', *The Wall Street Journal*, 6 August 2011, http://online.wsj.com/article/SB10001424053111903454504576486752134553990.html

88 Freedman, P. and Goldstein, K., 'Campaign Advertising and Voter Turnout: New Evidence for a Stimulation Effect', *The Journal of Politics*, 64(3), pp. 721–740.

89 Crugnale, James, 'Janeane Garofalo to Keith Olbermann: Cain Hides the Racist Elements of the Republican Party', 29 September 2011, http://www.mediaite.com/tv/janeane-garofalo-to-keith-olbermann-herman-cain-hides-the-racist-elements-of-the-republican-party/

90 Gehrke, Joel, 'Schultz says "break" is a "southern racist term"', broadcast of the Ed Show, MSNBC, 14 October 2011, http://campaign2012.washingtonexaminer.com/blogs/beltway-confidential/ed-cain-says-what-white-gopers-want-hear

91 Schneider, Matt, 'Chris Matthews: Newt Gingrich's "Racial Politics Is Doing Bad Things For This Country"', broadcast of *Hardball* with Chris Matthews, MSNBC, 12 May 2011, http://www.mediaite.com/tv/chris-matthews-newt-gingrichs-racial-politics-is-doing-bad-things-for-this-country/

92 Fiorina, Morris P., 'What Culture Wars?' *Wall Street Journal*, 14 July 2004, http://www.hoover.org/publications/hoover-digest/article/6699

93 Mead, Walter Russell, 'The Christianist Nightmare: It's Just a Bad Dream', *Via Media*, 20 September 2011.

94 Stein, Sam, 'Sharon Angle Floated "2nd Amendment Remedies" to our "Harry Reid Problems"', *The Huffington Post*, 16 June 2010, http://www.huffingtonpost.com/2010/06/16/sharron-angle-floated-2nd_n_614003.html

95 Hinderaker, John, 'Paul Krugman, Buffoon', Powerline, 11 January 2011, http://www.powerlineblog.com/archives/2011/01/028118.php

96 'They Have Blood on Their Hands', Daily Kos, 9 January 2011, http://www.dailykos.com/story/2011/01/09/934737/-They-Have-Blood-On-Their-Hands

97 Schwarz, Gabriella, 'Message from Senators: Tone It Down', Political Ticker, CNN, 9 January 2011 http://politicalticker.blogs.cnn.com/2011/01/09/message-from-senators-tone-it-down/

98 Shafer, Jack, 'In Defense of Flamed Rhetoric', *Slate*, 9 January 2011, http://www.slate.com/id/2280616/

99 'Bloodshed and Invective in Arizona', *New York Times*, 10 January 2011, http://www.nytimes.com/2011/01/10/opinion/10mon1.html?_r=1

100 Progressive bloggers are still trying to claim that 'angry' Republicans spout 'violent' rhetoric: see Katz, Jackson, 'Romney, Gingrich and the Two Visions of Ronald Reagan', *The Huffington Post*, 16 December 2011, http://www.huffingtonpost.com/jackson-katz/romney-gingrich-and-the-t_b_1152570.html

101 Halperin, Mark and Harris, John F., 'The Way to Win: Taking the White House in 2008', excerpted in the *Washington Post*, 3 October 2006, http://www.washingtonpost.com/wp-dyn/content/article/2006/10/03/AR2006100301030_3.html

102 'Media Alert: Now casting the hottest politicos in the nation', 24 October 2011, http://www.doronofircasting.com/blog/media-alert-now-casting-hottest-politicos-nation; http://www.partypoliticscasting.com/

103 Debord, Guy, *Society of the Spectacle*, (Rebel Press: London 1992) p.5.

104 Chomsky, Noam, 'What Makes Mainstream Media Mainstream', October 1997, http://www.chomsky.info/articles/199710--.htm

105 Miller, Sean J., 'Romney: Obama "one of the most divisive in history"', *The Hill*, 17 September 2011, http://thehill.com/blogs/ballot-box/gop-primaries/119437-romney-obama-one-of-the-most-divisive-in-history

106 Found on DemocraticUnderground.com, 26 July 2006, http://www.democraticunderground.com/discuss/duboard.php?az=view_all&address=102x2415275

107 Vowell, Sarah, *Assassination Vacation*, (Simon and Schuster: London, 2005), p.192.

108 Obama, Barack, 'Reagan Saw that We Are All Patriots', *USA Today*, 24 January 2011, http://www.usatoday.com/news/washington/2011-01-23-ronald-reagan-president-obama_N.htm

109 Pitney, John J., 'The Reagan Years: Not as Civil As We Think', Encyclopedia Britannica blog, 3 February 2011, http://www.britannica.com/blogs/2011/02/the-reagan-years-not-as-civil-as-we-think/

110 Sexton, John, 'Response to Krugman's Claim About Violent Rhetoric (Updated)', Verum Serum, 23 March 2010, http://www.verumserum.com/?p=13622. (Yes, that date is right; Democrats were complaining about 'uncivil behavior' from Sarah Palin nearly a year before the shootings.)

111 Sexton, John, 'Memo to Paul Krugman and Rep. Van Hollen: My Search Was Not in Vain (Updated)', Verum Serum, 31 March, 2010, updated 11 January 2011, http://www.verumserum.com/?p=13647

112 Hoft, Jim, 'Breaking: Daily Kos Put a Bullseye on Giffords in 2008', The Gateway Pundit, 10 January 2011, http://www.thegatewaypundit.com/2011/01/breaking-daily-kos-put-a-bulls-eye-on-rep-giffords-in-2008/

113 Smith, Ben, 'Obama Brings A Gun To A Knife Fight', Politico, 14 June 2008, http://www.politico.com/blogs/bensmith/0608/Obama_brings_a_gun_to_a_knife_fight.html

114 Orr, Jimmy, 'Sanford disappears, Kerry makes Sarah Palin joke', The Christian Science Monitor, 25 June 2009, http://www.csmonitor.com/USA/Politics/The-Vote/2009/0625/sanford-disappears-john-kerry-makes-sarah-palin-joke

115 'Non compos mentis', No Looking Backwards, 18 February 2008, http://massbackwards.blogspot.com/2008/02/non-compos-mentis.html

116 'Hate-o-Crat Eliminationism: Leftists Move to "Get Rid of Republicans Entirely"', American Power, 27 March 2010, http://americanpowerblog.blogspot.com/2010/03/hate-o-crat-eliminationism-leftists.html

117 Taranto, James, 'Get a Little Bloody', *The Wall Street Journal*, 23 February 2011, http://online.wsj.com/article/SB10001424052748703775704576162533209090102.html

118 Lord, Jeffrey, 'Kanjorski on Gov. Elect Scott: 'Shoot Him', 9 November 2010, http://spectator.org/blog/2010/11/09/kanjorski-on-gov-elect-rick-sc

119 Sarah Palin Facebook post, 'America's Enduring Strength', 12 January 2011.

120 (Quoted in) Thrush, Glenn and Haberman, Maggie, 'Sarah Palin's "Blood Libel" Claim Draws Criticism', Politico, 12 January 2011, http://www.politico.com/news/stories/0111/47490.html

121 Ibid.

122 Geraghty, Jim, 'The Term "Blood Libel": More Common Than You Might Think', National Review Online, 12 January 2011, http://www.nationalreview.com/campaign-spot/256955/term-blood-libel-more-common-you-might-think

123 Whittington, Mark, 'Threats of Violence Mark Wisconsin Protests', Yahoo News, 19 February 2011, http://news.yahoo.com/s/ac/20110219/pl_ac/7895742_threats_of_violence_rock_wisconsin_union_protests

124 Stranahan, Lee, 'Ignoring Death Threats To Wisconsin Politicians is Media Bias', Big Journalism, 15 March 2011, http://bigjournalism.com/lstranahan/2011/03/15/ignoring-death-threats-to-wisconsin-politicians-is-media-bias/

125 Buchanan, Paul G., 'A Word From Afar: Campaign Rhetoric As An Invitation To Violence', The Scoop (NZ), 28 October 2008, http://www.scoop.co.nz/stories/HL0810/S00373.htm

126 Sheppard, Noel, 'Bill Maher Tees Up Sen. John Kerry's Virulent Anti-Republican Campaign Speech', 8 October 2006, http://newsbusters.org/node/8175

127 Thrush, Glenn, 'Secret Service: Threats Against Obama No Greater Than Under Bush, Clinton', 3 December 2009, http://www.politico.com/blogs/glennthrush/1209/Secret_Service_Threat_level_against_Obama_no_greater_than_under_Bush_Clinton.html

128 Adorno, Theodor and Horkheimer, Max, 'The Culture Industry: Enlightenment as Mass Deception', http://www9.georgetown.edu/faculty/irvinem/theory/Adorno-Horkheimer-Culture-Industry.pdf

129 Rogers, Patrick and Gleick, Elizabeth, 'Barack Obama's big night: Fireworks and Family', *People*, 29 August 2008, http://www.people.com/people/article/0,,20222391,00.html

130 McArthur, John R., 'Palin Using Her Child as a Political Prop', Harper's Magazine, 17 September 2008, http://harpers.org/archive/2008/09/hbc-90003564

131 Roberts, John, CNN broadcast, 29 August 2008, http://newsbusters.org/blogs/matthew-balan/2008/08/29/cnn-s-john-roberts-palin-might-neglect-her-disabled-infant

132 Jacobs, Tom, 'Sex Appeal May Have Hurt Sarah Palin', Miller-McCune, 4 March 2009, http://www.miller-mccune.com/blogs/news-blog/sex-appeal-may-have-hurt-sarah-palin-3905/

133 Carpentier, Megan, 'Which Came First: The Objectification Of Sarah Palin, Or The Mistrust In Her Competence?' Jezebel, 5 March 2009, http://jezebel.com/caribou-barbie/

134 Cohen, Roger, 'The Texas Gipper', *The Washington Post*, 15 August 2011, http://www.washingtonpost.com/opinions/the-texas-gipper/2011/08/15/gIQA2SQGHJ_story.html

135 Mooney, Alexander, 'Obama backer compares Clinton to "Fatal Attraction" character', CNN Political Ticker, 12 May 2008, http://politicalticker.blogs.cnn.com/2008/05/12/obama-backer-compares-clinton-to-fatal-attraction-character/

136 Langer, Gary, 'Exit Polls: Economy, Voter Anger Drive Republican Victory', ABC World News, 2 November 2010, http://abcnews.go.com/Politics/vote-2010-elections-results-midterm-exit-poll-analysis/story?id=12003775

137 Lowen, Linda, '2010 Election – How Did Women Do in the 2010 Election?', 1 August 2011, http://womensissues.about.com/od/thepoliticalarena/a/2010-Election-How-Did-Women-Do-In-The-2010-Election.htm

138 Burton, Jonathan, 'Eight GOP women brave Middletown's political climate', The Middletown Press, 24 October 2011, http://www.middle-townpress.com/articles/2011/10/24/news/doc4ea4a7d6b550b604346499.txt

139 Quinnipiac Poll, 24 March 2010, http://www.quinnipiac.edu/x1295.xml?ReleaseID=1436

140 Rosin, Hanna, 'Is the Tea Party a Feminist Movement?' *Slate*, 12 May 2010, http://www.slate.com/id/2253645/

141 Bruce, Tammy, 'Why Tea Party Women Lead the Charge', *The Guardian*, 19 October 2010, http://www.guardian.co.uk/commentisfree/cifamerica/2010/oct/19/tea-party-movement-sarahpalin

142 60 Minutes broadcast, 22 June 2010, http://www.cbsnews.com/video/watch/?id=6607715n

143 Doniger, Wendy, 'All Beliefs are Welcome, Unless They Are Forced on Others', *The Washington Post*, 9 September 2008, http://newsweek.washingtonpost.com/onfaith/panelists/wendy_doniger/2008/09/all_beliefs_welcome_unless_the.html

144 The 'balloon head' comment came from the 25 January 2011 edition of *Hardball* and the nut case comment from the 19 January 2011 edition of *Hardball*, broadcast on MSNBC, http://www.huffingtonpost.com/2011/01/25/chris-matthews-michele-bachmann-balloon-head_n_814033.html; http://newsbusters.org/blogs/geoffrey-dickens/2011/01/19/sheriff-civility-aka-chris-matthews-calls-michele-bachmann-nut-cas

NOTES

145 'Michele Bachmann, A Special Kinda Moron', Moronwatch, http://moronwatch.blogspot.com/2011/01/michele-bachmann-special-kinda-moron.html

146 Gorney, Cynthia, 'Too Young to Wed: The Secret World of Child Brides', *National Geographic*, June 2011, http://ngm.nationalgeographic.com/2011/06/child-brides/gorney-text

147 'CNN Reliable Sources' broadcast, *CNN*, 7 September 2008, http://transcripts.cnn.com/TRANSCRIPTS/0809/07/rs.01.html

148 Carpenter, MacKenzie, '"Mommy Wars" Reignited in Debate over VP choice', *Pittsburgh Post Gazette*, 3 September 2008, http://www.post-gazette.com/pg/08247/908943-470.stm

149 Anderson, Kellie, 'Joe Biden's Tragedy: The Car Accident that Changed Senator Biden's Life', American Affairs, 3 October 2008, http://www.suite101.com/content/joe-bidens-tragedy-a71587

150 'PREVIEW: Access Exclusive – Barack Obama & Family Chat With Maria Menounos', Access Hollywood, 7 July 2008, http://www.accesshollywood.com/preview-access-exclusive-barack-obama-and-family-chat-with-maria-menounos_article_10226

151 Parker, Kathleen, 'Sarah Palin should beware of exploiting her youngest child', *The Washington Post*, 14 February 2010, http://www.washingtonpost.com/wp-dyn/content/article/2010/02/12/AR2010021204006.html?sid=ST2010021202633

152 Littman, Malia, 'Palin's Appealing "Morals"', Malia Littman: The Rebuttal to the Rogue, 16 March 2010, http://malialitman.wordpress.com/2010/03/16/palins-appealing-morals/

153 'Sarah Palin: Pimping Out Trig One Speech at a Time', FeministyMama, 12 October 2008, http://feministymama.blogspot.com/2008/10/sarah-palin-pimping-out-trig-one-speech.html

154 Treacher, Jim, 'Liberal Website Mocks Disabled Toddler', *The DC Trawler*, *The Daily Caller*, 21 April 2011, http://dailycaller.com/2011/04/21/liberal-website-mocks-disabled-toddler/

155 Smith, Olivia, 'Sarah's choice: Palin considered having abortion when she became pregnant with son Trig', *New York Daily News*, 17 April 2009, http://articles.nydailynews.com/2009-04-17/news/17921169_1_trig-gas-conference-sarah-palin

156 Harmon, Amy, 'Prenatal Test Puts Down Syndrome in Hard Focus', *The New York Times*, 17 May 2009, http://www.nytimes.com/2007/05/09/us/09down.html?pagewanted=all

157 Callender, James T., 'The Sally Hemings Accusation', *The Richmond Recorder*, 1 September 1802, available at http://www.pbs.org/jefferson/archives/documents/ih195822z.htm

158 Opie and Anthony Show, 14 May 2011, http://www.youtube.com/watch?v=qD-UC0eXVGE

159 May, Caroline, 'Comedian on Bachmann: I would "f*ck her angrily"', 16 July 2011, http://dailycaller.com/2011/07/16/comedian-on-bachmann-i-would-fck-her-angrily/

160 Baird, Julia, 'Too Hot to Handle', *The Daily Beast*, 2 July 2010, http://www.thedailybeast.com/newsweek/2010/07/03/too-hot-to-handle.html

161 Gutierrez, Lisa, 'Mike Tyson: Yeah I hit a woman, but I'll never do it again', *The Star*, 22 April 2009, http://www.kansascity.com/2009/04/22/1156248/mike-tyson-yeah-i-hit-a-woman.html#ixzz1YzaQDvCg

162 Brown, Larry, 'Mike Tyson Doesn't Think Glen Rice Banged Sarah Palin Hard Enough', 15 September 2011, http://larrybrownsports.com/gossip/mike-tyson-doesnt-think-glen-rice-banged-sarah-palin-hard-enough/87379

163 Nolte, John, 'Spur-of-the-Moment?: *Rolling Stone* Interview Contradicts *Jimmy Fallon Show* Drummer's Post-Bachmann Debacle Statement', 8 December 2011, http://bighollywood.breitbart.com/jjmnolte/2011/12/08/spur-of-the-moment-rolling-stone-interview-contradicts-jimmy-fallon-show-drummers-post-bachmann-debacle-statement/

164 Jessica G., 'Why Sarah Palin Incites Near-Violent Rage in Normally Reasonable Women', *Jezebel*, 8 September 2008, http://jezebel.com/5045934/why-sarah-palin-incites-near+violent-rage-in-normally-reasonable-women

165 Dowd, Maureen, 'Playing All the Angles', *The New York Times*, 16 October 2010, http://www.nytimes.com/2010/10/17/opinion/17dowd.html?_r=1&ref=opinion

166 Taranto, James, 'Palinoia, the Destroyer', *The Wall Street Journal*, 19 January 2011, http://online.wsj.com/article/SB10001424052748704590704576091962633206964.html?mod=rss_Today per cent27s_Most_Popular

167 Gross, Michael Joseph, 'Sarah Palin: The Sound and the Fury', *Vanity Fair*, October 2010, http://www.vanityfair.com/politics/features/2010/10/sarah-palin-201010

168 McEwan, Melissa, 'This is So the Worst Thing You're Going to Read All Day', Shakesville, 1 September 2010, http://shakespearessister.blogspot.com/2010/09/this-is-so-worst-thing-youre-going-to.html

169 Monika Bauerlein on Twitter: http://twitter.com/#!/MonikaBauerlein/status/22686010893

170 Smith, Ben, 'Saying Anything About Palin', Politico, 1 September 2010, http://www.politico.com/blogs/bensmith/0910/Saying_anything_about_Palin.html?showall

171 Loesch, Dana, 'Explosive Email Shows Anti-Palin Author McGinniss, Random House Likely Published Literary Hoax (Updated)', Big Journalism, 22 September 2011, http://bigjournalism.com/abreit-bart/2011/09/22/explosive-email-shows-anti-palin-author-tricked-random-house-into-publishing-literary-hoax/

172 Opensecrets.org, a project of the Center for Responsive Politics, http://www.opensecrets.org/pres08/search.php?cid=N00006424&name=%28all%29&employ=Random+House&state=%28all%29&zip=%28any+zip%29&submit=OK&amt=a&sort=A

173 Marks, Peter, 'Without You I'm Nothing: Bernhard's Acid Reflex', *The Washington Post*, 12 September 2008, http://www.washingtonpost.com/wp-dyn/content/article/2008/09/11/AR2008091103625.html

174 Thompson, Katherine, 'Sandra Bernhard Cut from Benefit After Gang Rape Joke', *The Huffington Post,* 1 October 2008, http://www.huffington-post.com/2008/10/01/sandra-bernhard-cut-from_n_131091.html

175 Hall, Colby, 'Montel Williams Suggests Michele Bachmann Should Stab Herself', Mediaite, 4 September 2009, http://www.mediaite.com/online/montel-williams-suggests-michelle-bachmann-should-stab-herself/

176 'Madonna to Sarah Palin: I will kick her ass', available at YouTube, http://www.youtube.com/watch?v=3o1zhXQXXAY

177 Paglia, Camille, 'Fresh bloody for the vampire', Salon, 10 September 2008, http://www.salon.com/2008/09/10/palin_10/

178 CBS Evening News with Katie Couric, 30 September 2008, http://www.cbsnews.com/stories/2008/09/30/eveningnews/main4490618.shtml

179 'The Second Great Awakening and Rise of Evangelism', http://xroads.virginia.edu/~ma95/finseth/evangel.html

180 Taibbi, Matt, 'Mad Dog Palin', *Rolling Stone,* 27 September 2008, http://www.alternet.org/election08/100551/mad_dog_palin_/

181 Taibbi, Matt, 'Michelle Bachmann's Holy War', *Rolling Stone*, 22 July 2011, http://www.rollingstone.com/politics/news/michele-bachmanns-holy-war-20110622

182 All assertions from Hudson, John, 'Rolling Stone's Bachmann article: The hit piece that hit itself', The Atlantic Wire, 24 June 2011, http://www.theatlanticwire.com/business/2011/06/rolling-stones-bachmann-article-hit-piece-hit-itself/39260/

183 Lizza, Ryan, 'Leap of Faith: the Making of a Republican Front-Runner', *The New Yorker*, 15 August 2011, http://www.newyorker.com/reporting/2011/08/15/110815fa_fact_lizza

184 See Domenech, Ben, 'In Bachmann Attack, Lizza Smears Francis Schaefer', http://thisisanadventure.com/2011/08/in-bachmann-attack-ryan-lizza-smears-francis-schaeffer/ and John Schroeder, 'Bachmann on Trial – so much for vacation', 9 August 2011, http://www.article6blog.com/2011/08/09/bachmann-on-trial-so-much-for-vacation/

185 Pearcy, Nancy, 'Dangerous Influences: The New Yorker, Michele Bachmann, and Me', Human Events, 12 August 2011.

186 Hofstadter, p. xxvi.

187 Cummings, Jeanne, '2008 election costliest in US History', Politico, 5 November 2008, http://www.politico.com/news/stories/1108/15283.html

188 Zengerle, Patricia, 'Billion-dollar Obama to run moneyed campaign', Reuters, 4 April 2011, http://www.reuters.com/article/2011/04/04/us-usa-election-obama-analysis-idUSTRE7330NY20110404

189 Cardowski, Scott, 'The $4 Billion Election: a few media companies are set to feast on campaign ads', *Fortune*, 4 February 2010, http://money.cnn.com/2010/02/04/pf/broadcast_ads_elections.fortune/index.htm

190 'Ideology/Single-Issue Sector Totals to Candidates', Center for Responsive Politics, 2008 campaign finance reports, http://www.opensecrets.org/pres08/sectors.php?sector=Q

191 Ibid.

192 Hofstadter, Richard, 'The Paranoid Style in American Politics', *The Paranoid Style in American Politics and Other Essays,* (Vintage Books: 2008)

193 Marcotte, Amanda, 'Blog for choice: I'm pro-choice because I love life', Pandagon.net, 22 January 2010, http://pandagon.net/index.php/site/blog_for_choice_im_pro_choice_because_i_love_life

194 Sister Toldjah, '"Twin reduction": Our pro-death, vanity abortion culture in a nutshell', SisterToldjah.com, 10 August 2011, http://sistertoldjah.com/archives/2011/08/10/twin-reduction-our-pro-death-vanity-abortion-culture-in-a-nutshell/

195 Tate, Ryan, 'Chris Dodd: OK, I allowed the AIG bonuses', Gawker, 18 March 2009, http://gawker.com/5174458/chris-dodd-ok-i-allowed-the-aig-bonuses

196 Cook, John, 'Meet Chris Dodd, the Senator from AIG', Gawker, 18 March 2009, http://gawker.com/5173647/meet-chris-dodd-the-senator-from-aig

197   Healy, Patrick D., 'Clinton Seeking Shared Ground Over Abortions', *The New York Times*, 25 January 2005, http://www.nytimes.com/2005/01/25/nyregion/25clinton.html

198   Ibid.

199   Campbell, David E. and Putnam, Robert D., 'Crashing the Tea Party', *The New York Times*, 16 August 2011, http://www.nytimes.com/2011/08/17/opinion/crashing-the-tea-party.html

200   Clement, Scott and Green, John C., 'The Tea Party, Religion and Social Issues', 23 February 2011, http://pewresearch.org/pubs/1903/tea-party-movement-religion-social-issues-conservative-christian

201   King Jr, Neil, 'Daniel's "Truce" call finds strong support in WSJ poll', *The Wall Street Journal*, 2 March 2011, http://blogs.wsj.com/washwire/2011/03/02/danielss-truce-call-finds-strong-support-in-wsj-poll/

202   'Economy trumps social issues in conservative SC', Associated Press, CBS News, 11 November 2011, http://www.cbsnews.com/8301-505245_162-57323175/economy-trumps-social-issues-in-conservative-sc/

203   CBS News/*New York Times* poll, 19–24 October 2011, http://www.pollingreport.com/prioriti.htm

204   Quick, Bill, 'The Gingrich Who Stole Santa Santorum's Sleigh', Daily Pundit, 10 December 2011, http://www.dailypundit.com/2011/12/10/the-gingrich-who-stole-santa-santorums-sleigh/

205   Lavender, Paige, '2012 Election: Where GOP Presidential Candidates Stand On Evolution', *The Huffington Post*, 18 August 2011, http://www.huffingtonpost.com/2011/08/24/2012-election-gop-candidates-evolution-_n_934045.html#s333313&title=Jon_Huntsman

206   Falcone, Michael and Saenz, Arlette, 'NH Mother Uses Child as a Prop to Question Rick Perry on Evolution', *ABC News*, 18 August 2011, http://abcnews.go.com/blogs/politics/2011/08/nh-mother-uses-child-as-a-prop-to-question-rick-perry-on-evolution/

207   Reeve, Elspeth, 'The Rick Roll: Perry Backs Teaching Creationism In Public Schools', *The Huffington Post*, 18 August 2011, http://www.theatlanticwire.com/politics/2011/08/perry-supports-teaching-creationism-public-schools/41462/

208   Richards, Jay and Klinghoffer, David, 'Answering the Dreaded Evolution Question', *The American Spectator*, 24 June 2011, http://spectator.org/archives/2011/06/24/answering-the-dreaded-evolutio

209   Rovzar, Chris, 'Matt Damon Wants to Know If Sarah Palin Believes There Were Dinosaurs 4,000 Years Ago', *New York Magazine*,

10 September 2008, http://nymag.com/daily/intel/2008/09/
matt_damon_wants_to_know_if_sa.html

210 Bauer, Gary, 'Presidential Candidates Weigh In on Evolution Debate',
CNN, 27 August 1999, http://articles.cnn.com/1999-08-27/politics/
president.2000_evolution.create_1_evolution-and-creationism-evolution-
debate-local-school-boards?_s=PM:ALLPOLITICS

211 'Edwards on Evolution', *Fun Murphys: The Blog*, 6 June 2007, http://www.
funmurphys.com/blog/archive/001406.html

212 Bailey, Ronald, 'Evolutionary Politics', *Reason Magazine*, 8 January 2008,
http://reason.com/archives/2008/01/08/evolutionary-politics

213 Luo, Michael, 'Romney Elaborates on Evolution', *The New York
Times*, 11 May 2007, http://thecaucus.blogs.nytimes.com/2007/05/11/
romney-elaborates-on-evolution/

214 Madsen, Lincoln, 'Joe Biden for President', Lincoln Madsen blog, 7 April
2008. http://lincmad.blogspot.com/2006/04/joe-biden-for-president.html

215 Myers, PZ, 'Mitt Romney, Theistic Evolutionist...and this is supposed
to be a good thing?', *Pharyngula*, 12 May 2007, http://scienceblogs.com/
pharyngula/2007/05/mitt_romney_theistic_evolution.php

216 Buckley, William F., 'How Is It Possible to Believe in God?', *Morning
Edition*, NPR, 23 May 2005, http://www.npr.org/templates/story/story.
php?storyId=4656595

217 Shaw, Jazz, 'Creationism, Evolution, and Politics', Hot Air,
30 January 2011, http://hotair.com/archives/2011/01/30/
evolution-creation-and-politics/

218 Morning Edition Broadcast, NPR, 4 August 2005, http://www.npr.org/
templates/story/story.php?storyId=4784905

219 Engber, Daniel, 'Creationism vs Intelligent Design', Slate, 10 May 2005,
http://www.slate.com/articles/news_and_politics/explainer/2005/05/
creationism_vs_intelligent_design.html

220 Cook, John, 'Rick Perry Gives Up the Ghost on the Intelligent
Design Lie', *Gawker*, 18 August 2011, http://gawker.com/5832243/
rick-perry-gives-up-the-ghost-on-the-intelligent-design-lie

221 Uncredited, '2010: The Vote: K-12 Education', *San Angelo Standard Times*,
11 September 2010, http://www.gosanangelo.com/news/2010/sep/11/
this-series-examines-important-issues-to-texans/

222 Meyer, Stephen, 'Intelligent Design is Not Creationism', *Daily Telegraph*,
28 January 2006

223 Haydon, Harry, 'Beauty Murder Gaffe by Tory MP', *The Sun*, 25 April
2009, http://www.thesun.co.uk/sol/homepage/news/article2396443.ece

224 (Quoted in) Boyle, Alan, 'The Candidates on Science',
     MSNBC.com, 3 January 2008, http://cosmiclog.msnbc.msn.
     com/_news/2008/01/03/4351229-the-candidates-on-science

225 Braun, Stephen, 'Palin Canny on Religion and Politics', *The LA Times*,
     28 September 2008, http://articles.latimes.com/2008/sep/28/nation/
     na-palinreligion28

226 Tierney, John, 'Social Scientist Sees Bias Within', *The New York Times*, 7
     February 2011

227 Edgeton, Doug, 'Local columnists say stem educa-
     tion if fuel for economic growth', 6 November 2011,
     http://www2.journalnow.com/news/2011/nov/06/
     wsopin02-doug-edgeton-and-ed-kitchen-guest-columni-ar-1578423/

228 'Direction of country' poll, Real Clear Politics, http://www.realclearpoli-
     tics.com/epolls/other/direction_of_country-902.html

229 Hoover, Michael, 'The Whiskey Rebellion', TTB.gov.

230 'The Critical Period: America in the 1780s', *Digital History*, http://www.
     digitalhistory.uh.edu/database/article_display.cfm?HHID=281

231 Wilder, Ingalls, *The Long Winter*, quoted on http://jezebel.com/5061793/
     the-long-winter-cold-comfort-or-in-which-i-dont-even-try-to-fight-the-
     metaphor?tag=finelines

232 Fimrite, Peter, 'Newsom says S.F. Won't Help With Raids', *San Francisco
     Chronicle*, 23 April 2007

233 Pollan, Michael, *The Omnivore's Dilemma*, (Penguin: London, 2006), p.229

234 CNBC *Squawk Box* Broadcast, 19 February 2009

235 'The Tea Party: Brewing Up a Movement', Knoxnews.com,
     23 September 2010, http://www.knoxnews.com/videos/detail/
     the-tea-party-brewing-up-a-movement/

236 Reynolds, Glenn Harlan, 'Tax Day Becomes Protest Day', *Wall Street
     Journal*, 15 April 2009

237 Akbar, Ali, 'Dear Morgan Freeman... An open letter from our Publisher',
     Tea Party Brew, 24 September 2011, http://teapartybrew.com/
     opinion/2011/09/dear-morgan-freeman-tea-party-is-not-racist/

238 Madison, James, Federalist Paper 46, first published in the Tuesday,
     January 29 1788 issue of the *New York Packet*.

239 Althouse, Ann, 'Why Talking about "States' Rights" Cannot Avoid the
     Need for Normative Federalism Analysis', *Duke Law Review*, Vol. 51.,
     (Duke University, School of Law: 2001), p.363+

240 MacKay, William R., 'Legitimacy in a Federal System', Fed Forum, http://
     federalgovernance.co/archives/volume2/FG_VOL2_ISS1_MACKAY.pdf

241 Brettel, Karen, 'Egan Jones Cuts US Rating, Cites High Debt Load', Reuters, 18 July 2011, http://www.reuters.com/article/2011/07/18/rating-bonds-eganjones-idUSN1E76H0ZH20110718

242 Kandangath, Anil, 'Where did my tax dollars go?', http://www.wheredid-mytaxdollarsgo.com/tax_payers

243 Jones, Jeffrey M., 'Debt and Gov't Power Among Tea Party Supporters' Top Concerns', Gallup, http://www.gallup.com/poll/141119/debt-gov-power-among-tea-party-supporters-top-concerns.aspx

244 Rago, Joseph, 'Obama and the Narcissism of Big Differences', *The Wall Street Journal*, 6 August 2011, http://online.wsj.com/article/SB1000142405 311190345450457648675234553990.html

245 Newport, Frank, 'Tea Party Supporters Oppose Debt Agreement 68% to 22%', Gallup. 4 August 2011, http://www.gallup.com/poll/148841/tea-party-supporters-oppose-debt-agreement.aspx

246 Merline, John, 'The Austerity Myth: Federal Spending up 5 per cent This Year', Investor's Business Daily, 17 October 2011, http://news.investors.com/Article/588254/201110170805/The-Austerity-Myth-Federal-Spending-Up-5-This-Year.htm

247 Mardell, Mark, 'Tea Party: Right-wing "nutters" or mature adults?', BBC News, 25 July 2011, http://www.bbc.co.uk/news/world-us-canada-14285831

248 Raban, Jonathan, 'Sipping with the Tea Party', *The Guardian*, 16 October 2010, http://www.guardian.co.uk/world/2010/oct/16/tea-party-movement-jonathan-raban

249 Sessions, David, 'The Christian Right in Disguise?', *The Daily Beast*, 18 August 2011, http://www.thedailybeast.com/articles/2011/08/18/tea-party-is-it-the-christian-right-in-disguise.html

250 Akbar, 'Dear Morgan Freeman...', http://teapartybrew.com/opinion/2011/09/dear-morgan-freeman-tea-party-is-not-racist/

251 Robinson, Eugene, 'Racism and the Tea Party Movement', *Real Clear Politics*, 2 November 2010, http://www.realclearpolitics.com/articles/2010/11/02/race_and_the_tea_partys_ire_107805.html

252 Wehner, Peter, 'Obama, The Tea Party, and the Incivility of Race Politics', *Commentary Magazine*, 4 March 2011, http://www.commentarymagazine.com/2011/03/04/obama-the-tea-party-and-the-incivility-of-race-politics/

253 Boyle, Matthew, 'NPR Executives Caught on Tape Bashing Conservatives and Touting Liberals', *The Daily Caller*, 16 March 2011, http://dailycaller.com/2011/03/08/npr-executives-caught-on-tape-bashing-conservatives-and-tea-party-touting-liberals/#

254 Shepard, Alicia C., 'NPR and Diversity – NABJ Says NPR Must Do Better', NPR Ombudsman's column, 29 October 2009, http://www.npr.org/blogs/ombudsman/2009/10/npr_and_diversity_nabj_says_np.html

255 Dixon, Kim, 'Tea Party Brining Cash in to the 2012 Elections', Yahoo News, 12 October 2011, http://news.yahoo.com/tea-party-bringing-cash-2012-elections-164408092.html

256 'Just when you thought you couldn't face another sermon, Jesse Jackson arrives', Scrapper Duncan, 15 December 2011, http://blog.scrapperduncan.com/

257 Owen, Paul and Batty, David, 'Student tuition fees protest – Wednesday 9 November 2011', *The Guardian*, 9 November 2011, http://www.guardian.co.uk/education/blog/2011/nov/09/student-tuition-fees-protests-live-blog

258 Miles, Chris, 'What the Tea Party and Occupy Wall Street Have in Common', PolicyMic, http://www.policymic.com/article/show?id=1916

259 Fields, Michelle, 'Protest Turns Violent Outside Washington Convention Center', *The Daily Caller*, 5 November 2011, http://dailycaller.com/2011/11/05/chaos-video/

260 McCain, Robert Stacy, 'Smelly Hippies Get Ripped Off', The Other McCain, 28 October 2011, http://theothermccain.com/2011/10/28/smelly-hippies-get-ripped-off/

261 Posted 6 November 2011, http://www.twitlonger.com/show/e1lppd

262 Carney, Timothy P., 'Is David Axelrod lying about lobbyists...', *The Washington Examiner*, 31 October 2011, http://campaign2012.washingtonexaminer.com/blogs/beltway-confidential/david-axelrod-lying-about-lobbyists

263 Uchitelle, Louis, 'The Richest of the Rich, Proud of a New Gilded Age', *The New York Times*, 15 July 2007, http://www.nytimes.com/2007/07/15/business/15gilded.html?pagewanted=all

264 Buffett, Warren, 'Stop Coddling the Super-Rich', *The New York Times*, 14 August 2011, http://www.nytimes.com/2011/08/15/opinion/stop-coddling-the-super-rich.html

265 'Warren Buffett, hypocrite', *The New York Post*, 29 August 2011, http://www.nypost.com/p/news/opinion/editorials/warren_buffett_hypocrite_E3BsmJmeQVE38q2Woq9yjJ#ixzz1WRoIlYSf; also, Gabbay, Tiffany, 'How Much is Buffett's Berkshire Hathaway Back-Tax Bill Exactly? About $1 Billion', *The Blaze*, 30 August 2011, http://www.theblaze.com/stories/how-much-is-buffetts-berkshire-hathaway-back-tax-bill-exactly-about-1-billion/

266 Transcript of President Obama's Buffett Tax address, Talking Points Memo, 19 September 2011, http://tpmdc.talkingpointsmemo. com/2011/09/full-text-president-obamas-buffett-tax-address.php

267 Stephanopolous, George, 'David Plouffe on Protesters, Herman Cain, Senate Jobs Vote', 11 October 2011, http://abcnews.go.com/blogs/ politics/2011/10/david-plouffe-on-protesters-herman-cain-senate-jobs-vote/

268 'A dramatic shift in America', *Google*, http://i.imgur.com/Z4toA.gif

269 McAullif, Michael, 'Occupy Wall Street's Message: Senate Democrats Say It Will Dominate 2012 Elections', 3 November 2011, http://www.huffing- tonpost.com/2011/11/03/occupy-wall-street-message-senate-democrats- 2012-elections_n_1074168.html?ref=mostpopular

270 Kalman, Nick, 'Giuliani: "Obama Owns Occupy Wall Street"', *Fox News*, 4 November 2011, http://politics.blogs.foxnews.com/2011/11/04/ giuliani-obama-owns-occupy-wall-street

271 Congressional Budget Office, 'Trends In the Distribution of Household Income Between 1979 and 2007', http://www.cbo.gov/doc. cfm?index=12485

272 Meyer, Bruce, and James Sullivan, 'The Material Well Being of the Poor and the Middle Class Since 1980', AEI Policy Research, 25 October 2011

273 Gordon, Robert, 'Misperceptions about the Magnituded and Timing of Changes in American Income Inequality', *The National Bureau of Economic Research*, September 2009

274 Kaplan, Steven, 'Wall Street and Main Street: What Contributes to the Rise in the Highest Incomes?' (University of Chicago, 3 March 2009)

275 Salam, Reihan, 'Thoughts on Airline Luxury and Inequality', *National Review Online*, 21 November 2011, http://www.nationalreview.com/ agenda/283745/thoughts-airline-luxury-and-inequality-reihan-salam

276 Goodman, Bonnie, 'How did the present alteriantive minimum tax come into existence?', *History News Network*, 20 June 2005, http://hnn.us/ articles/11819.html

277 Harsanyi, David, 'You Want More Equality? Support More Capitalism', *Reason Magazine*, 2 November 2011, http://reason.com/ archives/2011/11/02/you-want-more-equality-support

278 Anderson, Kenneth, 'The Fragmenting of the New Class Elites, or, Downward Mobility', The Volokh Conspiracy, 31 October 2011, http://volokh.com/2011/10/31/ the-fragmenting-of-the-new-class-elites-or-downward-mobility/

279 'Michelle Obama Lauds Community Service', Associated Press, 13 May 2009, http://www.msnbc.msn.com/id/30723084/ns/us_news-giving/t/ michelle-obama-lauds-community-service/

280 Drew, Christopher, 'Why science majors change their minds (it's just so darn hard)', *The New York Times*, 4 November 2011, http://www.nytimes.com/2011/11/06/education/edlife/why-science-majors-change-their-mind-its-just-so-darn-hard.html?pagewanted=all

281 Johnson, Ryan, 'Plenty of Jobs, Not Enough Skilled Workers', Grand Forks Herald, 4 November 2011, http://www.grandforksherald.com/event/article/id/220362/

282 Baum, Geraldine, 'Student Loans add to angst at Occupy Wall Street', *LA Times*, 25 October 2011, http://www.latimes.com/news/nationworld/nation/la-na-occupy-student-loans-20111026,0,7388368.story?page=2

283 Pareene, Alex, 'A New Declaration of Independence', 31 October 2011, http://www.salon.com/2011/10/31/a_new_declaration_of_independence/singleton/

284 'The pension disaster's Birmingham: cops assault student protesters at UC Davis', Republci of Costa Mesa, 20 November 2011, http://republicofcostamesa.com/2011/11/20/the-pension-disasters-birmingham-cops-assault-student-protesters-at-uc-davis/

285 Madison Lucy, 'Who will benefit from Obama's student loan plan?', *CBS News*, 26 October 2011, http://www.cbsnews.com/8301-503544_162-20126172-503544/who-will-benefit-from-obamas-student-loan-plan/

286 Sabato, Larry J., 'The 2012 election will come down to seven states', *The Wall Street Journal*, 6 September 2011, http://online.wsj.com/article/SB10001424053111903918104576504520213848188.html

287 Dahl, Melissa, 'Youth vote may have been key in Obama's win', MSNBC, 5 November 2008, http://www.msnbc.msn.com/id/27525497/ns/politics-decision_08/t/youth-vote-may-have-been-key-obamas-win/#.Trb_WWDafps

288 Lopez, Mark Hugo, 'How Hispanics voted in the 2008 election', 5 November 2008, http://pewresearch.org/pubs/1024/exit-poll-analysis-hispanics

289 'Will Mitt Romney kill the Tea Party?', Hot Air, http://74.84.198.233/headlines/archives/2011/10/14/will-mitt-romney-kill-the-tea-party/

290 Edsall, Thomas B., 'The Future of the Obama Coalition', *The New York Times*, 27 November 2011, http://campaignstops.blogs.nytimes.com/2011/11/27/the-future-of-the-obama-coalition/